MW00610936

Praise for

THE POWER OF INSTINCT

"A masterclass in understanding and leveraging the instinctive mind, this book dismantles traditional notions of consumer behavior and persuasion. Invaluable for CMOs and any leader navigating the future of marketing."

—Raja Rajamannar, CMO, Mastercard, and bestselling author of *Quantum Marketing*

"Zane cracks the code on human decision-making by showing us how to bypass the conscious mind and create a lightning bolt to your business. This is the must-read marketing book of the decade."

—Linda Kaplan Thaler, Advertising Hall of Fame, founder of the Kaplan Thaler Group, and bestselling coauthor of *The Power of Nice* and *Grit to Great*

"Zane's Growth Triggers® approach was instrumental in revolutionizing our brand strategy during my tenure as CMO at Aetna. It not only shaped our brand positioning and messaging but guided our prioritization of investments in customer experience—resulting in significant enhancements in market share and satisfaction levels. The techniques in Zane's book have universal applicability to foster extraordinary business growth across industries."

—David Edelman, Harvard Business School professor and former CMO, Aetna

"If you enjoyed *Blink* by Malcolm Gladwell and Daniel Kahneman's *Thinking, Fast and Slow*, Zane's book is another game-changer that will immediately impact how you think and act. Whether you're a start-up founder, growth-oriented CMO, seasoned CEO, or anyone seeking to move your priorities forward, *The Power of Instinct* will help you unlock the untapped potential of the instinctive mind."

—James M. Citrin, leader, Spencer Stuart Board and CEO Practice, and bestselling author of *You're in Charge, Now What?*

"A groundbreaking work that illuminates the hidden influences that drive our instinctive decisions and the formula for consistent financial growth. It's a playbook for success in business and life."

—Farnoosh Torabi, host, *So Money*, and author of *A Healthy State of Panic*

"A compelling blend of behavioral science and marketing strategy, this book is a must-read for anyone aiming to create lasting business and brand success."

—Michael Platt, director, Wharton Neuroscience Initiative, and author of *The Leader's Brain*

"This is not your average marketing book—it's a brain-bending, rule-breaking manifesto that challenges norms and shifts your perspective on the science of persuasion and influence."

—Jonah Berger, Wharton professor and bestselling author of *The Catalyst*

THE POWER
of INSTINCT

The New Rules of
Persuasion in Business
and Life

LESLIE ZANE

PUBLICAFFAIRS
New York

PublicAffairs
Hachette Book Group
1290 Avenue of the Americas, New York, NY 10104
www.publicaffairsbooks.com
@Public_Affairs

Printed in the United States of America

First Edition: June 2024

Published by PublicAffairs, an imprint of Hachette Book Group, Inc. The PublicAffairs name and logo is a registered trademark of the Hachette Book Group.

The Hachette Speakers Bureau provides a wide range of authors for speaking events. To find out more, go to hachettespeakersbureau.com or email HachetteSpeakers@hbgusa.com.

PublicAffairs books may be purchased in bulk for business, educational, or promotional use. For more information, please contact your local bookseller or the Hachette Book Group Special Markets Department at special.markets@hbgusa.com.

The publisher is not responsible for websites (or their content) that are not owned by the publisher.

Triggers®, Brand Triggers®, Growth Triggers®, Image Triggers®, *Distinctive* Brand Triggers®, Brand Connectome®, and Brain Branching® are registered service marks of Leslie Zane Consulting, Inc.

Verbal Triggers™, Instinctive Advantage™, Taste Triggers™, Auditory Triggers™, and Olfactory Triggers™ are common law service marks of Leslie Zane Consulting, Inc.

Print book interior design by Amy Quinn.

Library of Congress Cataloging-in-Publication Data

Names: Zane, Leslie, author.
Title: The power of instinct : the new rules of persuasion in business and life / Leslie Zane.
Description: First edition. | New York, NY : PublicAffairs, [2024] | Includes bibliographical references and index.
Identifiers: LCCN 2023046887 | ISBN 9781541703858 (hardcover) | ISBN 9781541703872 (ebook)
Subjects: LCSH: Instinct. | Persuasion (Psychology) | Decision Making—Psychological aspects. | Marketing—Psychological aspects.
Classification: LCC BF685 .Z36 2024 | DDC 650.1—dc23/eng/20240308
LC record available at https://lccn.loc.gov/2023046887

ISBNs: 9781541703858 (hardcover), 9781541703872 (ebook)

LSC-C

Printing 1, 2024

To my incredible parents, Charlotte and Pierre Picot, who taught me to have a healthy disrespect for authority and that I could accomplish anything I set my mind to

People don't buy because of need or loyalty;
they buy on instinct.

CONTENTS

INTRODUCTION

Human beings are unpersuadable. They are obstinate. Closed-minded. Skeptical. Resistant to change. By the 1980s, brand managers on the baby care team at Johnson & Johnson had been trying to revive their sagging business for years. Private label brands, with a similar-looking teardrop logo, and Mennen Baby Magic had taken market share. In response, Johnson & Johnson tried launching new products, promoting them as something that could be used by babies and adults, and created emotional campaigns like "Because you never stop caring"—nothing worked. Market share was down, and no one seemed to have a solution. Obviously, this was a problem. With the possible exception of Tylenol, Johnson's baby shampoo was the crown jewel of the consumer and pharmaceutical giant. And something was amiss. Throughout most of the life of the company, the formula for advertising baby products was like wallpaper: a repeating image of young mothers holding their babies in the traditional Madonna-and-child pose. Anything else was heresy. However, as a young member of the baby care marketing team, I had noticed something. When a *dad* pushed a stroller down the street, moms' heads would turn.

I dug into quantitative trends and found that fathers were getting more involved in caregiving. I tested attitude statements and found that moms' fixation with dad tenderly caring for baby performed at the very top of the heap. So I put on my high heels, scarf bow tie, and skirt suit—the 1990s female version of men's power suits—and marched into my boss's office. "I know what we need to do to fix the business," I told him. He looked unenthused, but I wasn't fazed. "We need to put the first dad in a baby care commercial." I smiled triumphantly, expecting a lightbulb to pop up over his head or fireworks to stream through the sky. This was *it*. A once-in-a-lifetime idea.

With two words, the wind was sucked right out of my sails: "You're crazy." Before I could interject, he was on a roll. "It's moms who buy these products, *not dads*. We have no research to suggest moms want to see dads taking care of babies, and even if we did, there's no evidence this would help the business." With that, he led me out of his office.

But I continued to push the idea, advocating for it at every turn. I explained how we could be the first company in the baby care category to take this untraditional POV. Still no takers. Then came my performance review that year, which included a comment that I will always remember: "Leslie is too passionate about putting fathers in advertising and this demonstrates an overfocus on executional marketing, rather than strategic thinking." While at Bain & Company, at Harvard, and at Procter & Gamble afterward, I had been told that strategic thinking was my superpower. In fact, I had defined myself by it. Reading this sentence in my review was devastating. But I didn't stop. I brought the idea up at team meetings, during one-on-ones, at the water cooler. I became obsessed.

Whether they ultimately relented because they genuinely believed in my idea or because they had grown exhausted of me, no one will ever know, but they went ahead and finally put the first father in a Johnson's baby shampoo commercial. And you know what? It was the highest-scoring commercial in the company's history. The business started moving again. Management was thrilled.

I had found my first supercharged cue—a back door into consumers' unconscious minds that has the power to change the trajectory of a business. Dad, instead of mom, giving baby a bath leveraged familiar associations—caring, tenderness, nurturing—but it did so in a fresh, distinctive, and unexpectedly powerful way. Now the brand was not only caring, it was progressive. The ad spoke to men's sensitive side, showcasing the type of hands-on husband every mom wanted, while giving mom a much-appreciated break. The stark contrast between a strong male body and a fragile, tender baby was also visually captivating and seeped into people's minds, building memory structure. On the surface, the ad was selling baby shampoo, but unconsciously, it was conferring all of these positive associations onto the brand, a phenomenon that had a direct connection to sales.

The experience led me to a stark realization. We cannot *convince* anyone of anything, no matter how we try. People's choices are not based on conscious thought. They don't make decisions because of facts or even perceived need. They don't buy products or services on loyalty or emotion. The vast majority of decisions come from the center of instinctive choice that resides in the unconscious mind, from our preferred brand of bottled water to the presidential candidate we vote for. It's like a lightbulb turning on in a pitch-black room—our eyes widen, and everything just clicks, no thought required. To simplify the complexity of human decision-making, I refer to the brain's two distinct mechanisms as the conscious and unconscious mind. While of course there is only one brain that operates holistically, it's the unconscious mind that exerts the most influence on our everyday decisions.

But this is a counterintuitive idea to many. That's because the belief in conscious decision-making has had a long reign. Nowhere is this idea more entrenched than in the world of marketing and advertising, an industry worth more than $350 billion in the US alone. Marketing departments, ad agencies, and a constellation of research and consulting firms have been built to sway audiences using rules developed back in the middle of the twentieth century, before anyone recognized how we actually make decisions.

These old rules of marketing have penetrated our societal understanding of everything we do, from how we sell products and services to how we form an argument. And they are deeply entrenched. Even kids recognize these rules as unspoken law. When my son was running for class president at age twelve, he insisted his posters had to stand out with a unique message and visual. That rule—part of

Marketing 101—is inherent in the societal manual we all have in our minds about how to market anything. But in reality, the human brain is hardwired to connect with the *familiar*, not the unique.

Traditional marketing, and its influence on our greater culture, has led us astray, causing us to believe the conscious mind is persuadable, that the classic rules of marketing are infallible. But I'm here to tell you they're not. This is because the conscious mind is skeptical, aware it's being marketed to and resistant to change. Moreover, the conscious mind only accounts for roughly 5 percent of our decisions, as suggested by Harvard Business School professor Gerald Zaltman and behavioral economist Daniel Kahneman. Think about that for a moment—a staggering 95 percent of our choices are made by our unconscious mind. Still, every aspect of the business, political, and advertising worlds relies on this conscious model of marketing. These ideas are institutionalized, taught, and practiced everywhere, from P&G's marketing department to MBA programs worldwide. This approach is like selling to a brick wall.

For over fifty years, marketers have followed this traditional model of persuasion: muster more arguments, bombard people with messages, spend more than competitors, and you'll dominate the market. But we have entered a new age: *the Age of Instinct*. And like other culturally transformative eras in history, from the Renaissance to the Industrial Age to the Tech Revolution, all spurred by tremendous progress in a particular sphere, this one is no different. Today, that progress has taken place in our understanding of the human brain. And the effects are felt in all areas of contemporary life—from the economy to politics, and education to health care.

The truth is hard for many people to swallow: the traditional conscious-model approach to marketing is dead. In fact, businesses, politicians, nonprofits, and leaders of all stripes are following a method that's not only out-of-date and largely ineffective, it works *against* our brains. It's no wonder so many marketing and advertising efforts have a low return on investment. It helps explain why the top one hundred advertisers' business growth declined by 4 percent from 2009 to 2019. You can only shout at people so long until they stop listening, or pile on discount after discount until you're giving your product or service away for free. It's time to throw out the old persuasion model and embrace a new one, a model based on the way the brain actually works.

BEHAVIORAL SCIENCE COMES OF AGE

After starting my career in marketing at Procter & Gamble, then later moving to Johnson & Johnson, I quickly realized that when you're on the inside of big corporations, you are expected to follow conventional marketing orthodoxy. My ideas were different from everyone else's. I maintained that what people *say* in research is unreliable, telegraphic cues are more effective than direct persuasion, and successful brands have multiple associations for consumers, not one defining identity trait. These ideas and my research were slowly coalescing into a model, one that was entirely different from the conventional marketing model, and which went directly against the core of the P&G training. It did not go over well.

Like most unconventional thinkers, particularly women, when I voiced these unorthodox beliefs, I was often dismissed. But I kept at it. I felt I had to. At many of the companies I worked for early in my career, a number of brands in the portfolio had sluggish growth. No one seemed to understand why. Here I was at the center of the marketing capitals of the world, working for companies renowned for their brand management, yet no one knew how to consistently grow business. If they didn't know how to drive sustainable growth, then who did?

I watched one brand manager after another try to crack the mysteries of customer conversion and business growth with hit-or-miss results. They were overreliant on promotional incentives, like coupons, buy-one-get-ones (BOGOs), and customer reward programs. And they blindly accepted what consumers reported in research, even though time and time again, marketplace results didn't pan out. I saw the same thing happen in political campaigns: the polls pointed in one direction, but voting went another way. No one was any closer to discovering the essence of what actually made someone choose a brand, vote for a candidate, or support a particular cause.

So I went to the consumers. I listened carefully as they spoke confidently about reasons they were loyal to the brands they bought, and noticed that when I observed their actual behavior in, say, a grocery store, those reasons seemed to fly out the window. Here, they went on autopilot. Their choices were instinctive, automatic. No contemplation. No "reasons." They just reached. They explained why they picked up the same brand of soap or cereal every time they went to the store, but in reality, that was a rationalization that took place *after* they made their choice. In research, what people said was their reason for choosing a brand rarely aligned with the true drivers of their choice. The same was true when they donated to certain charities or voted for one political party over another. Something greater was at play.

In 1995, I left the corporate world to start Triggers®, the first-ever strategy firm founded on the principles of behavioral science. Triggers is also the first brand strategy and research firm founded by a woman that still exists today. Since then, my colleagues and I have worked closely with the very Fortune 500 companies I had left, helping them consistently change their customers' and clients' instinctive purchase behavior. Together, our team of expert strategists has guided top companies from McDonald's and Pernod Ricard to PepsiCo and Mars toward driving faster, more sustainable growth. The results speak for themselves: when clients precisely execute our recommendations, they see growth rates two to three times those of the prior year.

But that doesn't mean it has been easy. In many ways, we were about twenty years ahead of our time. We were talking about cognitive shortcuts that work at the unconscious level well before behavioral science started to seep into business and popular culture. Dan Ariely's *Predictably Irrational* wouldn't come out until 2008, and Daniel Kahneman's *Thinking, Fast and Slow* didn't appear until 2011.

When they did, they didn't really change how leaders ran their businesses. Behavioral economics was still viewed as this niche practice that was interesting but not essential to building brands.

Over the past decade, however, interest in behavioral science has exploded. Every top consulting firm and ad agency has behavioral scientists on speed dial, if not on the payroll. It is much more common to see Fortune 100 companies tracking the components of mental availability—situational salience, category relevance, and distinction—to measure their brand health. But most of these approaches are still focused on theory; it's no wonder that 42 percent of behavioral scientists say they are having difficulty applying the practice in organizations.

We were fortunate enough to have real life as our laboratory. We also had the rare privilege of working with the most forward-thinking marketing and insights leaders, executives frustrated by the status quo in pursuit of a reliable way to achieve bold change. Trusted by clients across industries to fix their greatest brand challenges, we had no choice—we had to change competitive and non-users' brand behavior. There was no time for theory, just action. That's how we learned what actually worked. We set out to uncover the secret to how humans choose, and we found it: the command control center of people's decisions. And with that discovery, we realized we all have the power to change anyone's mind—even when their instincts seem to be entrenched. By utilizing the built-in, physical, neural pathways that form associations and memories in our brains, and building new ones, it's possible to influence the choices people make to drive success in any arena.

WE ARE ALL MARKETERS

Without fail, every day, each one of us tries to "sell" something to someone else. Maybe that's a product or a service. But it could also be an idea at work or in the classroom, where to eat on date night, or what proposals to vote for or against in the upcoming midterms.

Or maybe it's our personality, skills, or experience. In effect, we are all marketers. Whether you are trying to grow your business or your personal brand, get your candidate elected, or get people to buy into your idea or contribute to your social cause, you need to approach the process as if you were building a brand.

For your brand to be accepted and grow in the marketplace, it must first grow in consumers' minds. This critical link is starting to change dynamics across companies. Approximately 85 percent of CEOs don't trust their CMOs because they think they're too focused on splashy creative, not business performance. Indeed, many leaders consider brand development efforts to be a separate discipline that has little direct impact on revenue and share growth. These notions couldn't be further from the truth. Building a large, thriving brand in the mind is the difference between financial success or failure.

From the beginning, my team and I began using cognitive shortcuts in marketing and advertising to help get competitive users to switch to our clients' brands. We showed that people's choices were not consumer driven as much as they were "brain driven." By creating mental availability for our clients, in which their potential customers would recognize or think of their particular brand when considering a purchase, we ensured they were top of mind. Blue-chip clients were stunned by the performance of the new approach. After forking over millions to large global consulting firms (one thousand times our size) without moving the needle, they finally, and quickly, were driving market share gains at a fraction of the cost and effort.

We weren't focused on the battle for shelf space out in the marketplace or even for share of voice in advertising—we were focused on winning the competitive battle in their customers' minds, ensuring their brand gained the Instinctive Advantage™ over the competition. The theory of competitive advantage assumes that we make decisions based on the actual costs and differentiation of products and services. Well, we don't. Though the real world influences us, the only reality that matters is the one that exists in our heads.

Competitive advantage was developed at a time when business leaders thought people make conscious decisions based on reality. But perception beats out reality every time. Gaining the instinctive advantage is the evolution of competitive advantage, based on applied behavioral science, which shows you can become the first choice in any sphere by reaching people's instincts. By shedding the old way of thinking and adopting the new rules of instinctive behavior, you can change the trajectory of your personal brand, your business performance, your life.

ACCESSING THE INACCESSIBLE

More often than not, organizations run into trouble because they aren't aware of what's going on in their consumers' unconscious mind. Negative associations accumulate in people's minds, typically relative to other offerings or trends—and the brand fails to evolve and stay meaningful. Slowly, the brand becomes consumed by negative associations, the brand's footprint shrinks, and revenue growth starts to decline. Most business leaders see this decline as a product of outside forces: the economy, the stock market, a global recession.

The truth is that there are plenty of examples of companies that *are* able to gain share in spite of bad times, driving growth even in the face of a new competitor that's on fire. The secret is to grow your brand in your prospects' unconscious mind. But if you're not paying attention to how your brand is faring in their unconscious, you're not going to know what's going on with your brand until it's too late. The unconscious, or instinctive, mind is the first place it happens. The marketplace is the last place it shows up. In a big way.

In the following pages, I provide my science-backed, field-proven methodology for targeting the area of the mind that's responsible for decision-making. As a brand strategist and behavioral science practitioner who has dedicated my professional life to understanding how people make choices, I lay out the first and only systematic process for expanding a brand's physical presence in people's minds.

That's right: the more neural connections an idea takes up in the brain, the more power it has. Our straightforward approach has allowed companies across industries to leverage the memories and associations of consumers to increase sales, and now you can use it to accelerate the success of anything you're working on. Throughout these chapters, I show you how to grow the physical size and salience of your Brand Connectome® (pronounced "kuh-NEK-tome"), the command center for instinctive choices that resides in the unconscious mind.

What people want most is validation—they want to be told that they are right. That's why the only way to succeed is to leverage familiar anchors in people's memories that work with, instead of against, the mind. This is not some type of subliminal advertising. And it certainly doesn't happen by creating a more emotional communication. You do it by planting a seed, nourishing it, and growing its physical footprint—in people's minds. As the tree grows—the Brand Connectome—so will your business, cause, or idea, ensuring success over the long term, and a foolproof approach to getting people to buy, vote for, and do what you want.

The health and size of the Brand Connectome in consumers' minds has a direct correlation to a company's growth and the health of its profit and loss statement (P&L). When positive associations in consumers' minds reach a certain point, they buy your brand on "autopilot." This explains why some personal brands achieve sustainable growth, and others don't. In the political arena, this phenomenon explains voters automatically pulling the lever for the same party in election after election. And for companies, that means a healthy, growing Brand Connectome is absolutely crucial to financial goals. By adding positive associations through Growth Triggers®, any brand, candidate, or idea can become the go-to, automatic choice. Does that mean they choose you 100 percent of the time? Of course not. Consumers typically buy multiple brands in a category. But this approach ensures that your brand will have more mental availability than your competitors and become your audience's first choice more of the time.

This book is more than an inside look at the marketing industry or the latest pop psychology—it provides the definitive understanding of and rules of engagement for the hidden forces that shape our world. A scientific way to use the power of instinct has profound implications for anyone who wants to scale businesses or movements faster, using fewer resources while making a greater impact. But success requires a new set of instructions. In each chapter, I share the new rules, all of which I have used to help new brands take off and enable established-but-struggling companies to execute dramatic turnarounds. Once you know the rules, you will see the world through a different lens. As a pioneer of applying behavioral science to practical situations, I have seen it work time and time again in business, politics, and even selling ideas. I've also witnessed companies fall flat on their faces when they've refused to break away from the marketing tenets of the past.

Although my experiences are rooted in helping Fortune 500 companies, the techniques I provide are applicable to improving personal effectiveness, marketing a small business, championing a cause or candidate, or getting into the college of your choice. This book discards the worn-out rules of traditional marketing and persuasion, crafted over fifty years ago when it was believed that the conscious brain influenced decisions. But it doesn't work that way. We may think we control our decisions, but we do not. That's why we need a new set of principles rooted in the understanding that the unconscious brain is king. Unlike the old rules, these new instinct-based principles work *with* people's brains instead of *against* them to change behavior faster and more effectively. Understanding this concept will not only help you build your own brand, it can also help you recognize when people are preying on your unconscious mind, trying to get you to make a choice that might harm, instead of help, you.

Whether you're an entrepreneur trying to build the next unicorn, a job hunter looking to land a higher-paying job, a freelancer pitching projects, or someone who wants to build their personal brand, even become a social media influencer, you need new rules. If you're a Fortune 500 CEO, CGO, or CMO with tough growth objectives or head of insights who is tracking the brand mind share, mental availability, or health of the brands you manage, this book will finally give you the means to substantially move your metrics. Think of it as the first operating manual for marketing to the unconscious mind. Using these rules, you can accelerate the pace of any opportunity—getting people to buy, vote, or contribute on autopilot—time and time again. This easily replicable approach ensures that when the choice is made, it is no choice at all—it's instinct.

Chapter 1

THE CONSCIOUS MARKETING MODEL IS DEAD

INSTINCT RULE: Traditional persuasion is an uphill battle, which is why you need to take the backdoor route.

na's presentation had not gone as she'd hoped. Walking into her sprawling corner office, dressed in a sharp white suit, she closed the door, let out a heavy sigh, and drifted toward the window, seeking a moment of respite as she took in the striking views of Central Park. Growing up in a South Carolina mill town, she'd always dreamed of living and working in New York City. But now, looking out at the greenery tucked into Manhattan's grid of skyscrapers, she wondered if she'd made a mistake.

Ana had recently joined one of the top three cosmetic companies in the US, believing she'd been hired to shake things up. Once the market leader of the half-trillion-dollar beauty industry, the company's public slide from the number-one to the number-three spot had not been pretty. During the job interview with the president of the company's North American operations, her would-be boss detailed how the brand was overdue for repositioning. He wanted fresh ideas, innovative approaches, and someone who would "jump-start growth." He thought she could be that someone, and when she left the interview, Ana, a rising industry star, agreed.

In that morning's presentation, she had argued the company's celebrity supermodels were too inaccessible. What the brand needed was to go behind the scenes of the models' lives, exposing their personal beauty challenges, to counteract the "They wake up gorgeous" misconception and make it clear that the company's cosmetics were enhancing their appearance. Ana had refined the presentation for weeks, tweaking every little detail. Worried her boss would catch wind of what she was working on before she had a chance to make her case, she kept the idea close to her vest. When she got up in front of the president and the rest of the executive leadership team, she felt confident the presentation covered all the important points and would make a real impression. The president's response was tepid at best. He pushed back, saying, "We tried something similar three years ago and it failed—consumers didn't want to see our models without makeup on."

So she doubled then tripled down, trying to argue those points as best she could. She provided market research with page after page of facts and figures, graphs and tables that supported her recommendation. It was all to no avail. The president was convinced it wouldn't work. He said he just "wasn't seeing it." And the more Ana tried to convince him, the more intractable he became. The rest of the executive team stayed silent.

Back in her office, looking out her picture window, Ana suddenly had an epiphany. There wasn't something wrong with her idea; there was something wrong with how she had presented it. She decided she would not approach the next presentation with an abundance of facts, figures, and research, trying to persuade her boss over to her side. Instead, she would approach selling her plan the same way she launched a new brand in the marketplace. This was simply a different type of marketplace; she just needed buy-in from her boss instead of from the consumer. She would create a marketing campaign around her idea.

Her first stop in the campaign, which she called "Revolutionary Beauty," was Research and Development, where she learned about the product technology that keeps color applied on lips for eight hours. No competitor had made this breakthrough yet, a significant development Ana felt had been overlooked. "This technology is gold," she told the department's VP, who happily agreed. She then moved to Sales, where the priority was to generate a continuous stream of news to drive customer traffic into stores like CVS and Walgreens. Ana explained that "Revolutionary Beauty" paid homage to the brand's legacy as an innovator while tipping its hat to the need for the industry to evolve. Specifically, the campaign would provide a breakthrough benefit—stay-on lipstick color that makeup influencers could share with their audiences, which would send them running to the cosmetic aisle of drugstores across the country. The sales director liked what she heard. Up next was the company's legal counsel. An attorney's perspective would normally only be needed to ensure no trademark violations, but the attorney was a personal and trusted friend of the president of the North American division, who appreciated being solicited for his input. Ana shared her vision.

When the day of the presentation arrived, instead of a typical PowerPoint, Ana started with a visual of the company's beloved celebrity supermodel spokesperson standing at the peak of an imposing mountain. Wearing a shirt emblazoned with the company's logo, her hair blowing in the wind, the well-known supermodel hoisted a large gold number one over her head. Farther down the slope, hikers wearing shirts with the logos of competitors struggled to catch up.

A few people in the room chuckled. The president nodded and said, "That's where we want to be—at the top." Before she turned to the next slide, the president mentioned he had been hearing positive things about Ana's idea. Ana smiled before explaining the campaign around the new stay-on color technology and how it would build market share, not just in lipstick but also in lash, eye shadow, and foundation, three categories in which competitors currently had the advantage. She ended with expected press coverage that the company would receive. As hypothetical positive headlines flashed on the screen, she could see people in the room smiling, including her boss.

You can say Ana effectively persuaded her boss—but persuasion had nothing to do with it. During her first presentation, Ana had piled on facts, figures, and every manner of persuasive argument, but those only made her boss more resistant to her recommendation. The second time around was altogether different. Her boss easily accepted the telegraphic symbols and visuals she used. Cues from the company's golden years created familiarity and comfort. Imagery of the company's spokesperson climbing the mountain associated the company—and, of course, the boss—with achievement. It was as if they snuck in through the back door, bypassing all of the boss's objections on the way. By piggybacking on positive associations in his memory, Ana's recommendations flowed into his mind without resistance.

One after the other, iconic cues in her presentation layered positive associations on top of an existing foundation that had been built by the "word around the office." Still, Ana didn't necessarily have to build consensus first through R&D, Sales, and the company attorney. Tapping into these influencers was only one way to affect her boss. For example, if her boss had been open to it, she could have collaborated with him early, building the plan together in a series of meetings. No matter the approach, the boss needed repeated positive exposures to Ana's idea (early and often) in order for the neural network of the idea to physically grow in his mind. But this wasn't simply about frequency of messaging. It was about content.

Why did the other members of the executive team nod along this time? Ana had increased the neural network of positive associations for her plan in their minds prior to the meeting. Essentially, they came to the presentation positively biased toward the idea. Although Ana's overall recommendation was the same, the way she presented it this time was radically different. Ana shifted her boss's decision from rejection to acceptance and created buy-in from the entire executive team by appealing to their hidden brain.

As Ana discovered, whether it's the marketplace of ideas around the office, the marketplace of politics, or the marketplace of your child's school or the college you're applying to, they all operate in the same way. To succeed, you have to connect with the audience's unconscious mind. But the old rules of marketing tell us otherwise, negatively affecting our chances of success in whatever marketplace we're operating in. And even if some of those rules worked in the past, when there was less competition and less noise in the marketplace, they are no longer relevant in the Age of Instinct.

There is a myriad of companies that thrived at one point in time using old marketing tactics, but whose growth gradually, or quickly, slowed down, stopped, or declined. In fact, a recent study showed that of 3,900 brands analyzed over a three-year period, only 6 percent were able to gain market share, 60 percent of those were able to sustain those gains, and fewer still were able to accelerate after their initial growth. This trend is seen with hundreds of top-name brands, across every category, leaving marketers worldwide scratching their heads.

THE FALLACY OF PERSUASION

The conscious persuasion model employed by marketers is based on three things: more, more, and more. Think about it: Retail and grocery stores offer more coupons. Politicians, more arguments about their positions. Health care and Big Pharma? More data via clinical trials. Lawyers provide more evidence. And most brand managers and ad agency leaders believe you have to spend more to make an impact.

This focus on "more" creates a world in which marketers are constantly yelling in their audience's faces, pushing them to buy, prodding them to choose what they're offering, in an attempt to convince them to do their bidding. But truth is, this either goes in one ear and out the other or turns people off altogether. Still, this model is employed by marketers and ad agencies across the world, tricking most of us into thinking it is the best way to convince someone to vote for a political candidate, contribute to a cause or charity, or sell a house. The thought is if they only shout louder, spend more, and make better arguments, the customer will surely yield, give in, and comply. This is supposedly how to "persuade" the conscious mind. But the conscious mind is obstinate. In fact, it's unpersuadable.

This model may be more visible in social media digital marketing than anywhere else. Companies believe that in order to sell their wares today, they must maintain a 24/7 dialogue with consumers. If they don't keep up the barrage of social media posts and digital ads, they worry they'll be left out of these "ongoing conversations" and their competitors will prevail. But with such an active digital ecosphere, their message is more likely to get lost than heard. The average American in 2022 saw between four thousand and ten thousand ads per day, double what they were exposed to in 2007. In a never-ending search for more content, more interactions, more likes, a brand's reputation can even take a hit as their message gets watered down or disappears in the chaos of thousands of ads.

Meanwhile, these companies spend millions, hoping the more money they throw out there, the more attention they'll generate. It adds up: In 2022, US companies spent a total of $56 billion on social media advertising. Worldwide, brands spent over $173 billion on social media ads, an amount projected to reach nearly $385 billion by 2027. But this model of "more" is a relic from the past, part of the failed traditional marketing approach. Aimed at the rational, conscious mind, it's the wrong technique because, in reality, that's not the part of the brain that's in control. Still, marketers and business leaders have spent the past ten decades trying to persuade people to use their brands, products, and services through an array of techniques from an outdated playbook. They can't help but follow the old rules. It's not their fault. They were trained on them; they moved up the corporate ladder with them. They have become ingrained in our collective understanding of how marketing works. The problem is, they were developed in a world that had a radically different understanding of how the brain works.

At Harvard Business School, we were taught that competitive advantage comes from either being the low-cost provider, having product differentiation, or focusing on a particular niche. Seems reasonable, but it leaves out the most important driver of all: perceptions. Highly differentiated, even superior, brands don't always get that credit in the marketplace; time and time again they are beat out by parity products with *perceived* superiority. That's the ultimate competitive advantage because it exists in people's minds. Another well-established principle, life cycle theory, proposes that brands and products exhibit higher growth when they're younger and slower growth as they age. But there are many exceptions to the rule. Brands that have been kicking around for fifty to one hundred years—like Coca-Cola, Target, and McDonald's—can still go through a growth spurt.

Similarly, many research tools that metrics leaders rely on, from brand health tracking studies to the Net Promoter Score (NPS) (a metric of customer advocacy based on how likely a consumer is to recommend a brand they have used before), are founded on questions people answer with their *conscious mind*. Despite what they say, consumers have no idea why they buy the brands they do, which means their answers to research polls, surveys, and focus group questions are largely unreliable. Recognizing the limitation of such conscious approaches, the field of neuromarketing has come up with a number of offerings, from brain scans, such as EEGs and fMRIs, to emotion tracing and facial-expression coding.

Unfortunately, these new tools have some gaps of their own. Though they go beyond the conscious persuasion model, they don't tell us what's really going on "behind the scenes." Brain scans, for example, are great at showing how a stimulus affects a person's brain—such as a certain portion lighting up when the person experiences empathy, sadness, or a sense of community—but they don't explain *why*. Why does looking at a certain image cause us to feel joy? Unless we look at the underlying associations, we simply cannot know. These newer techniques are encouraging, as they begin to move the research community toward a greater emphasis on the unconscious mind. However, they don't provide quite enough insight into the network of memories and associations that influence a person's decisions.

The truth is, changing people's perceptions and behavior is not about emotion. It's about memories. It's not about coding people's facial expressions in response to stimuli. That's external. It's not about attributes. It's about understanding the associations that live on our neural pathways. Moreover, every technique traditional marketing uses to drive business—from inundating people with social media posts to promotional incentives—is aimed at changing the conscious mind. None of the traditional techniques focused on persuading the conscious mind, nor the new techniques that purport to have the inside track on the brain, have proven fruitful in consistently driving growth and market share.

THE PATH OF GREATEST RESISTANCE

Facts don't have the power to affect our decisions as much as we'd like to think. What we are happy to believe, however, is information of any kind that confirms our worldview, that which we can consciously point to when we want to prove to others, and ourselves, that we're right. This confirmation bias is the foundation of the social media echo chamber that has contributed to such division in US politics and society. The more we hear or read a point of view that confirms our own, the more we click on it, the more we interact with it. Meanwhile, we reject ideas that don't conform to our worldview.

The more we click, the more entrenched our point of view becomes and, as a society, we grow more and more polarized. In the same way that Gaston used inflammatory rhetoric ("The Beast will make off with your children...he'll come after them in the night") to incite the crowd of the poor provincial town in *Beauty and the Beast*, getting the townspeople to light their torches and hunt down the beast, Facebook fuels angry mobs online. Obviously, this presents a problem: If people are so stuck in their ways that they are unwilling to listen to another point of view, how can we ever expect to change someone's mind, preference, or behavior?

By working *with* the unconscious mind, you can tap into people's existing memories and affect their decisions. In the process, you take the path of *least* resistance. Professor Adam Grant, author of *Think Again*, has come to a similar conclusion when considering two different mindsets. In the adversarial mindset, a person takes on the role of preacher, politician, or prosecutor when communicating with others or making an argument. This mindset leads people to spout their point of view without listening to the other party involved. In essence, this is the conscious persuasion model at work, *pushing* the audience toward a choice. Grant contrasts this mindset with one that is collaborative, in which people take on the role of a scientist. Here, people listen with curiosity and maintain a sense of humor to try to find deeper meaning and a common ground. Not surprisingly, the collaborative mindset is more effective in changing people's choices.

Though Grant makes some excellent points, he stops short of explaining exactly why the collaborative mindset works and how we can use it to affect people's decisions. What's really going on here is that, instead of working *against* the *conscious* mind, a collaborative mindset works *with* the *unconscious* mind, influencing people's instinctive behavior by connecting with what already exists in people's minds. The collaborative mindset leverages how our brains work; the adversarial mindset works against it.

For example, in 2020 when the long-running, beloved host of *Jeopardy!*, Alex Trebek, tragically died of pancreatic cancer, Sony Pictures tried out a parade of guest hosts to replace the irreplaceable. They were trying to find the right formula, but they took on an adversarial mindset, utilizing a conscious persuasion approach. Remember what that approach relies on? That's right, *more*.

One day, they tried out football star Aaron Rodgers. Another, the iconic journalist Katie Couric. Anderson Cooper had a chance as well. For viewers, it was a little like whiplash. The results spoke for themselves: audience ratings kept sliding, from 6.1 in January of 2021 to 4.8 in May. Producers assumed the scores were a reflection of the viewers' interest in each new host. But that was not the case. Rather, as audience ratings declined, a gradual deterioration of the *Jeopardy!* brand was taking place in viewers' minds.

You can understand why *Jeopardy!*'s producers initially gravitated toward these celebrities. They needed a substitute; why not make it someone famous? The thought was likely that a famous person would resonate with the audience as a known entity, and even make the show more popular. But what they missed was that the new hosts had *nothing* to do with *Jeopardy!* fans' cumulative memories of the show. They weren't a fit. *Jeopardy!* needed to *ease* their audience into a new host—creating an evolution of the brand rather than a disruption with the past. Instead, every time they tried out another new host, they actually created cognitive dissonance with viewers' existing image of the brand. The audience was confronted with something new that didn't quite compute with their existing notion of *Jeopardy!* Not only were none of these people Trebek, most of them seemed entirely foreign to the show.

By making major changes to their beloved brand, instead of building on what already existed, *Jeopardy!* went against the audience's expectations. It was like entering your favorite, most comfortable room in your house and suddenly finding it filled with different furniture. With each new host, audience ratings declined a little further, which management interpreted as an evaluation of each new host. But our understanding of instinct suggests that each daily score wasn't a judgment of each host at all. Rather, the declining ratings were a case of what I call "brand atrophy"—a loss of Brand Salience in the audience's minds. And the more time went on, the more faded the memory of Trebek's show became. What Sony needed to do was choose a person based on one simple criterion: Who had the strongest connection to Trebek and the show? Instead of trying to cram new hosts down viewers' throats—the adversarial approach—they had to find someone whose association with the show, and specifically Trebek, led to feelings of familiarity and continuity. They needed to bypass viewers' instinct to reject any new host ("None of these people are Trebek") and influence their unconscious minds.

One guest host fit the bill: the well-known former *Jeopardy!* contestant Ken Jennings, who still holds the record-setting seventy-four-consecutive-games win, worth a total of $2.52 million, on the show. Though Sony ultimately landed on a cohost model, including award-winning actress Mayim Bialik, Jennings was hailed as saving *Jeopardy!* in 2022 when he was chosen as the second cohost. He was recognizable and had history with the show. Any die-hard fans who watched his winning streak in 2004 saw him standing next to Trebek seventy-four games in a row.

Trebek had been the face of the *Jeopardy!* brand since 1984. Introducing a totally new face would be like relaunching the brand. It would be as if Disney switched from Mickey Mouse to Snoopy, or Aflac switched from their famous white duck to Big Bird. But by bringing fans another familiar face, there was already an existing association between Jennings, the show, and its former host. When Jennings appeared as the host, existing memories about him kicked in, and viewers were automatically biased toward him. Positive bias is at the root of any brand preference—whether for your favorite TV show or your go-to political party—and it is based on cumulative memories, either positive or negative. Again, when you leverage a positive bias, you take the path of least resistance. That's because you are piggybacking your idea, opinion, or product onto associations the person you're trying to influence already has. This approach is so much easier than starting from scratch.

When we typically think of memories, we think of something wispy or amorphous. But in reality, the memories and associations that exist in our minds are scientific, measurable. It might have become habit for the marketing industry to rely on conversions, clicks, and eyeballs as a bellwether of consumer preference and action, but none of these metrics actually help predict what consumers are going to do next. The fundamental reason people choose one brand over another, or prefer one TV host over another, has to do with *the space it takes up in our brains.* It's all physical.

OUR PHYSICAL BRAIN

Our understanding of the human brain has evolved immensely over the past fifty years. Prior to the 1960s, it was thought that the brain was much more static than it is known to be today. In fact, scientists believed that the brain's physical structure could only change when we were infants and children. By the time we reached young adulthood, they thought that was it—our brain's structure was pretty much permanent, incapable of change. But with advances in technology, cross-field collaboration, and a growth of neuroscience research, that theory fell apart. And with the discovery of stem cells in the adult brain in the 1990s, scientists began to think that neurogenesis, in which new neurons are formed in the brain, was possible. Neurogenesis in the hippocampus is now believed to play a major role in our memory, mood, and ability to learn new things.

Neurogenesis is just one facet of neuroplasticity, our brain's ability to physically change as a result of new inputs, information, and overall experiences. This means our neural networks can be altered or reorganized, and new ones can grow. Though there is more than one type of neuroplasticity, when our brain's physical structure changes as a result of something we've learned, that's called *structural plasticity.* Structural plasticity takes place throughout our lives as we continue learning. So the physical structure of the adult brain can be changed, and it actually happens all the time.

There is the well-known example of London taxi drivers, whose intimate, specified knowledge of the twisting, tangled streets of the city stimulate their brain development. A five-year study that concluded in 2011 showed that, through training, these cabbies' hippocampi actually became larger than average. As described by one cabbie when asked what it's like when they pick up a fare and are given a destination, "It's like an explosion in your brain. You see it instantly." The test to become a London cab driver is known as the Knowledge of London, an exam so difficult, it has been referred to as "the hardest test, of any kind, in the world." Memorizing the city's every street (all twenty-five thousand of them), landmark, and monument, from the largest to the most minute, takes up so much physical space in the brain, other gray matter is crowded out. Research actually shows that London cabbies' short-term memory is worse than a control group's, as is their ability to form new associations via visual information. It seems that the Knowledge dominates their brain to the exclusion of all else. When such drivers retire and no longer need to use the Knowledge, their hippocampi begin shrinking back to average. Bottom line: when people learn something new, their brain grows.

Every meaningful interaction with an idea, one in which the idea is made memorable and "sticks" in our mind, rewires our brain; the same goes for any "sticky" interaction with a company, brand, or TV show. Learning about a company's CEO in a documentary, growing up with a mom loyal to a certain juice, seeing a captivating post on social media—any meaningful encounter changes the physical structure inside our heads. In the process, memories and associations form.

When it comes to making choices, the brain isn't a neat and orderly database. Nobody consults an internal list of pros and cons for each available option before deciding on a car, tube of whitening toothpaste, or job candidate. Instead, all of our choices are based on associations and memories that live on the neural pathways of our brains. These pathways create vast interconnected vectors of neural activity.

As explained by Geoffrey Hinton—a former engineering fellow at Google Brain and cognitive psychologist, known as the "Godfather of AI"—these vectors interact with one another, leading to one's instinctive preferences and behaviors. And instincts are driven by what the human brain does extremely well: analogical reasoning. It was previously thought that our brains are akin to "deliberate reasoning machines," but in reality, Hinton explains, the human mind is constantly making analogies between trillions of associations, memories, images, sounds, and more, rapidly coming to intuitive conclusions. Artificial intelligence (AI) works in a similar way. In fact, it's this enlightened understanding of how the human brain operates that enabled the massive leap forward in AI technology. AI operates on an analogic model, mirroring how the human brain and the Brand Connectome work. But while large language models, such as the one first popularized by ChatGPT in November 2022, have half a trillion to a trillion connections, Hinton points out that "our brains have 100 trillion connections."

This unconscious decision-making, now thought to control 95 percent of the choices we make all day long, has minimal conscious thought involved. It's dictated largely by these neural networks. In fact, our conscious thoughts are believed to be more of an after-the-fact rationalization of what we feel and do intuitively. That is why the conscious persuasion model favored by traditional marketing is so ineffective at changing minds. If you simply tell someone what they should believe, whom they should vote for, or what product is better than another, they won't listen, and you'll make no impression on these networks of interconnected vectors. What you need to do instead is go in that back door—the unconscious mind—by actually changing the physical neural pathways in people's brains. When you're able to do that, their choices become instinctive—the holy grail of creating preference for a particular brand.

INSTINCTIVE BRAND PREFERENCE

Most people think of a brand as a logo, product, or service. In addition, they might think of marketing campaigns or ad copy, that targeted ad that popped up in their social media feed. That's pretty much the extent. But this view is entirely too limited. A brand is everything that it is connected to. It's not just the product or logo, it's all the connections the brain has created about the brand—it could be the people who work at the company, the consumers who use the brand, and a myriad of images, ideas, and memories the brand brings to mind. Simply put: *a brand is known by the associations it keeps.*

No matter your brand, you need to think about it in a way that's larger than what's right in front of you. Otherwise, it will always remain small and confined, which is the exact opposite of what you should aim for—you want large and sprawling. Or in behavioral science parlance, you want *salience*, the ability to stand out above all other options. As people's brains are pounded by choices left and right every single moment of every day, the salience of your brand is the primary determinant of whether or not it receives attention and, in the end, is chosen.

Salience is created by having associations that reach far beyond a well-designed logo or a flashy ad. These associations must relate to things people actually care about and that are meaningful in their lives, whether presently or in the past. And you want to have tons of them, so many connection points they overpower even the mere possibility that your target audience would dare do anything but select your brand. When your brand has this abundance of positive associations, you create a larger physical footprint in the brain, leading to what I call *instinctive brand preference.*

Instinctive brand preference is automatic, repetitive purchase behavior. This is when people make your brand their "go-to." They buy it over and over again without thinking, as if they are on autopilot. For example, in a grocery store, this autopilot purchase behavior means your customer reaches for Coke or Pepsi, Colgate or Crest every time they are in the aisle or looks for that particular Goya logo on a can of black beans. It's as if they can't even see the other options. They don't have to do an ounce of soul-searching to make the decision and they certainly aren't comparing your product to any other. They just reach blindly and throw that gallon of water and can of beans right in the cart. According to Triggers' managing director and former Havas and BBDO exec Morgan Seamark, it's so unconscious, they might as well be *sleep-shopping.*

This is the most profitable type of purchase because it happens with little in the way of incentives, promotions, or other marketing support. Coupons, discounts, or other promotions are expensive and produce little to no long-term payoff. Sure, they can produce a short-term bump in sales, but such incentives do almost nothing for your brand long term because you are essentially trying to buy consumers' loyalty. Instinctive brand preference, however, is the result of creating true loyalty organically, connecting with your audience at that unconscious, instinctive level. Instinctive brand preference is not specific to products or services; the same idea can be applied to watching your favorite TV show, determining which political party you vote for, accepting a start-up business idea or pitch, or choosing what town or state to live in.

Brands that do this best survive the test of time by creating giant ecosystems that touch multiple aspects of people's lives. Nike, for example, is a go-to athletic brand because it has more connections to more touchpoints in people's minds than any other sports brand. Associated with perseverance, grit, style, and importantly, success, it has its own massive neural network in people's minds. With 650 sponsorship deals across 140 leagues and organizations, the Nike swoosh is omnipresent in all the places you'd expect it to be—and perhaps some where you wouldn't. It is of course emblazoned on sneakers, baseball caps, jerseys, and uniforms of more aspirational sports figures and teams than any other brand, but with Nike having become an international fashion brand, partnering with the likes of Kim Jones of Dior and Rei Kawakubo, the founder of Comme des Garçons, the logo also pops up in the top fashion shows. Nike stages scavenger hunts using a dedicated app for limited-edition kicks, attracting the most devoted sneakerheads of all ages, and museums, such as the Rubell in Miami, have held exhibits featuring designer versions of their shoes—the swoosh always front and center. And Nike creates as much fanfare about its new SNKRS "releases" as Steve

Jobs did with the iPhone introduction. This excitement fuels their shoes to become part of the cultural conversation around art, technology, and business; its Brand Connectome goes way beyond sports.

When negative associations enter into people's neural pathways, which they invariably do with any business, Nike immediately addresses them, so they are unlikely to stick. For example, in the 1990s, Nike came under increased scrutiny for their suppliers' labor practices in Southeast Asia, which included underpaid workers, child labor, and poor and unsafe working conditions. The company responded to this negative PR by establishing greater oversight and transparency, regular inspections of their facilities, a code of conduct for suppliers, and other related measures. Such positive associations were added to much of the public's mind, and they were able to go on enjoying the brand as they had before. That's not to say the company has remained entirely clear of controversy, including in 2020 when it was found that one of Nike's suppliers, Qingdao Taekwang Shoes Co. in China, had been using forced labor, with hundreds of ethnic Uighurs being sent to work there by local authorities. But with all of the positive brand associations out there, this news seemed to go fairly unnoticed.

Another go-to sports brand is the Yankees, extending well beyond the game of baseball itself and leading to its dominance, and $6 billion valuation. The most valuable team in baseball (though Mets fans would bristle at the notion) is careful to build positive associations with their brand that span generations of fans. They elevate their players to near superhero status, making connections between those past and present and creating one large vector stretching across fans' minds. Each new generation of Yankees players stands on the shoulders of those who came before them. Aaron Judge, widely considered the Yankees' best player (winner of the American League MVP in 2022) is an evolution of the star era of the earlier 2000s, with players like Derek Jeter and Mariano Rivera.

This connection is made for fans through the respect the team gives to players of the past, with public rituals like retiring the jerseys and numbers of top players, which turns them into beloved icons. Monument Park, located in Yankee Stadium's center field, acts as a museum to past players, reinforcing their heritage so that it's not lost. When Aaron Judge was anointed the Yankees' captain, the designated jersey (featuring a Nike swoosh, by the way) was given to him with Derek Jeter at his side. The brand is essentially continuous. By never fully breaking with the past, new players continue the brand, just with some new faces. They avoid the *Jeopardy!* problem discussed earlier by continually reinforcing their heritage so it stays in fans' collective memory.

Does this mean that the Yankees can rest on their laurels? Of course not. No brand can. If fans grow mistrustful of leadership—keep in mind, the owner and coaching staff are part of a team's network of associations—and question whether they are truly dedicated to winning or just the money, even a revered brand can suffer damage, resulting in a devaluation. The fact that the Yankees remain the preeminent, most valuable brand in sports, though they haven't won the World Series since 2009 (a date that stands out in our family's memories, as we took our two sons, giddy with excitement, out of school to attend the ticker-tape parade in Lower Manhattan), proves that what matters is not actual superiority but perceived superiority, which is far more important.

As discussed, competitive advantage is limited. Success for a brand does not come from actual or tangible superiority, it comes from perceived superiority—a well-managed, large, positive physical presence in the mind. But perceptions require constant upkeep and nurturing. By pursuing new top players and keeping the former ones alive in their neural networks, the Yankees can create continued salience and remain the instinctive brand preference for millions.

Brands like Nike and the Yankees go beyond product categories and sports teams to become worlds unto themselves, pulling us inside. In the process, they create customers of all ages for life. But you don't need to be Nike or the Yankees to become the go-to choice. By understanding how brands grow in the human brain, you can build your start-up, political candidate, or social cause rapidly—and make an impact sooner than you think. But in order to do so, you must first leave the old rules of conscious, persuasion-based marketing behind and start using a new set of rules that help you harness people's instincts. To become your audience's go-to, you need to build your *Brand Connectome* and grow its presence in their brains until it takes up so much physical space, they reach for your brand on autopilot.

Chapter 2

THE INSTINCT CENTER

INSTINCT RULE: You don't control your choices.
Your Brand Connectome does.

R ound-rimmed metal glasses. A lightning-bolt-shaped scar on a forehead. With these two simple sentences alone, you likely know who and what I'm referring to. If you're even a casual fan, the mesmerizing theme song from multiple movies might be swirling in your head. Maybe you're picturing the books' intricate front covers or the opening scenes. Connections to witchcraft, wizardry, and a wealth of imagination are likely bubbling up. By opening a book, flipping on a screen, visiting a theme park, store, or any of the locations around the UK where the movies were filmed, you can become part of this magical universe. A whole fantastical world unto itself awaits readers, viewers, gamers, and children and adults of all ages.

But this magical universe almost never saw the light of day. *Harry Potter and the Philosopher's Stone* was rejected by more than twelve publishers before being acquired by the London-based Bloomsbury Publishing. When asked why J. K. Rowling's masterpiece had been turned down so many times, the author's first literary agent,

Christopher Little, said it was due to a number of reasons, including its length and setting—the boarding school was thought to be too exclusive for readers. "Over the period of nigh on a year," explained Little, "the book was turned down by more or less every major publishing house in the UK." Rowling trudged on.

Her proposal eventually came across the desk of the chairman of Bloomsbury, who passed the first chapter of the book on to a trusted beta reader—his eight-year-old daughter, Alice. When Alice sat down to read the first chapter, she was sucked into a world she didn't want to leave. When she finished, she immediately asked her father for the rest of the manuscript. Bloomsbury decided to publish the book, but even then, they had no idea of its potential when it was released in 1997. Rowling's editor at Bloomsbury, Barry Cunningham, even suggested Rowling get a part-time job because she would never be able to make a living as an author of young adult books. Suffice it to say, Cunningham was wrong.

An unassuming little kid with a mysterious past in a coming-of-age story with magical, dreamy twists and turns. Fantasy and magic have of course been part of art, literature, and film long before the late 1990s, but Harry Potter caught the public's imagination in a way that has made the brand endure and grow over the past two-and-a-half decades. Ubiquitous, it has become known throughout the world, a franchise worth roughly $40 billion. That value is only expected to grow, not just with the multibillion-dollar franchise's current offerings, but with multiple spin-offs—prequels like *Fantastic Beasts: The Secrets of Dumbledore*, the theatrical sequel *Harry Potter and the Cursed Child*, and 2023's *Hogwarts Legacy* role-playing computer and video game.

Though many books are turned into movies, toys, and franchises, none has ever achieved the level of Harry Potter's success. What is different in this case? How did J. K. Rowling capture the imagination of so many readers, and why does every reader who enters the tale keep coming back time and again? Moreover, how is the franchise able to stay relevant and continue influencing generations of readers? I first read the books to my son when he was a little boy, and I was astounded by how effectively they pulled both of us in, along with hundreds of millions of other children and adults alike.

The same thing had happened with eight-year-old Alice. When Cunningham saw how strongly his daughter connected with the book, he decided to publish it. What he missed was that the adult brain operates the same way as a child's brain when it comes to making connections and associations. That's true of most successful children's properties, from *Sesame Street* to Disney. They are successful because they leverage connections in both the adult brain and the child brain, just on different levels, causing them to be beloved by people of all ages. When it comes down to it, a brain is a brain. We are all human, and our brains generally operate the same way.

Harry Potter was a good story, sure, but that's not why the books were so successful. There have been plenty of other young adult fantasy novels and children's books with strong narratives that build magical worlds and introduce a cast of intriguing characters: Madeleine L'Engle's *A Wrinkle in Time*, J. R. R. Tolkien's *The Hobbit*, C. S. Lewis's *The Lion, the Witch and the Wardrobe*. These are classics, and all of them spawned their own movies, plays, toys, and TV shows— but unlike the first Harry Potter book, none of them sold 120 million copies. *The Hobbit* is at least 20 million copies shy. Meanwhile, *A Wrinkle in Time*, published in 1962, has sold just 10 million. The entirety of the Chronicles of Narnia, of which *The Lion, the Witch and the Wardrobe* is one of seven books, has sold around 100 million copies. All seven of the Harry Potter books together have sold roughly a half billion. Further, when these franchises expanded into film and TV, none of them earned a total of $9.6 billion at the box office, the combined revenue of all thirteen of the Potter and related movies.

Like Potter, these are all great stories. They feature heroes that go through trials and tribulations and come out transformed. They have magic, intrigue, incredible settings. And they are adored by fans the world over. However, their success pales in comparison with Potter's. Something else is clearly going on.

The Potter books' success actually came from Rowling's ability to create a vast, sprawling world that hit more touchpoints in our brains than any of these other authors' books. These touchpoints are the result of connecting Potter's world to every aspect of our everyday lives, as if his world were superimposed on top of ours. Potter's world feels immediately familiar, especially for kids. But the students' parents, classrooms, teachers' lessons, and school sports are all a fantastical mirror image of our own reality. A parallel universe with that of "Muggles"—Potter parlance for us non-witches and non-wizards—emerges, one in which a tree can have emotions, a book can carry on a conversation with you, a portrait is literally alive, people can travel through fireplaces, and the streets of London hide a whole wizarding world if you just know where to look.

Each aspect of Harry Potter's world has a clear corollary in our own but has been elevated to a fantastic level. In *The Lion, the Witch and the Wardrobe*, the reader enters a magical world—one that is nothing like ours—through a wardrobe. In the real world, we don't use wardrobes to travel—we drive a car or ride a bus...or take a train. In Harry Potter, Platform 9 3/4 is our Amtrak platform, a typically dreary, dead zone we're forced to hang around in while we wait to board. But in Potter, there's a secret passageway to access the train that whisks Harry and his friends off to Hogwarts School of Witchcraft and Wizardry. When they arrive, Dumbledore, the headmaster, awaits them, the wise principal we never had but always wanted. The school operates like the ones we attended ourselves, with classes, lunchtime, semesters, vacations, cliques of students, and favorite teachers, but none of us ever took a Defense Against the Dark Arts lesson or met ghosts in the girls' bathroom.

Hogwarts is split up into "houses"—Gryffindor, Hufflepuff, Ravenclaw, and Slytherin—familiar because they're so much like our college fraternities or sororities. But here, "rushing" is out. The Sorting Hat chooses where we go. The sport of choice is Quidditch, which Rowling based on American basketball, complete with goals, refs, and spectators, only it's played in the air on broomsticks. With all four houses competing against one another, the game's pageantry and patriotic pride create a neural connection straight to our Olympics or Super Bowl.

Everything is familiar in Potter's world, but nothing is what it seems. It's a place where anything can happen, but it's anything but obscure or foreign to readers. Every aspect of this sprawling ecosystem is relevant to some part of our lives, connecting directly with ideas, associations, and memories we already have. Harry Potter's success was inevitable—long before the first movie was even made. That's because Rowling created a tremendously salient Harry Potter world that took over people's minds long before it took over the marketplace. It was then a natural step for Heyday Films, Disney executives, candymakers like Jelly Belly, and toy makers like Lego and Mattel to latch on and use the license for everything under the sun.

The most successful brands of any kind take the same approach. They create an all-encompassing world that has outsized salience in the mind. When you enter, you learn that this brand's world has its own rules, a particular set of values, a distinctive setting, certain types of people or characters, sometimes even its own language, like "Patronus" or "*Accio*" in Potter's. Now some could argue Potter is an outlier, impossible to replicate. But the truth is, tremendous wins are within reach in any field when you start understanding what made the book such an unbridled success. Recognize the pattern and you can incorporate the same approach in building your business, personal brand, or college application.

Google followed a similar pattern when creating their many offices and campuses, both domestic and international. Instead of just thinking about functionality, Google's campuses are designed for maximum engagement. The tech giant's modern architectural designs, colorful decor, Tinkertoy-like furniture, and endless comfy seating options are just the beginning. Google also provides a complete array of elements to engage employees on aspects of their personal lives: kitchens full of healthy food, dry cleaners, treadmills, Razor scooters to travel between buildings, and even sleeping pods.

This environment is an all-encompassing, colorful world, a catalyst for work, play, collaboration, and innovation. Add their notorious intramural software development competitions (Google's answer to Quidditch), health consultations, stress-relieving massages, and the "Googley" personality traits they look for in recruiting employees, and you have an immersive world that people clamor to get into. Consistently ranked as one of the best places to work, they receive upward of three million job applicants per year.

In the past, HR and business leaders bracketed these elements as "company culture," but in an era where employee retention is a growing challenge, it's much more useful for companies to think about creating an *immersive brand world*. Just like Potter's, you want to develop a world that automatically draws people in by visually communicating its brand identity and engaging them on as many multidimensional levels as possible. It all comes down to following the instinct model—creating elements in your brand that connect to familiar pathways in the mind—and touching multiple aspects of people's lives. The more touchpoints the better. Such ubiquity is the result of a myriad of connections in the physical brain, enhancing the salience, relevance, and clarity of a brand. For your brand to be an unbridled success, it has to have so many connections to people's lives that it mushrooms in their minds. Simply stated, the only way to grow your brand financially out in the marketplace is to first have it grow in people's minds, sprouting from a tiny seed into a giant sequoia growing your Brand Connectome.

THE BRAND CONNECTOME

A connectome is essentially a map of all the neural pathways and connections in the human brain. First developed in 2005, the idea, and term itself, was inspired by scientists' attempts to build a human genome, a sequencing of the human genetic code. In 2009, the National Institutes of Health funded a five-year program called the Human Connectome Project to "map" the human connectome.

The project's goal was to help scientists understand how we make decisions. This mapping provides a complex, and colorful, look into how our brains operate, unlike any before, and helps scientists research and treat health issues such as stroke, depression, and attention disorders.

As it turns out, within the human connectome, every brand, idea, and concept has its *own* network of associations and memories. These cumulative associations and memories, both positive and negative, become inseparable from the brand over time, forming a physical network of neural pathways that I coined the Brand Connectome, and introduced to the public in an article I wrote with Wharton professor Michael Platt. The human connectome—consisting of all the brain's wiring—is the command control center of the mind, dictating who we are and our points of view. The Brand Connectome is the command control center for the brand decisions we make on autopilot every day, whether in the supermarket, online, or in the voting booth.

Every brand has its own connectome. Within the larger human connectome, you can pull out any brand—whether a political candidate, an idea, a country, or a place to go on vacation—and look at its pattern of associations and memories in our mind. These memories and associations live on huge interlocking vectors in our brains. When taken together, they dictate our instinctive behavior. But understanding what resides inside the Brand Connectome is where it really gets interesting. The associations that lie on these pathways are the key to uncovering why some people choose Coke and others Pepsi, some vote Republican and others Democratic or Independent, and certain people run to get vaccinated while others opt out.

Some of the cumulative associations and memories in these physical networks go as far back as childhood. As the neural pathways connect one memory to the next, a complex web of interconnected memories related to a brand forms in your brain. It's these multidimensional associations and memories—imagery, symbols, experiences, and impressions—that, taken as a whole, unconsciously influence your choices. The more positive associations you make with a particular brand, the more neural pathways you form, growing the brand's connectome. The biggest brands, like Apple, McDonald's, or Google, are those with the most robust Brand Connectomes in our gray matter. That's why when most people go to buy tissues, they automatically choose Kleenex, or pick up Band-Aids for a cut, Clorox for stains in white garments, and Drano for a clogged sink. Many don't even realize these are brand names, not the generic term for the products themselves (tissues, bandages, bleach, and drain cleaner). They just reach.

Just as every person, place, or thing can be seen as a brand, each has its own Brand Connectome, from consumer products like Pepsi and Coke to B2B companies like Morgan Stanley or Goldman Sachs, from your corner deli to political candidates, and from causes like stopping climate change to entertainment franchises like Harry Potter. Some Brand Connectomes are larger and more positive than others, creating salience and connection. Those that are smaller or negative have little to no impact on decision-making and don't get chosen. The most effective brands physically take up the most space in our heads. As in a game of Monopoly, whoever owns the most real estate in the brain and has the largest physical footprint wins.

Over time, we unconsciously absorb information about certain brands, companies, and people. Every memorable sight, taste, and smell and every person, place, and idea connected with them become *glued* to their Brand Connectome in our brains. Think of a brand like Pepsi or Coke as the central node of the neural network. These impressions accumulate, sprouting from that node into an entire ecosystem of branch-like associations. Then we make split-second decisions in the moment based on those accumulated impressions. The long and short of it is simple: You don't control your choices. Your Brand Connectome does.

Once a brand is launched, it takes on a life of its own inside consumers' memories—organically growing or shrinking depending on the rise and decline of positive and negative associations.

The Brand Connectome forms from the associations that the consumer makes with the brand. If your mother used Prego tomato sauce while you were growing up, the idea of your mom will be physically connected to Prego in your brain, along with the chicken parmigiana, mozzarella pizza bites, and other favorite dishes she made with it. If your favorite uncle took you to Carvel after school every Friday, that treasured experience and the distinctive swirl created by the soft-serve machine will be a physical part of your Carvel Connectome, along with any other related associations.

The goal, therefore, is to increase the size of your Brand Connectome by continuously adding positive associations. Like much of my philosophy behind the power of instinct, the effectiveness and long-term success of a connectome comes down to growth. When we hear about a new brand from someone we respect (a coach, role model, or admired friend), see a brand's ad in a venue that's part of our lifestyle or rituals (think the Gatorade logo at your local stadium), or are exposed to a point of view that's different from our own, our brains grow. Without such growth, we can become narrow-minded and stuck in our ways. In that sense, a growing brain is a thriving brain, which leads to healthier, more broad-minded perspectives and behaviors.

Picture a seed. Now, this seed can stand in for any type of brand: a company, industry, or product; a restaurant, shop, or café; a political candidate, party, or cause; a diet, exercise routine, or mindfulness practice; a CEO, athlete, or musician; a piece of art, music, or literature—pretty much anything you can think of. This seed is planted in your mind the first time you are exposed to it. Your brain has to form new neural pathways that stretch out across its terrain. Like the nutrients in soil, sun, and water, the more associations you add to a connectome, the more its roots spread and its branches sprout. In time, or even quickly, that connectome grows and, if done right, becomes a whole ecosystem of positive associations for a brand. When your tree covers more of your audience's brain and connects with many familiar touchpoints in people's lives, it creates true mind share.

MIND SHARE

Mind share is a term marketers have thrown around since the Stone Age. One standard definition is the relative public awareness of a particular phenomenon. Others define it as "the attempt to make a company, brand or product the first one that comes to mind when a customer thinks of a particular market." Until now, though, no one understood what mind share really was, how to measure it, or the process to achieve it. Making a brand the first one to come to people's minds with consistency always seemed like a conceptual desire, something that might forever remain out of reach.

Turns out, mind share is not conceptual at all, it's physical. Byron Sharp and Jenni Romaniuk of the Ehrenberg-Bass Institute describe mind share, what they call Brand Salience, as "the propensity of the brand to be noticed or come to mind in buying situations." But until now, no one really understood what lies beneath salience. Turns out, for a brand to have salience (to be the first a consumer thinks of), it must have the most robust Brand Connectome in the category in which it competes; again, it's the *size* of these neural networks that matters most. When a brand's physical footprint is so large that it eclipses the Brand Connectomes of competitors, it dominates the memories of the audience to the point that it becomes the first thing they ask for or reach for. It becomes their go-to, automatic choice. Salience is the outcome—the Brand Connectome is the underlying command control center you must manage to influence this critical metric.

Companies have long used awareness of their brand relative to that of competitors as a proxy for mind share, a one-dimensional view. It's not enough for a brand to be well known or well advertised—it needs to have a myriad of diverse associations. Salience is the modern evolution of mind share, and a more useful way to think about brand building. Create the largest (most salient), most positive, and distinctive connectome you possibly can, and you will become the go-to choice in your category.

Take M&M's, for example. Its connectome is enormous, and it has salience on par with Harry Potter. The company has created an M&M's universe in its own right, one that has touched count-less aspects of people's lives since the product's first release in 1941. However, its endurance should come as something of a sur-prise: an artificially colored, artificially flavored, candy-coated hunk of milk chocolate in an era of raw cacao, whole foods, and nutri-tious snacks. Think about it—even Cookie Monster has gone health conscious. Looking at current cultural trends, M&M's sales should be in decline. Instead, in 2021, it was a $990 million brand, grow-ing at 7.7 percent per year, all thanks to its ever-evolving Brand Connectome.

Forrest Mars came up with the idea for M&M's in 1930, inspired by a favorite snack of Spanish Civil War soldiers. Moving from fox-hole to foxhole throughout the countryside, soldiers often brought along small pieces of chocolate featuring a hard candy shell. They were especially convenient as they didn't melt easily, a fact Mars would later use in the famous M&M's tagline "Melts in your mouth, not in your hand." A somewhat similar candy existed at the time in England, but Mars secured a patent for a hard-coating chocolate shell process in March 1941, and production started soon after. The seed of M&M's Brand Connectome had been planted.

Though there were some innovations, like the creation of peanut M&M's in 1954, the brand continued on without much change until the 1980s, when it started making headway in the global market. That decade also saw the introduction of Christmas M&M's, the im-petus for the many holiday versions of the candy that would become a staple of the brand for years to come. They even made their way to space, as they were included on NASA's space shuttle missions in the 1980s by special request of the crew. By then, the seed had sprouted, and the connectome was growing. But it wouldn't be until the '90s that the connectome would be in full bloom.

The best-selling chocolate candy brand in the United States, M&M's has enduring revenue and market share that are only par-tially due to its candy-coated products; in fact, the product itself is quite flawed for twenty-first-century food trends. But careful management and continuous nurturing of its large and ever-expanding Brand Connectome has enabled it to stay relevant, maintain salience, and grow revenue for decades. Though the company introduced two M&M's characters in the 1950s, they were not central to the company's marketing until the '90s, when the idea was expanded to create a whole cast. The distinct white *m* on each candy—originally introduced in black in 1950, and then updated to white in 1954—gave the candy its long-standing, recognizable logo, but the characters, featured on packaging and in commercials, brought the little hard-shell candy to life.

In a strategy more representative of an entertainment company than consumer packaged goods, each character has been developed to have its own personality, its own foibles, its own back story. Undeniably part of the M&M's connectome, the characters humanized the brand in a way that a static, lifeless piece of candy never could have. Many brands have mascots. Kellogg's Frosted Flakes has Tony the Tiger, introduced in 1952. Energizer has their hyperactive bunny, who's been "going and going" for over thirty-five years. But neither of these longtime mascots, nor many others, were developed as fully and with as many human traits as the M&M's characters. The controversy that erupted over the M&M's "spokescandies" in 2023, after they received a facelift, further shows how viscerally people felt about these characters and the instinctive connection they had come to have with them.

Still, M&M's characters are far from the only piece of the puzzle when it comes to the M&M's connectome. M&M's did what many brands fail to do—it kept expanding its Brand Connectome so it would stay relevant in a world that was becoming healthier. In the 1990s to the 2000s, M&M's started to position itself as less of a candy and more of a full-on snack. They cleverly came out with a whole range of innovations that helped cultivate the "snack" side of the brand, such as peanut butter M&M's and pretzel M&M's. This added a type of permissibility association the brand didn't previously have—there was real food value in there, not just candy and the occasional peanut. Instead of promoting the candy exterior, the marketing focus shifted to what was inside the shell: smooth peanut butter, a crunchy pretzel. A brilliant package graphic featured the orange M&M going through an X-ray machine revealing a pretzel underneath its candy coating, immediately conveying the candy's food value and the company's ingredient transparency.

Related to permissibility, the company created recipes and accessories, like measuring spoons and mixing bowls, that linked M&M's to baking. This worked on two levels: this was real food, not "just a piece of candy," but it also wired people's brains to connect M&M's with a wholesome activity, often enjoyed between a parent and child, or grandparent and grandkids. They roll out the dough, throw the M&M's in, watch the cookies rise in the oven, and then after letting them cool on the rack, snack away together. Of course, M&M's doesn't need to tell you any of this—your brain already has a whole host of positive associations connected to baking, so it's piggybacking on an existing network. Now when you see a package of M&M's Baking Bits, there's that physical connection in your brain that associates the brand with the positive feelings of baking with Grandma. You don't think of M&M's as artificially colored or processed because wholesome associations dominate your connectome. It's easy to see why our instinctive behavior is to reach for that package of M&M's over another snack: it's innocent indulgence.

M&M's branches have continued spreading, growing in areas that once probably seemed unlikely, but that we now take for granted. Take sports teams. You can go online and buy M&M's that are branded with your favorite football or baseball team logo, and you can pick up some themed apparel while you're there. What does candy really have to do with baseball? Not a whole lot per se, but baseball is a beloved American tradition, and the Red Sox or Yankees fan in your life will be happy to receive a bag of branded M&M's sporting the team's signature colors. If that bag lands in your lap, you will start associating the brand with your favorite team as well. And as many of you may know, some sports fans are rabid. There's a tremendous passion for one's home team. Some of the same passion you have for the Sox, or whoever, is then unknowingly transferred over. Again, this is all physical, rewiring your brain and affecting your instinctive brand preferences.

And the connections carry on: when the characters appear dressed in the garb of the Statue of Liberty or done up like a Buckingham Palace guard, they connect with viewers' sense of national pride. Or when Ms. Green is shown as a Marilyn Monroe figure in the famous shot of her dress floating up on the city sidewalk, or when she and her other "spokescandies" are pictured imitating the cover of the Beatles' multiplatinum-selling *Abbey Road*, these new associations are made. Our favorite movie stars, rock stars, actors—they're all added to that big, bold M&M's Brand Connectome. M&M's also offers a variety of celebratory package designs and product colors tailored to the different seasons and, as mentioned, holidays—red and green for winter; red, white, and blue for the Fourth of July; and more.

By connecting the brand to all of these familiar beloved aspects of our lives, positive associations are conferred back on M&M's. Even as you've read this section of the chapter, it's been at work. Maybe you never saw an M&M dressed up as a Beatle, but now, in your brain, there's a pathway between the Beatles and M&M's. There's one between the brand and Marilyn Monroe too. And between M&M's and fresh-baked cookies.

As the brand extends its reach, the brain now makes a connection between those two points. And new neural pathways are being laid that are slowly extending M&M's Brand Connectome so it becomes larger, larger, and larger still. It's like a forced connecting of the dots forming those new interconnected pathways. Now instead of having one association—"it's just a candy"—it has many more, thousands even, an explosion of connections: a gigantic, dominating ecosystem. As a result, these associations create a virtual "buffer of goodness" around the artificially colored candy, elevating its stature and salience to an iconic, go-to snack—even in the face of this health-conscious cultural wave. And all these diversified touch-points into our lives taken together—from baking and patriotism to beloved celebrities and sports teams—make M&M's a permissible, instinctively preferred choice.

But what if you're a small company or start-up? You don't need to be a brand the size of M&M's to create instinctive choice. Even if you're still getting your sea legs, you can build a Brand Connectome that rivals any of the big players in your category. Start by monitoring your established competitors' connectomes. By studying the associations people have with your competitors, you can understand their vulnerabilities. This allows you to figure out your angle on how to position your business, cause, or idea.

In many ways, a small brand just starting out has an advantage as it can be deliberate about defining its connectome. If you consciously develop your brand's connectome from inception, you can better track its growth and manage its trajectory. Further, unlike legacy brands that have connectomes full of years of cumulative associations, both positive and negative, yours is a clean slate. This means you can be more precise about which marketing and communications will achieve your desired goal.

When done right, it's almost as if the brain becomes consumed with this overwhelming quantity of associations, taking up so much space that the brand becomes the instinctive choice. Therefore, to gain true mind share and get people to make the decision you want, you must grow your connectome in their brains, sprouting and tending new branches and roots, growing those neural pathways. I call this process *Brain Branching*®.

BRAIN BRANCHING

The brain is a learning machine. When the brain learns something new and meaningful about a brand, those new associations get added to existing dendrites, or branches. But when the branches fill up, that new information has no place to go. So new branches must sprout to hold those additional associations, a process of dendritic arborization. Like a plant sprouting new leaves, Brain Branching signifies a brand's health—it means the brand is alive, adding new memories and associations, evolving and growing. If an abundance of associations is added, the brand owns more of the brain's memory structure, causing the brand to become the instinctive preference.

For example, most everyone knows about the "incumbency advantage," in which political incumbents are more likely to win reelection than their opponents. This trend has held in US presidential elections going back to George Washington's reelection in 1792. The advantage can also be found throughout Congress, including in the 2020 election, where 93 percent of incumbents won their respective races. Similarly, between 1964 and 2022, the US House reelection rate averaged 93 percent; the US Senate, 83 percent. These stats likely come as no surprise. Incumbents receive years of exposure during their time in office, building their public reputation. This repeated exposure—the equivalent of millions in free advertising—is certainly one reason incumbents are hard to beat. But it's not the only reason.

During their time in office, presidents take on greater stature and importance, the result of, once again, positive associations. We regularly see them interacting with global leaders at the highest possible level, speaking at the UN, and signing bills in the Oval Office. During their State of the Union address, they stand in front of Congress in the House chamber of the US Capitol building, massive black-and-white marble columns behind them, the American flag hanging down in reverence, gold fasces on either side. These symbols have intrinsic associations of stability, democracy, perseverance, and endurance—in fact, they are some of the most aspirational symbols we have. When sitting presidents appear with these symbols, implicit associations are conferred upon them. Because a brand is known by the associations it keeps, these associations elevate the importance and respect we have for incumbents. It's as if our mind puts them on a pedestal.

The same goes for members of Congress. Seeing them give a speech from behind the dais, meet with community, state, and national leaders, appear at decisive hearings—all of these associations continue to create new physical connections in our minds. The more we see them in these positions of power, and in a positive light, the more these branches are going to spread. Connotations of strength, leadership, and importance are all being physically transplanted into our brains. No wonder incumbents are so difficult to beat. The only time they are likely to lose an election is if their connectome has taken on a large amount of negative, as compared with positive, associations.

The more positive touchpoints, the more elevated the audience's perceptions of a candidate will become. That's why when President Obama was running for his second term, he appeared on shows like *The View* and *Jimmy Kimmel Live!* Meanwhile, his wife, Michelle, gave out the Best Picture award at the Oscars in 2013, via video. Obama's team must have intuitively known that these additional touchpoints would broaden the relevance of Obama's connectome beyond government into popular culture—more branches sprouting off. It's hard to top. As the branches splinter out, it's almost as if they take over the mind, removing the old, bringing in the new, sheltering the connectome from harm (or from your opponent's attacks). But incumbents are not the only individuals who can succeed by growing a large, robust connectome. The same can happen with any personal brand. And anyone who wants to build their personal brand can learn a lot from studying the rise of the GOAT.

Before Gwyneth Paltrow's goop, Chip and Joanna Gaines's Magnolia, or Jessica Alba's the Honest Company, there was Oprah. Oprah Winfrey is arguably the first celebrity to have extended her individual brand into a true lifestyle brand. Getting her start as an evening news coanchor on a local Nashville station, Oprah had a charismatic, conversational style that immediately caught audiences' attention. It was no surprise *The Oprah Winfrey Show*, which hit the air in 1986, quickly replaced Phil Donahue's as the number-one syndicated daytime talk show.

The reason is simple. To the viewers, Oprah's intimate style felt like a friend coming over for a chat in their living room. She was someone they could trust, and who would confide in them in return. She was earnest about her personal struggles with weight loss, willing to talk about the sexual abuse she suffered as a child, and unafraid to speak her mind on a host of topics. In viewers' minds, Oprah was not just a talk show host or a celebrity, but a confidante. By positively exposing the human brain to the same person over and over again, growing the connectome in the process, viewers began to feel an almost familial connection to Oprah. And in a way, Oprah *literally* became part of them as she entered into their brains' memory structure.

Though that explains Oprah's initial rise, that's not what led to her extraordinary success. Just like Harry Potter and M&M's, she diversified her brand beyond entertainment to many other aspects of our lives. This caused her connectome to grow not just in viewers' minds, but in the general public's. She became a spokesperson for WW (formerly Weight Watchers); established a world-renowned book club; founded the Oprah Winfrey Charitable Foundation, which has donated $400 million to different causes; created a magazine; and as if one TV show wasn't enough, started a whole television network. People took her nutrition suggestions, recipes, and dieting tips as gospel. Her book club exposed us to the best and brightest authors. With the "Oprah" stamp of approval, a book could witness an average sales increase of 420 percent one week after it appeared on her show.

Oprah's branches extend in so many directions, they are hard to count, each one hitting another touchpoint in our lives. Her brand is multidimensional, physically dominating our neural pathways. You may be a loyal viewer or have never watched a full episode of the show, you may be fifteen or ninety-five, you may live in the US or Afghanistan—it doesn't matter. Oprah's connectome is so encompassing, she is known throughout the world. She was, and remains, both aspirational and inspirational, a woman who started with little and by the early 2000s was the first Black female billionaire and the leader of a mega-media empire. But somehow, she still feels like she's one of us. It's no wonder that in a poll conducted by *PBS News-Hour*, NPR, and Marist, leading up to the 2020 US presidential election, half of registered voters said they would vote for Oprah if she were running against the incumbent. If she had run, who knows? With a connectome as robust and multidimensional as hers, it might just have been enough to thwart the incumbency advantage.

In Oprah, it's possible to see how sowing seeds across the whole field, not just planting in one spot, allows a brand to branch out across the brain. The same goes for an incumbent hitting multiple touchpoints in the minds of the public. Candidates who have built their connectome over years have a tremendous advantage, while newer players have to scramble to break in and try to establish their brand quickly. Celebrities like Oprah are so incredibly successful because they too have been able to grow undeniably positive, large connectomes. But Oprah started just like everyone else—as a seed that no one knew. That's the remarkable thing about Brain Branching in action. Anyone can make it happen as long as you follow the rules. Again, it's all about making connections. To thrive, you must continue growing, branching your brand out in the public's mind. By physically layering associations across the brain, you create unbelievable salience, becoming the go-to no matter how crowded the field may be.

It all starts with that first seed—whether the opening chapter of a book, the hard coating of a chocolate shell, a political campaign, or a job at a local TV station. At the start of this chapter, I wrote the only way to grow your brand financially out in the marketplace is to first have it grow in the public's mind, sprouting from a tiny seed into a giant sequoia. But there's a somewhat lesser-known tree, at least for Western audiences, that may be a better analogy than a sequoia. Thimmamma Marrimanu—a banyan tree more than 550 years old in southeast India that holds religious significance for Buddhists, Hindus, and practitioners of other Eastern religions—features the world's largest canopy, which spreads out across more than five acres.

When viewed from above, the tree's massive canopy dominates the landscape, a symbol of persistence, life, and growth in an otherwise dry, arid land. The branches spread out in all directions, intertwining with each other to create its own forest, despite being just one lone tree. Underneath, its vast network of roots spreads throughout the soil. This tree has not persisted on its own—the local forest department carefully nurtures it, encouraging young roots to spread and larger roots to continue growing. Your Brand Connectome can grow and prosper like Thimmamma Marrimanu, but you have to keep adding water, soil, and nutrients. If you don't, your brand will never reach its full potential.

Chapter 3

THE SHORTCUT TO INSTINCTIVE CHOICE

INSTINCT RULE: You can't force people to buy your brand, but you can change their instinctive behavior.

n entire product line of cheese—in all types, shapes, and sizes—and you would be hard pressed to find a single cow on any of them.

In the mid-'90s, a major cheese company seemed to be operating on an unstated principle: we will avoid cows, dairy farms, and barns on all packaging and advertising. Instead of focusing on where their cheese came from, they marketed convenience with a major push into pre-shredded cheese, and a series of product innovations that took the market by storm. Shredded cheese made mealtime, and even snack time, easier, simpler, and of course, faster for busy parents across America. Who has the time to get out the grater and shred a block of cheese when the kids are clamoring for nachos?

The company bagged up shredded cheese in all manner of customized variations—mozzarella for pizza night, a signature cheese blend for tacos, pepper jack for a kick to your eggs in the morning—and sold millions of units. But by focusing virtually all their advertising and promotional efforts on these precut shreds and resealable plastic bags, new unintended associations slowly accumulated in consumers' minds, unbeknownst to the heads of the company. Over time, these associations turned into implicit barriers: this pre-shredded, pre-bagged product was not real cheese at all, but some highly processed, unnatural, plastic-filled concoction. The brand had been losing market share ever since.

Maybe they refused to place cows on their packaging because they associated them with the smell of manure, or dirtiness, or even global warming (cows are, after all, the number-one agricultural source of greenhouse gas emissions into our atmosphere). Or maybe they felt the company needed to stay away from what they considered generic dairy iconography. Unfortunately, the decision by one of the largest cheese companies in the world to not use "source imagery"—visuals of where your food originates—left a giant opening.

Meanwhile, almost every private and store label manufacturer—from Aldi (Happy Farms) and Safeway (Lucerne Dairy Farms) to Kroger—came out with their own cheese brands, placing red-and-white dairy barns, silver silos, and Holstein cows all over their packaging. These brands managed to take a significant chunk of market share away from the long-standing company. Though consumers originally felt the brand's product was superior to the store label varieties, and were willing to pay the price differential, they started believing these store-brand cheeses were just as good, maybe even better. Still, no cows.

Ask consumers what images of cheese they find most appealing—which ones they like best—and they will point to the stretchy topping on a piece of pizza, gooey slices bursting out the sides of a burger, or a forkful of melted deliciousness in the perfect bite of lasagna. But ask the same consumers what *superior* cheese looks like and the images stored in their minds are completely different. Visuals of cheese wheels and wedges universally come to mind, along with cows, dairy farms, and grassy fields under bright blue skies. Even the locations are the same—rural Wisconsin, pastoral Vermont, and other places close to the source of cheese, all of which they equate with high quality.

With no mandate restricting them, private label brands jumped into source imagery with both feet. As positive associations of dairies, cows, and real cheese were added to the Brand Connectome of store-brand cheeses, a myriad of neural pathways sprouted. Little by little, store and private-label cheese connectomes became physically larger—as quality and expertise associations increased, their salience in the mind grew. Private-label cheese became consumers' instinctive go-to choice, while the company's connectome became laden with negative associations and less salient. It's hard to believe this could happen. The company was one of the first to sell cheese to the masses in the US; its dairy expertise is irrefutable. But when it comes to the unconscious mind, reality doesn't matter—it's all about perception and the resulting associations.

Consumers don't need advertising to tell them what these images mean, or that a particular brand of cheese is more wholesome, natural, and authentic. American culture has already done that work for them. The associations have been ingrained in our memories over our lifetimes. By associating itself with dairy farms and cheese wheels and wedges—which feel authentic and close to the source of real dairy, placing them on a pedestal in our minds—a brand, whether well established or new to the market, can piggyback on those connections. These are not fleeting emotions. Rather, the brand is tapping into implicit associations already written into our neural pathways. This is the path of least resistance—piggybacking on what is already in the mind. Importantly, the emotional connection we feel with a brand or product is an *outcome* of all these positive associations, not an input.

Since the mid-2000s, psychologists such as Daniel Kahneman have opened our eyes to the irrational nature of decision-making.

In Kahneman's case, *Thinking, Fast and Slow* went mainstream, providing the public with a new understanding of behavioral science. The entire marketing and advertising industry jumped on the bandwagon, but they jumped to the wrong conclusion. Since people make decisions irrationally, they reasoned, we need to communicate *emotionally* to them.

But emotional connection doesn't work that way, and this concept has remained one of the most persistently misunderstood aspects of marketing. There is no such thing as brand love. A bond is not created by overtly expressing an emotion, and it has nothing to do with messages that are humorous, wistful, or sentimental, no matter how clever. Emotions are fleeting—laugh at something and then the feeling is gone—they don't seep into people's memory structure. Instead, you have to tap into existing associations that people already hold in their minds and link them with your brand—that's what creates emotional connection.

The company did ultimately start using imagery of wedges and wheels of cheese and prominently featuring the words "Natural Cheese" across their packaging. Though this approach helped pull back in some customers that had been lost to the private labels, the company's market share never quite returned to their highest levels. What they should have done throughout their transition to emphasizing "convenience" was incorporate the dairy farm and superior cheese imagery as well. For example, they might have depicted a master cheese maker carving a piece of cheese off the wheel, showing where those shreds of cheese actually came from. If these images and ideas had been presented together, they would have communicated "natural" and "convenient" simultaneously, an effective layering of multiple messages that could have expanded salience.

Contrary to popular opinion in the industry, emotion just doesn't work. You can't force people to love your brand, just like you can't force someone to love you. And it's not just love—any overtly emotional ad will fall flat if it doesn't create lasting positive associations.

That includes humor. When done right, humor can be a strong way to build your brand and cause it to seep into memory structure. But ad agencies often prioritize getting a laugh over building salience. This results in ads where humor overwhelms the brand and its benefits. Let's take the 2023 Super Bowl. Quiznos spent millions to create and run their "Spongmonkeys" ad, featuring little furry creatures singing about the sandwich shops' subs. Though the ad generated some chuckles, it failed to drive business. The same happened with Skittles that year. Their "Skittlepox" ad showed Skittles lovers contracting a contagious disease in which the multicolored candies appeared all over their faces (and are even eaten off of them). But because the ad didn't convey Skittles' great taste or the joy of the candy, it wasn't worth the spend. When humor or silliness overtakes the story, nothing meaningful seeps in about the brand and its actual benefits.

But if you understand how the Brand Connectome and positive associations drive choices, you can get people to change their behavior instinctively, so they choose your brand over and over again in any field. When you connect your brand with ideas your audience cares about, only then do you break into their instinctive brain. In the case of cheese, consumers increasingly care about natural over processed food and sourcing that is fresh off the farm versus out of the factory. That doesn't mean they consciously think about these aspects when they go to pick out a nice Roquefort at the supermarket; these associations are stored in their memory. And as discussed, to drive growth in the marketplace, you have to grow the presence of these associations in the customer's unconscious mind. To do that, you need *Growth Triggers®*.

GROWTH TRIGGERS

Growth Triggers are succinct codes or cues packed with a slew of positive associations. Concise shortcuts, they telegraph these positive associations and rich meaning using any of our five senses.

These supercharged images, words, sounds, smells, and even textures trigger the memories, impressions, and good feelings that already exist in our minds. Like a Trojan horse, they can then sneak new ideas into our minds undetected because they rely on something familiar to us. Once inside our heads, they explode with positive associations and meaning, latching on to different parts of the brain and expanding their reach across its terrain. Growth Triggers can be used in communication, customer experience, and products to build more successful innovations.

In effect, Growth Triggers need no explanation. That's why they're so efficient from an advertising and communication standpoint. The cows, dairy farms, and wheels and wedges related to the cheese category are perfect examples—they have so many positive associations and such elevated status in our brain, we are drawn to them instinctively. They are also universal across consumers. If a cue is only effective with a small slice of the audience or a particular group of people, then it's not a Growth Trigger at all.

By forming a connection between your brand and these cues, you can rapidly grow your connectome's physical footprint in your target's brain. Emotion, however, fails to do that. Heartfelt or humorous messages, no matter how clever, don't create a strong bond with consumers because they are fleeting. And they don't stick in people's memories. Emotional connection doesn't actually occur by expressing emotion. It only happens when the Growth Triggers a brand uses are a match with the ideas that already exist in your target audience's mind.

As you may recall from the Introduction, when I finally persuaded my boss at Johnson & Johnson to put dads in a Johnson's baby shampoo ad, I found my first supercharged cue. Dad tenderly caring for a newborn communicated a host of positive associations, including the strong, sensitive father, and Mom finally getting a break. Such cues are essential to gluing positive associations to your brand, idea, cause, or product. So though it might seem counterintuitive, the key to creating emotional connection is not to *express* emotion but rather to use familiar cues packed with positive associations that the brain already understands.

A limited number of fundamental cues exist for every category and brand. That means for your brand to grow, you want to own the category's Growth Triggers, not just the ones specific to your brand. Lose these important markers, and you lose the category. With the major multinational cheese brand, the most powerful cues and codes in the category were wholesome, natural, close-to-the-source dairy imagery, many of which they had stopped leveraging. It's no wonder private and store labels were making inroads. When a consumer sees a brand with these cues, there is a match—a lightbulb moment—between what the brand stands for and what the shopper already has in their brain. It's like two pieces of a puzzle coming together, interlocking with one another. Instinct takes over. No need for a lot of advertising spending. No coupons necessary. The package design alone does the work.

But Growth Triggers apply to much more than visual packaging. A variety of sensory cues can supercharge every touchpoint with your audience: written communication, social media, advertising, live events, even a CEO's speech or an earnings call—any point of contact is an opportunity. Look for creative ways to leverage Growth Triggers: Why do you think Laughing Cow cheese comes in a wheel, made up of individual wedges?

GROWTH TRIGGERS ALREADY EXIST IN OUR MINDS

Growth Triggers already exist. They're out there—you just need to find them. Many are embedded in specific categories, and once you understand what you're looking for, you will start seeing them everywhere. Take financial services. The introduction of online trading, the birth of fintech, and the ever-changing markets continue to drive growth every year. According to Investopedia, the end of 2021 saw the financial services market reach $22.5 trillion, a growth rate of 9.9 percent from the previous year. Today, the financial services sector makes up 20 to 25 percent of the world economy. New players are emerging all the time just to get a slice of the ever-growing pie.

Robinhood is one of them. Started in 2015, the company is at the forefront of commission-free trading of stocks, ETFs, and crypto-currencies, all via a mobile app. The mission of the company is "to democratize finance for all"—and they have branding to match. Their logo is a simple, abstract green feather, like the one said to have adorned the folk hero's hat. Robin Hood, known to most everyone as a fighter of tyranny who steals from the rich and gives to the poor, is invoked in this image. The feather summons the idea of enabling access to wealth for anyone.

The feather is so effective because it's just a snippet—an incredibly condensed, succinct cue—as the best Growth Triggers are. The company doesn't need Robin Hood's hat; the feather is enough. A snippet of a recognizable visual allows our brain to complete the rest of the picture and make Robinhood's desired connections. This activity is fun for the brain. People's minds seek to fill in the blanks, to make the associations on their own. By giving people a little piece of the puzzle that their brains solve, it's as if they and the company are in cahoots, working together to create the full meaning. The company did not create the meaning or the positive associations—popular culture had already done that work for them. Well-known folklore memorialized Robin Hood in at least ninety books going back to the nineteenth century. More than twenty movies about the storied outlaw who steals from the rich and gives to the poor have been produced, with Hood played by everyone from Errol Flynn in 1938 to Russell Crowe in 2010.

Another example can be found in Heinz ketchup. Though ubiquitous, over time the condiment became associated with highly processed, manufactured food while consumers were becoming more health conscious about their eating choices. Natural was in; processed was out. In response, Heinz aimed to remove the growing negative associations. How'd they do this? By reminding consumers of the ketchup's source: bright red, juicy, fresh tomatoes.

The marvelously creative "Slices" ad featured the famous Heinz ketchup glass bottle, sliced up like a tomato, with a sprig of a green stem in place of the bottle's typical white cap. The image was emphasized with the tagline "No one grows ketchup like Heinz." The bottle, the tomato, and the tagline—each one a Growth Trigger of its own—called upon positive associations of fresh, juicy red tomatoes, like picking the summer's first from your garden, right off the vine.

When consumers saw this image, it immediately clicked, changing the perception of Heinz ketchup from a highly processed, manufactured condiment to a natural food in a nanosecond. The image piggybacked on viewers' preexisting neural pathways in which sliced, ripe tomatoes have overwhelmingly positive associations. If that wasn't enough, the tagline further emphasized the concept— Heinz ketchup is not *manufactured*, it is *grown*. Just like Robinhood, Heinz did not create these associations. They were already out there in people's minds.

And Growth Triggers are not just reserved for messaging. They work exactly the same way in product innovation. It's well established that nine out of ten new products fail, a stat that every marketer and business leader knows. One of the best ways to flip that stat around and launch consistently successful new products is to harness consumer behavior that already exists. A great example is Kellogg's Special K Red Berries, launched in April of 2001. It was a game changer. The cereal was so successful, Kellogg's had to initially ask retailers *not* to promote the product because the company was unable to produce enough of the cereal to meet growing demand. According to the *Wall Street Journal*, in 2002, Kellogg beat General Mills out for the number-one spot in the US cereal business.

Why did this product innovation work so well? Special K looked to existing human behavior. Slicing fresh fruit on top of cereal is a frequent morning ritual among millions of people. But going to the store and buying fresh strawberries is not always convenient. And they're a perishable item—you cut up a few one morning, throw the package in the fruit drawer in the fridge, and by the time you remember they've been hanging out in there, they've begun to mold.

Further, when you're in a rush in the morning, heading out the door on your way to work, you don't necessarily feel like you have the time to chop up the perfect strawberry slices. Sure, freeze-dried is not as good as the real thing, but through all the positive associations, it becomes a close second. Keeping a box in the cupboard for a quick, healthy breakfast becomes a no-brainer.

HOW TO FIND GROWTH TRIGGERS

Stimuli is the gateway to emotional connection, so having the right stimuli is everything in uncovering useful codes and cues. To find the right Growth Triggers, you want to consider stimuli that affect at least one of the five senses. If the customer can see it, hear it, touch it, taste it, or smell it, it can serve as a cognitive shortcut. In fact, it already does. All you have to do is recognize these mental heuristics when you encounter them and then incorporate them into all the marketing touchpoints you have.

IMAGE TRIGGERS®

Visual Growth Triggers (we call them Image Triggers) are the most powerful type of all—more powerful than words for learning. Visual processing of inputs is most important for memory formation. When you see an image, it is stored in your memory twice, as both a visual and a word, but a word is only stored once. Further, according to research by 3M, humans process images sixty thousand times faster than text. Like the green feather in Robinhood's logo, and dairy farms, cows, and cheese wedges—Image Triggers are any colors or icons that produce implicit associations. A common example is a tree. As consumers, we don't need to be told that a tree symbolizes life, growth, and protection—we automatically make those connections. As an Image Trigger, trees telegraph all those associations in a single visual.

Nike's "swoosh" is another example. The logo conveys speed, dynamism, and forward momentum. It calls to mind old cartoon characters like the Road Runner after he's fooled Wile E. Coyote, leaving a plume of dust in his wake and "speed lines" flying off his feathers. Nike's swoosh is something of a modern-day speed line, implying extremely quick movement. When placed right underneath the word "Nike," as if being placed under one's feet, a visceral association is made, remaining as powerful and effective today as it was fifty years ago.

VERBAL TRIGGERS™

Nike didn't stop at the swoosh. As legendary as its logo are three oft-repeated words: "Just do it." Nike's slogan, like Heinz's "No one grows ketchup like Heinz," is a verbal Growth Trigger. Like Image Triggers, verbal cues rely on existing connections—you don't have to explain them because they're already in our minds. The power of "Just do it" comes from the many positive associations we've already established. The statement communicates perseverance, commitment, and motivation without ever mentioning such words. When we hear this phrase, it immediately lands without our ever having to stop to think about it.

You can find verbal Growth Triggers in some pretty unlikely places, like *E pluribus unum* ("Out of many, one"), developed by Swiss American Pierre Eugene du Simitiere, who suggested the phrase be incorporated on the Great Seal of the United States in 1776, and which now proudly adorns the back of every US coin. Many verbal codes and cues are used in politics to gain support for, or against, certain public policies, such as "death tax" (versus "estate tax") or "climate change" (versus "global warming"). They also abound in social movements, like the 1960s' "Make love, not war." They have even been incorporated in murder trials. Criminal defense lawyer Johnnie Cochran's famous phrase "If it doesn't fit, you must acquit"—in reference to a glove his client, O. J. Simpson, was asked to try on during the trial—turned out to be a strong verbal shortcut. Further, much of the defense's approach focused on simple, familiar expressions the average citizen or juror could quickly and easily understand. For example, regarding DNA evidence, another defense attorney, Barry Scheck, characterized the contamination of the crime scene as "garbage in, garbage out," instantly calling into question all the evidence against Simpson.

Meanwhile, the prosecution was drowning the jury in data that was hard to understand and much less compelling than a simple, succinct phrase. Our brains are lazy. They don't like to work hard, which is why our split-second decisions are made by effective cognitive shortcuts. In the Simpson trial, jurors had a choice between reams of complex information they would have had to study thoroughly in order to make a judgment versus simple triggers that could be understood in a second. Going up against these powerful soundbites, the prosecution didn't stand a chance.

Verbal Triggers can be particularly useful in the customer experience. For example, customer associates at Chick-fil-A never say "You're welcome" when a customer at their counter says thank you. Instead, they say "My pleasure." This particular articulation conveys that the associate really wants to help the customer. The phrase comes from a heartfelt commitment to customer service, assuring the customer that the associate wants to be there and they enjoy their job. Companies today struggle to create elevating customer experiences, but a positive catchphrase can go a long way toward drowning out some of the mishaps that may arise through a customer's interaction with your company.

AUDITORY TRIGGERS™

Sounds produce immediate associations. Birds singing? Spring. Rejuvenation. Rebirth. The sun shining and flowers growing. The "whoosh" sound Microsoft uses to indicate when an email has been sent? It makes users feel like they are literally sending an envelope up an old-school mail chute—even if that's something they've never done in the real world—simply by pressing "send." The whole sensation is extremely satisfying. What's important to note is that this sound is hardwired somewhere in our brains. Maybe it goes all the way back to a time when we sent messages by pigeon and the "whoosh" as they took flight, a little note attached to their leg. Or maybe it's the sound of pushing an envelope into a mailbox. These cues get baked into our brains somewhere.

Music is another auditory cue. Much of contemporary music builds on sounds, styles, and themes that have come before, riding along on a huge connectome that has been growing for decades. In fact, the entire music industry relies on recognizable themes. Without these familiar strains, our mind would reject most new music. It's also why your favorite songs, even short riffs from them, produce instant emotional responses.

OLFACTORY TRIGGERS™

One of the go-to scents in the air fragrance category is called Clean Linen, which should come as no surprise. Everyone knows the sensation of placing their nose in a pile of fresh laundry. Maybe it reminds you of when your parents put warm sheets on your bed, right out of the dryer, before tucking you in. Or maybe you think of your grandmother hanging pristine whites out on a laundry line in her backyard on a sunny morning, the breeze wafting through them. As with all Growth Triggers, smells activate latent feelings, memories, and unconscious associations—but even more so. Scientists posit that memories connected with smells compared with other senses *evoke greater emotion.* Validating the narrator of Proust's *In Search of Lost Time,* who relives a childhood event after dipping his madeleine in tea, Pamela Dalton, PhD, MPH, of the Monell Chemical Senses Center, concludes the most powerful scents are those that were "initially experienced at a younger age."

Think of your favorite pine-scented candle from the store. You can almost hear your feet stepping lightly on pine needles covering a path through the woods, fresh cold air filling your lungs, a purity only found in nature. Your brain may jump to the winter holidays, time spent with family, curling up by a roaring fire. All of these associations tickle the back of your mind as you take a candle off the shelf in the home goods section of your favorite department store, remove the cap, and breathe in. Or maybe it's Bath & Body Works' relaunch of its '90s sensation Cucumber Melon, which not only brings to mind the crisp scent of fresh-cut cucumbers and fruit, it also raises nostalgic associations for a generation of women who spent their teenage Friday nights at the local mall, not a smartphone in sight, the Backstreet Boys playing in the background.

TASTE TRIGGERS™

Like smell, our sense of taste can produce incredibly powerful Growth Triggers. This comes as no surprise. Not only do we eat every day, many of our social experiences with family and friends are based around food and drink, creating a storehouse of associations in our minds. While every other snack bar company was mashing up their ingredients into an unrecognizable log, KIND left theirs intact. The bars are chunky and substantial. Biting into a KIND bar, consumers know what they are eating because they can see whole nuts, raisins, and seeds—all the joy of eating a handful of trail mix, but in a simple bar that can be consumed on the fly. That mouthfeel is undeniably satisfying, but equally as important is the implicit connection to the real-food movement. Like with cheese, shortening the distance to the natural source of the food creates positive associations.

TACTILE TRIGGERS

Think of the feel of a product in your hands or underfoot. Consider the closing of a cosmetic compact, with a click that feels hefty and substantial as compared with weak and ineffectual. One powerful tactile touchpoint used in today's packaging is kraft paper, a brown wrapping that immediately cues positive associations. When consumers hold brown, unbleached kraft paper, it creates a sensation of naturalness, making the product within feel more authentic and artisanal. People given the same piece of chocolate covered in three different wrappings will attribute different flavors and experiences with each. Nothing changed, mind you, except the packaging.

TRIGGERS FOR YOUR PERSONAL BRAND

Everyone today is trying to build their personal brand, whether online, at work, or in their personal lives. You may be applying to college, looking for a promotion at the office, or working on building buzz on social media for your personal coaching career. No matter what the goal, when you're actively trying to brand yourself—or in other words, sell *you*—Growth Triggers are just as effective as they are for large businesses and organizations. But most people approach personal branding in a random way. They don't have a system for how to do it effectively. They don't think about the markers that could supercharge their effort to move their career along more quickly.

Consider business thought leader Seth Godin and his trademark yellow glasses—a bright, visual cue that creates associations of intellect, curiosity, and a distinctive point of view. Godin has become so recognizable, thanks to those glasses and his closely shaved head, that he was cast to play himself on TV (on Showtime's *Billions*), cementing his status as a business icon. Likewise, you never know what Lady Gaga, a style chameleon, will look like next, but one image of her has stayed indelibly with us because of its powerful associations. Sporting her signature platinum-blonde wig and bright red lipstick, her look became a portal, evoking the golden age of Hollywood, from Marilyn Monroe to Jayne Mansfield, especially when singing Broadway classics alongside the late Tony Bennett. With that persona fixed in our minds, no matter how she transforms herself, her association with glamorous icons remains.

But you don't have to be Seth Godin or Lady Gaga to benefit from Growth Triggers. If you're applying for a job, for example, it's not enough to simply provide your credentials. Education, work experience, and skills may get you past the initial vetting, but beyond that, all the candidates likely have similar qualifications. So how do you distinguish yourself when the final decision very often comes down to instinct? Leverage existing connections in the mind of the decision-maker. Don't worry that you don't know the person.

Growth Triggers are universal, and the universality of associations, like the intellect and curiosity conveyed by Seth Godin's glasses, is what makes them so effective.

Remember Ana from the cosmetics firm? She showed up for her job interview in a sharp white suit, the same one she later wore to the presentation to the executive committee. Not only did Ana desire to project a stylish statement in an industry built around products that help you look and feel better, she wanted decision-makers to intuitively "feel" she was the right choice. Her suit played into this plan.

Everyone knows white clothes are impractical, and for Ana that was the whole point. No one would make that fashion choice by default. Like the perfect shade of lipstick, her outfit channeled intention and follow-through, underscoring her impressive résumé with these positive associations. Her choice also harkened to the suffragettes from the early 1900s who stormed the streets of New York City in white garb. The beauty industry is filled with smart, ambitious women and Ana banked on their positive associations to the historic campaign giving women the right to vote. Women in Congress understood this potency well when they arrived at the 2019 State of the Union address wearing white. The message they sent, without saying a word, was one of solidarity and the need for progress. And no wonder Kamala Harris made her first appearance after the 2020 election, as the first woman vice president, wearing a white trouser suit. The image went straight to the instinctive brain of everyone watching the historic moment.

Verbal Triggers, such as how you speak, are yet another way to build your personal brand. Whether you play up or down an accent, use certain phrases or language, or talk in a formal or informal way can all be cues for your audience's brains that you use to your advantage. Judith Humphrey, founder of the Humphrey Group and author of *Taking the Stage: How Women Can Speak Up, Stand Out, and Succeed*, suggests that if women want to be listened to in a professional environment, they should speak more slowly and in a lower register, "grounding" their voice. Often at work, women are perceived as speaking too quickly and at too high a pitch, which instinctively cues a lack of confidence. Maybe that's because they feel as if they need to get everything out then and there because the typically male-dominated workplace may lose interest, or not want to hear them out in the first place. (I can attest to that feeling firsthand from my early days in the business.) By slowing down, women show more confidence in what they're saying ("what I'm saying is worth lingering on"), and by grounding their voice, the weight of their words feels heavier and more important. To that end, speaking slow and low is a power-packed cue.

Don't overcomplicate it either. The most effective cognitive shortcuts are typically the simplest. Consider the yellow hard hat. When real estate executives show up at a site visit and don safety helmets, they're sending a clear message, and it's not at all about safety. The hard hat stands for hard work; the construction and road workers, for example, who physically build the foundation of our country. It causes the executives to seem like they're part of the team, on the ground, and in the mix, instead of sitting up in their penthouse offices, totally aloof. The helmet signals they know what they're doing, and they don't mind getting their hands dirty. That's why they will often roll up their shirtsleeves as well—another Image Trigger utilized by politicians, whether at groundbreaking ceremonies or in brochures during an election campaign. The rolled-up sleeves signal they're ready to put in the work and get things done for you, just like the people building the infrastructure across our cities and towns. All these associations are passed on to the executive or politician through this one visual cue.

While what you wear, or how you wear it, can become a Growth Trigger, there are other ways to build your personal brand. You can associate a specific expertise with your brand through the use of imagery and language. For example, Marie Kondo, the world-renowned organizing consultant and author, exploded into notoriety, not just because of her books, but because she imprinted her approach on the public's mind through a specific, boxlike organization technique, in which messy underwear, unkempt bras, and rumpled shirts are transformed into a still-life-like work of beauty. By showing a Kon-Mari drawer or closet over and over again, this method became associated with her expertise, and the audience was inspired to follow her approach in their own lives.

But why do we have to play all these games to get noticed and get buy-in and acceptance for our ideas? Why do we have to use triggers? You shouldn't have to change your voice, or put on an outfit or pair of glasses, or do anything more than present your credentials at a job interview. Right? If it were only that easy. We *do* need to do these things because that's how the world works. Maybe we shouldn't have to, but at the end of the day, the world operates this way for one simple reason: that's how our brains operate.

Communication is getting shorter and more rushed. People don't even text in sentences anymore, they just use acronyms. We've created a new language that lets us pack more meaning into parsimonious snippets. That's what Growth Triggers are all about. They are concise cues and codes that pack a punch. They're also thrifty. You don't have to state all the associations—the brain does that work for you based on our culture and prior learning. Contrary to what marketers and advertisers have been taught, you don't create emotional connection by expressing emotion. A quick laugh or tear simply isn't enduring.

And what people like can't be trusted. They may like a lot of things, but that doesn't necessarily drive them to action. (Sorry Facebook!) It may sound counterintuitive, but emotional connection doesn't occur by expressing a particular emotion. It happens through stimuli, in which Growth Triggers create a match with what exists in your target's mind. That moment when the two puzzle pieces come together *is* the elusive emotional connection that marketers and advertisers have been looking for. This is when your product becomes an *instinctive choice*, not something forced. And if someone chooses your product instinctively, their mind is already sold. They're reaching for it without thinking. In fact, they won't even see the alternatives.

Chapter 4

THE CURSE OF NEGATIVE ASSOCIATIONS

INSTINCT RULE: Market conditions aren't holding your brand back; negative associations are.

B y the early 2000s, McDonald's image had taken a hit. The publication of *Fast Food Nation: The Dark Side of the All-American Meal* in 2001 scrutinized fast-food companies' practices and food production, workers' safety, and impact on American health and society. Morgan Spurlock's 2004 documentary *Super Size Me* took direct aim at the health aspect of fast food and, in particular, the McDonald's menu and its "supersize" meals. Such books and movies were paired with a general anti-corporate trend of the time, with a new focus on eating and shopping locally, eschewing fast-food chains in favor of the town's corner café and the weekend farmers market.

But none of these factors negatively impacted McDonald's reputation as much as the videos that began circulating about the chain's chicken nugget and burger ingredients, including the dreaded "pink slime." One such video showed an intestine-like, bubblegum-pink goo oozing out of a large faucet, like some meat by-product soft serve. It went viral. That wasn't all: rumors about cow eyeballs, worms, horse, and mystery fillers in the meat, ammonia-treated beef, burgers that never decompose, and lab-made proteins all grabbed the public's attention. These claims led to the impression that the food McDonald's was serving was subpar or even unnatural. In other words, it was "fake" food.

Turns out this couldn't be further from the truth. The pink-slime videos? A hoax. The many "creative" ingredients people had called attention to? None of them are used in McDonald's products. Still, the company's reputation for affordable, fun family meals began diminishing as these negative associations took hold of consumers. And McDonald's response didn't help the situation.

McDonald's leaders started to recognize they had a real problem on their hands, and they reacted the same way any other company would: refute the negative allegations and tell the truth. Hoping to show what was really "behind the curtain," they created a series of videos inside their plants, revealing how their nuggets and burgers were made. One started out with the video's host standing next to a conveyor belt with workers at a Cargill food-processing plant (one of McDonald's suppliers), watching unprocessed raw beef move down the line. Within the first ten seconds of the video, before anything else has yet been said, he asks, "Are there lips and eyeballs in there, Jimmy? At what point in the process do we inject the pink slime?" Meanwhile, a new ad featured a customer walking up to a McDonald's kiosk and asking whether or not there really is pink slime in the company's signature chicken nuggets. They also publicly stated that their food does, in fact, rot—just ask the scientists.

The problem was that, rather than change people's minds about the rumors, these initiatives actually served to amplify the negative associations, causing them to stick and grow in people's minds. By highlighting the negatives—which were entirely false—they ended up alerting more people to the idea that there might be problems with their food. McDonald's took the bait and, by responding to and refuting the negative claims, unintentionally reinforced them. More people, including those who had never even seen the viral videos, now wondered whether something questionable was going on with McDonald's ingredients. Further declines in sales ensued, a direct reflection of the growing negative perceptions.

The company needed to change course, which isn't easy for a giant Fortune 500 firm to do. But in one of the most comprehensive and well-executed strategic initiatives in its history, McDonald's set the engine to full throttle and turned the ship around. They began promoting the realities of their food: their burgers are 100 percent USDA-inspected beef, their cows and chickens are raised on farms, all of their eggs are USDA Grade A. They began focusing on where their food came from and how it ended up on your tray or in your kid's Happy Meal. They promoted their suppliers, many of which are family-run operations, like a potato farm in Washington, an apple orchard in Michigan, and dairy farms in Illinois and Wisconsin. They also incorporated cognitive shortcuts like a fresh-cracked egg being transformed into their signature Egg McMuffin, providing associations of farm-sourced food, right off the griddle. This real-food strategy told a story that already existed but which the company hadn't been telling. By bringing this information to light, they began creating positive associations that stuck with consumers.

Left unchecked, negative associations can cancel out all the positives of your brand, creating a Brand Connectome consumed by negative associations. When that happens, instead of being the instinctive first choice, you become the last—or you disappear altogether. Most leaders believe their brand's growth is contingent on factors like their spending level, the category's growth rate, competitors' aggressiveness, and whether or not the economy is favorable. While these elements undoubtedly play a role and consume business leaders' attention to the point where they are the focus of weekly sales meetings and quarterly earnings reports, they don't play nearly as large a role in business growth as most people are led to believe. A fast-growing category means nothing if your Brand Connectome is a toxic wasteland of negative associations. And if you do not address the cumulative negative associations damaging your brand, you're obviously not tending to your connectome.

Few leaders take this fact into account because they're not tracking what's going on inside their target audience's unconscious mind. Then when they end up with low growth or an irrelevant brand, they often make the situation worse by trying to directly dispel or discount the negative associations. Despite their best intentions, these efforts inadvertently reinforce those associations rather than eliminate them. But the good news is there is a way to remove negative associations. The key to eliminating them and restoring growth is to overwhelm negative associations with positive ones. To understand how, and get your brand back on a growth track, you need to recognize how negative associations come to exist in the first place.

HOW NEGATIVE ASSOCIATIONS FORM IN THE BRAIN

Humans have a negative-bias disposition. Just look at social media. According to executive director and cofounder of the Center for Humane Technology Tristan Harris, a former design ethicist at Google best known for speaking out about the harms of social media, outrage "just spreads faster" than positivity. The AI used by platforms such as Facebook operates based on engagement—it doesn't discern between positive or negative, it just focuses on how to get the most clicks. As Harris points out, "The outrage stuff gets the most clicks, so it puts that at the top."

A study from Cambridge University found that when it comes to politics on social media, user engagement doubles with negative posts about the opposition, as compared with those that just celebrate a party's own views. But it's not social media alone. Online media in general exposes our bias toward negative information.

When we see headlines in any online media outlet, each additional negative word increases our likelihood to click through by 2.3 percent. In other words, consumers have a natural propensity to create negative narratives, whether warranted or not. As a leader of a business, cause, or any kind of brand, that means knowing the formula for taking down these negative associations isn't just nice to have but critical to survival.

Negative associations can come from just about anywhere, but the sources fall into two broad categories: direct and indirect. Direct sources might include a news report of contamination and a product recall, a pop star's scandal, or a politician's inappropriate remark when they thought their mic was off. They may also come from a company's messaging that has missed the mark and created controversy. These direct sources are easy to point to—they are out in the open, and you can see them coming a mile away. So when a Brand Connectome starts showing negative associations, it's no mystery where they came from. In McDonald's case, the direct sources were the viral videos about pink slime, which fueled a false narrative that took over people's unconscious minds.

Indirect sources are more nuanced and, in some ways, more insidious. They're often overlooked by brands because they are not out in the open. Rather, they are an interpretation people's brains make about a brand that has somehow gotten out of alignment with what the brand intends. Remember, since the brain operates on cues, it is constantly making interpretations based on signals and stimuli it encounters. If business leaders aren't actively monitoring their Brand Connectome, negative associations can accumulate in prospective consumers' minds without the leaders realizing it. While direct sources of negative associations may feel like an attack, indirect sources are more like a virus slowly and stealthily growing inside your brand. By the time their impact surfaces and shows up in your P&L, it can be harder to take corrective action.

Victoria's Secret is a perfect example. Founded in the late '70s, Victoria's Secret was the darling of retail for decades. The name came to conjure images of supermodels, flowing silk sleepwear, and premium—though skimpy—undergarments. Millions tuned in to watch the annual Victoria's Secret Fashion Show, broadcast on prime-time television for over twenty years, an entertainment spectacle featuring models in oversized angel wings and high heels walking the runway. Customers bought the brand's lingerie as sexy indulgences, whether for themselves or their partners. And overall, wearing the lingerie made women feel attractive, desired, and admired, at least in theory. For many, Victoria's Secret and femininity went hand in hand. But by the 2010s, a change in cultural trends was taking place, and Victoria's Secret seemed entirely blind to this reality.

That's not to say the signs weren't there. The feminist movement had been evolving throughout the lifespan of the brand. By the mid-2000s, the fourth wave of feminism had gone mainstream, focusing on not just equality but empowerment and greater social change. The #MeToo movement also brought to light systemic issues of sexual abuse in the entertainment industry and beyond, including in fashion. Equally important, women's roles in society and their financial independence were evolving by leaps and bounds. By 2014, more women were graduating from college than men. Between 1990 and 2022, over twenty million women entered the US workforce, reaching seventy-four million at the end of the thirty-two-year period; and women's median wages more than quadrupled between 1980 and 2021.

Afraid to deviate from what had worked in the past and failing to keep their finger on the pulse of these cultural changes, Victoria's Secret continued to churn out the same dated brand of femininity, Miracle bras and all. But indirect negative associations had done their damage. To many observers, the brand felt out of touch. What was once seen as sexy seemed distasteful, or worse. The company's brand became increasingly less relevant as new brands like Aerie, from American Eagle Outfitters, entered the market, focusing on comfort over carnality, and the athleisure trend, with companies like Lululemon and Alo Yoga, took hold. Further, more lingerie companies across the board began focusing on body-positive messaging.

The negative associations that accumulated in the Victoria's Secret connectome were a result of a brand that stood in stark contrast to the changing world. There was no direct attack on the brand, as in the case of McDonald's. No one put those negative associations in the Victoria's Secret Brand Connectome. Rather the situation developed indirectly; the brain created its own story about VS based on the contrast between the evolving social and cultural environment and the brand's one-dimensional representation of women. In time, direct sources would also come into play, as a number of scandals ensued over reports of employees and models being harassed and bullied, and chief executive Leslie H. Wexner's employment of Jeffrey Epstein for over a decade. This perfect storm of direct and indirect sources led to a 3.4 percent compound annual growth decline in revenue between 2016 and 2022.

Just like positive associations, negative associations about a brand can become embedded into our existing neural pathways and create new ones. If you're not paying close attention, a new narrative can take over your Brand Connectome too, the result of accumulated negative associations. The more often your audience is exposed to repeated negative information about your brand, the more extreme their position against your brand will become. Your brand can sustain tremendous damage—damage that you don't even know is taking place—from direct or indirect sources. Since we are more wired toward negative associations than positive ones, it tends to be more difficult to change negative associations than to create positive ones, but if you have the right tools, you can quash those negative associations more easily than you think.

The more important issue is that most business leaders aren't even aware that negative associations are the source of their business challenges. Survey and brand tracking research often tells business leaders everything is fine, so when growth starts slowing and their business starts losing market share, they're taken by surprise. We've seen customer satisfaction surveys show an 85 to 90 percent satisfaction score while the business is hemorrhaging cash and losing market share every day. It's like a punctured tire: you might not even recognize it's losing air until you rush out to your car one morning, already late to work, only to find you have a full-on flat. You probably wouldn't have had the same problem if you had changed the tire when you were supposed to.

This situation occurs with major companies all the time. Everything seems rosy until the numbers come in. Then, at board meetings, everyone has a different argument as to why growth is stagnant or declining. It's the competition. Or the economy. Inflation or the "Great Resignation." But what they are missing is the real root cause: accumulated negative associations. The reason they don't see them is because they're focused on the wrong data—Net Promoter Score (NPS) or brand-tracking attributes, but *not associations*. Metrics like NPS scores only look at conscious thought. And attributes are just a quality or feature of a brand that the business decides it wants to track, such as "a good value for the money" or "is good for the whole family." They are surface level and don't get at the story consumers' brains have created about the brand through the sprawling network of pathways that live in the instinctive mind. Associations, on the other hand, are multidimensional memories that seep into people's memory structure and go much deeper.

That's why traditional consumer surveys can be misleading. Tracking consumers' rating of attributes, such as "good-tasting," "has healthy options," or "has good quality ingredients," won't tell you anything you didn't already know. Of course, there's nothing wrong with tracking attributes per se. For example, it's good to know how your brand performs relative to the competition on standard measures. But getting good scores on those attributes is just table stakes. And tracking them to the exclusion of associations will cause you to miss what's really going on underneath. This leads to an incredible reality: most of the world's business leaders don't know their true purchase barriers and drivers because the data they collect is either about superficial attributes or clicks and impressions, all worlds apart from associations.

Still, it's easy to understand why business leaders rely so heavily on these metrics. They're rational, easy to track, tangible, and provide a bellwether against which you can compare your company with others in your industry. In contrast, associations are less rational, more nuanced, and more difficult to access and measure by most standard research methods. But if you don't monitor them, negative associations will grow like a virus in the mind, spreading all the time, undetected. To uncover those negative associations, you need to delve into people's memories and identify the connections the brain has made on its own that don't serve the brand well. If you're not paying close attention to them, negative associations can damage your brand without your realizing it. Since these associations are hidden from view and consumers are not even conscious of them, it's easy to miss what's happening to your Brand Connectome. And if those associations are predominantly negative, then the result is inevitable: negative growth.

THE NEGATIVE ASSOCIATIONS–NEGATIVE GROWTH CONNECTION

Nothing is worse for a brand than slow or declining growth. Whether an esteemed tech entrepreneur, a professional baseball team, a Fortune 100 company, or an employee who is well known and well liked around the office—if you're not growing, you're dying. Sounds dramatic, sure, but ask any actor whose star is fading who can't land gigs or make ends meet, and I guarantee that's precisely what they will say. There is a direct correlation between negative associations and stagnant or negative revenue growth. The two are indelibly linked. Think of negative associations as weeds in your well-tended garden, growing up around all the beauty you've taken the time and effort to cultivate and choking it out. Virtually every time a brand's growth is in decline, or lower than that of its competitors, you can trust that negative associations are at play, wreaking havoc in prospective buyers' minds, taking over and conquering the neural pathways in their Brand Connectome. And a large advertising budget won't solve the problem. Whether you spend $1,000 per year on advertising or $100 million, if your target has a lot of implicit barriers, they're not coming over to your brand.

For example, as recently as 2018, the Kohl's department store chain seemed to be dominating its market. As of February that year, the brand had 1,158 locations, consisting of 82.8 million square feet of selling space across forty-nine states. With around $19 billion in annual sales and a stock price that hit its all-time high that year at $70.11, it seemed poised to continue leading the market in the coming years, beating out its two main rivals, Macy's and Nordstrom, and outperforming others, including Gap and JCPenney. The company also had a slew of initiatives that indicated they were keeping up with modern trends. They had been an early entrant into online sales and e-commerce, launching Kohls.com in 2001. They offered free returns for Amazon purchases at locations throughout the country and aimed to attract the millennial market, with a focus on athleisure brands like Nike, Adidas, and Under Armour. Further, they began offering clothes curated by the media and tech company PopSugar, which had grown out of a pop-culture blog started in 2006. On the surface, it seemed that Kohl's was doing all the right things to stay relevant.

But four short years later, Kohl's found itself in a much different place. Market share was in decline and the stock price hit a low of $26.49. Meanwhile, an activist investment firm, Macellum Advisors, took a major stake in Kohl's in 2021 and wanted to overhaul the brand and upend the company, calling for a new board and potentially a new CEO. It turned out that between 2011 and 2022, Kohl's had lost a massive 17 percent of its market share, even though in 2018, it seemed to be at the top of its game. With the rest of the category growing by double digits, and Kohl's only at a 0.5 percent compound annual rate, it was only a matter of time until they would experience a major loss in market share. So who did that market share go to? It was eaten up by many of the companies you might have expected: discount stores like T.J. Maxx; big-box chains like Walmart, Target, and Costco; and not surprisingly, dedicated online retailers, specifically Amazon. But if Kohl's was an early mover in e-commerce and athleisure, and brought in designer product lines and pop-culture partnerships, how could this happen? Where did they go wrong?

In many ways, they ran into the same issue as Victoria's Secret. A sea of negative associations had flowed into Kohl's Brand Connectome without the company realizing it. Focused on innovation and new product lines, no one on the Kohl's leadership team was paying attention to existing perceptions of the master brand. Not even the marketers who were busy creating loyalty and rewards programs for existing customers. At the first sign of trouble, leadership needed to dig into the brand's associations, not the attributes surrounding it. Even if you believe your Brand Connectome has few negatives, it's probably time to take a second look. Don't let strong performance on traditional satisfaction surveys mislead you. Stagnating growth and declining market share, like that experienced by Kohl's, are red flags that your research isn't capturing what's really going on. Something is missing from the analysis. And that "something" is the negative associations, or implicit barriers, that can either make or break your brand.

But you won't find the highly nuanced associations that are causing your problems in the minds of your current customers. You have to go to your growth target—your prospective customers—for answers. In fact, even your growth target won't *tell* you what's wrong with the brand. You have to get beyond what they say and go deeper, collecting the implicit negative associations they connect with your brand. And you must always keep your eyes on cultural trends and the competition to find the positive associations they are developing in people's minds that you might be missing.

For Kohl's, negative associations had been accumulating in both existing and potential customers' minds. But to access the most aggressive growth, you must prioritize your growth target and make sure your brand projects the key drivers that audience needs to convert to your brand. We see politicians do this all the time as they jockey for one demographic or another's vote. But it's also the main way that consumer brands grow.

When your growth target's Brand Connectome has a higher ratio of negative to positive associations, revenue growth usually ranges from stagnant to declining. But as negative associations were accumulating in the Kohl's Brand Connectome from 2018 to 2021, no one in leadership seemed to be paying attention. Negative associations were slowly taking over the unconscious minds of competitive millennial users, and probably some existing consumers as well. But the decline had little to do with the products Kohl's sold and more to do with Kohl's brand associations.

All the partnerships and new designer product lines in the world won't overcome negative associations and drive business growth if people are not connecting with your brand in the first place. It would be like asking someone to come into your store while it's on fire to have a leisurely stroll around the aisles. You're not going to get any takers. But that's essentially what companies do all the time. They consistently try to drive growth by launching new products and line extensions, but if your brand is not in consumers' consideration set, new products won't change that, and they certainly won't reach their full potential. In other words, if a new user is turned off by the Kohl's brand itself, you've lost them at hello. They won't go to the Kohl's website or come into the store from the start, which means they will never experience those new product lines anyhow.

Kohl's negative associations were also a result of changing times, but unlike Victoria's Secret, this was more a change in fashion and style, not necessarily a cultural or social change. For years, Kohl's was the go-to for millions of middle-aged, middle-income moms throughout the US. But in time, that reputation took on new connotations. For a younger audience, the brand seemed to be passé.

Kohl's became associated with matronly styles, suburban fifty-something moms shopping for everyday clothing at discount prices. What had been touted as affordable for years was now seen as cheap and of poor quality, no better than any of their rivals—less fashion forward and more fashion faux pas.

A survey of Kohl's brand advertising between the early 2010s and the early 2020s shows a brand stuck in time. While similar retailers like Macy's and Target have continually upgraded their image as offering stylish, high-quality, designer-like looks for less, Kohl's master brand advertising put greater emphasis on affordability than quality. If you compared Kohl's advertising side by side with a discount store like Dollar General, you would be hard-pressed to tell the difference between the two. Even partnerships with more upscale companies, such as Sephora, weren't helping Kohl's because they failed to evolve their master brand image as their product line changed.

If Macy's and Target were communicating a higher-end, stylish image at a discount, but Kohl's was just conveying low prices, why would you go to Kohl's over the other options? People want to have their cake and eat it too. Despite their efforts to upgrade their product line, the Kohl's brand was not projecting any evolution at all. It was severely disadvantaged versus competitive options, and the business results followed suit. Without in-depth inspection of their master brand to uncover the negative associations that had spread across their connectome, Kohl's was unable to reach new markets or pull in competitive customers—one of the few surefire paths to growth.

Negative associations act as implicit barriers to growth. If the growth target's mind has been infected with negative associations—whether from direct or indirect sources—brands are going to have a difficult time getting them to come over to their side. But because most companies are unaware of these barriers, they assume the traditional factors are at play: being outspent by competitors, economic factors, and other issues they more or less can't do anything about. What they don't realize is that by tapping into the instinctive mind and overcoming negative associations, they could actually accelerate their company's revenue growth to a level that would be unachievable through the conscious route.

The benefits of tapping the Brand Connectome go beyond what you can accomplish for your business in the present. As a business leader or owner, taking a peek into the hidden minds of your growth target can actually help you *predict* where your revenue will be in the future. If there are a lot of implicit barriers in your growth target's minds, you're going to have a tough time driving growth. Every penny you spend on marketing trying to acquire new customers is going to run into a brick wall. In contrast, if you have a robust, positive Brand Connectome, your marketing efforts will reach your target unimpeded, perhaps even be positively received, and your business growth will be higher.

Essentially, the beauty of uncovering your brand's implicit associations and barriers is that you can use them to help predict and better calibrate your company's revenue projections. This gives your company the instinctive advantage in planning everything from your financial projections and supply chain management to hiring. And the benefits of this approach extend beyond a business or brand you already own. Evaluating the Brand Connectome in prospective customers' minds is a new best practice for companies and private equity firms evaluating the health of acquisitions *before* they buy them. They want to see if the business they're considering has negative associations—because of course the more it has, the harder it will be to grow and get a high return in a short amount of time. They're also calibrating the price they're willing to pay based on what they learn. Looking for implicit barriers is a new level of due diligence, the ultimate "look under the hood."

When a brand is in trouble and growth has stalled, companies have a list of predictable action steps. They fix their operations. Improve their customer service. Add apps. Fire their old ad agency and hire a new one. Switch ad campaigns, develop a new emotional tagline. They look everywhere for growth except the place where the answer truly lies: in the unconscious mind of the growth target. The downside of not doing so is simply too great. The longer a business is in decline, the higher the barriers of the growth target become, and the tougher it is to drive growth. But that's far from irreversible.

OVERWHELM THE NEGATIVES WITH POSITIVES

Many people believe that if their brand has a limited image or some negative barriers, they are stuck with them. As a result, they may be reluctant to embrace certain opportunities because they are not sure their brand equity can extend to the new offerings. This may be an alcoholic beverage company deciding not to wade into the waters of nonalcoholic spirits, or a bachelor deciding not to ask someone out on a first date. But nonalcoholic spirits sales increased 33 percent in 2021 (to $331 million), and if we've learned anything from rom-coms, the underdog always gets the girl (often after a dramatic makeover, highlighting his best inner qualities). What most people don't understand is that nearly any negative association can be removed. How is that possible? You can't reach into someone's brain and pull it out as if you were extracting a tooth. But you can do something as effective—and less painful.

Negative associations can be overcome by positive associations, as long as they're strong enough, or "sticky" enough. Every sticky association—negative or positive—rewires our brains. If someone whose taste you respect tells you a certain iced tea is the best they've ever had, that person is added to the drink's connectome in your brain. If you already have positive associations with the beverage, whether from digital ads you've seen or experiences you've had in the past, then they are further reinforced. But if someone reminds you that the tea's plastic bottle is the same kind currently filling up the ocean and destroying precious ecosystems, that negative association might also be added to the beverage's connectome, especially if you're just a casual fan.

If that particular tea has been your favorite all your life, however, this information may not affect your brain at all. Chances are, it won't even go into the brand's connectome in your mind. All of the positive associations you have in the connectome will force out this one new piece of information. That's because a rich, robust connectome filled with positive associations acts as a goodwill buffer, preventing negative associations from sticking. Similarly, enough strong, sticky, positive associations can overwhelm negative associations. Just consider any classic comeback story.

Comeback stories can be found all around us (and the public loves them): actors throughout the entertainment industry, whether Robert Downey Jr. or Brendan Fraser, sports figures such as Mike Tyson, TV personalities like Martha Stewart, and even historical figures such as Winston Churchill. For years, Churchill had been building a public persona, from his time as a young military officer to his best-selling books to his first seat in Parliament in 1900. But in 1922, long before he came to ultimate fame as prime minister in 1940, he lost his seat as the colonial secretary. Though he briefly returned to Parliament, by 1929, he and the rest of the Tory Party were voted out. Like many others, he was hit hard by the Great Depression, and he languished as a political outsider for years, though he continued writing and making speeches.

Over the years, negative associations accrued in the Churchill Brand Connectome, including that he was out of touch, in part due to his resistance to India's self-rule. He was considered a "Colonel Blimp" figure that could not be taken seriously; a person of poor judgment, a result of the Dardanelles fiasco during World War I, in which Churchill, as First Lord of the Admiralty, led a failed attack that resulted in 46,000 Allied troops' deaths; a man who was opportunistic and disloyal, as he switched back and forth between the Conservative and Liberal parties; a candidate unable to win an election; and a spendthrift with expensive taste in homes, food, and cigars. Churchill's friendship with unpopular figures created additional negative associations in the public's mind. These friends included the Irish MP Brendan Bracken, who many thought of as "phony," and Frederick Lindemann, his scientific adviser, who was considered so arrogant that *every* member of a research committee Lindemann was on quit, saying they couldn't stand him. Though it might be unfair, people, like brands, are known by the associations they keep.

But Churchill's public concerns about a conflict with Nazi Germany, and Britain's lack of preparedness to handle it, widely changed the public's and his colleagues' perceptions about him. He believed the rearmament of the German Air Force was a major threat to Britain, warning that by the end of 1936, Germany's air force would be 50 percent stronger than Britain's. Churchill also saw Hitler for the dangerous warmonger he was long before many of his colleagues were concerned. This foresight and senior statesman wisdom led to enough positive associations to place him back into mainstream politics, and at the highest level possible. Following his election as prime minister, he would go on to help lead Britain and the Allied forces to victory in World War II.

Professional athletes are also no strangers to the ability of positive associations to overwhelm negative ones. For example, golf sensation Tiger Woods had a spotless reputation when he first came into the public eye. His connectome was huge and full of positive associations: young, from a diverse background in a white-dominated sport, son of a veteran, amazing athlete, family man—a true American success story. However, in time, numerous affairs rocked his marriage and brought it to an end, followed by a hiatus from golf, and then years of injuries that affected his ability to play. In 2010, of seventy-one PGA Tour golfers surveyed, 24 percent believed Woods had used drugs, including human growth hormones. When ESPN polled sixty PGA Tour pros in 2016, 70 percent believed he would never clinch another major golf championship title. The following year, he was found asleep at the wheel of his car under the influence of painkillers. At that point, negative associations had taken hold: infidelity, sex addiction, drugs, washed up, and on steroids among them.

Then there was the comeback. Not only had Woods gone to a sex rehabilitation center after his widely scrutinized divorce, but over the years, he and his former wife, Elin Nordegren, were able to move beyond the past, developing a healthy relationship both as loving co-parents and friends. Meanwhile, in 2018, he won his eightieth PGA Tour, his first in five years, proving his peers wrong and regaining his spotlight. (Nothing removes negative associations better than winning.)

Though some negative associations may remain in his connectome today, his ability to move on from an incredibly tumultuous period of his life refilled his connectome with positive associations: persistent, gets back up when knocked down, true champion, loving parent, reconciled with his ex-wife, trying to be a better athlete and better person, grateful for a second chance. Even in 2021, when Woods was involved in a one-car accident in LA, questions around the cause—many of which could have led to negative associations— were quelled. The positive associations in Woods's Brand Connectome had become stronger and larger than the negative, and this new piece of information could not breach the buffer.

Positive associations are able to overwhelm negative ones due to how our brains work. The brain is a learning machine, and it acquires new information every day. New experiences cause some connections in our brain to strengthen, while others are removed, or "pruned" (in neuroscience, this process is known as *synaptic pruning*). That means negative associations are never truly entrenched. When positive new associations grow in our minds, they create new neural pathways, overwhelming the old negative associations, and in effect, crowding them out. This process can happen quickly or over time. As the negative associations become pushed down or subsumed, the positive associations flourish in the brain, growing that robust Brand Connectome. And as you know by now, that's when new instinctive behaviors take shape.

Think about political polls. In polling, voters *say* they care about the economy, jobs, health care, immigration, taxes, or social security.

But when they get inside the voting booth, they choose the candidate with the largest positive connectome in their minds. Just as we make most of our brand choices on instinct, our votes are based on cumulative memories connected to a party or candidate that may or may not have anything to do with their actual public policy or effectiveness. Again, the sad truth is that our brains are lazy. Conducting research on a candidate's voting record and policy platform takes work. So we make snap decisions based on associations, positive or negative. They may not be the best decisions, but they are definitely the path of least resistance for our brains.

Positive associations are always better than negative when growing your connectome, but don't forget that the size or salience of the connectome counts the most. The largest connectome tends to drown out the competition. A small positive connectome will still nearly always lose out to a large one, even if it has some negative associations, because the physical size of the connectome (your brand footprint) is what matters most. As long as you keep your connectome in order, growing those positive branches and in the process pruning the negatives, your brand will be more salient and positive than that of your competitors. The brand that's most prominent in the mind becomes the go-to choice. And the more you keep inundating people with positive associations about your brand, the more you diminish their negative associations and ensure they keep choosing it. This process can be applied to more than just selling a product or getting picked for a promotion—it can even help change our biases.

BRAND PREFERENCE IS ACTUALLY A BIAS

Brand choice is a bias. This isn't a judgment statement. It's a fact. When you reach for Pepsi over Coke, it means your Brand Connectome is positively biased toward Pepsi and negatively biased toward Coke. When you align with the Democratic Party over the Republican Party, it means your political Brand Connectome is positively biased toward Democrats and negatively biased toward Republicans.

A bias is nothing more than a predominance of positive associations toward one choice and a predominance of negative associations toward another. And though people think they are in conscious control of the choices they make, their biases are always at play.

Vaccinations, climate change, the best way to hard-boil an egg—any issue with at least two sides (and all issues have more than one) can be seen in this light. If you have more negative than positive associations in your mind about one side over the other, you have a negative bias that will affect your instinctive behaviors and decisions. These biases are all a result of our connectomes and the accumulated associations, either positive or negative, inside them, and they can be seen playing out in almost every area of life. Consider the political arena and the growing division between Democrats and Republicans. It's not that the polls are polarized—voters' connectomes are.

A loyal Republican's and a loyal Democrat's Brand Connectomes tend to be the mirror image of one another. Staunch Republicans have a Republican Connectome that is filled with positive associations, and their Democratic Brand Connectome is filled with negative associations. Republicans' Brand Connectome of their own party is made up of a majority of positive associations, and relatively few negative associations. Their Democratic Brand Connectome is the opposite: few positive, the majority negative. Not surprisingly, Democrats are the reverse. Loyal Democrats have a Democratic Brand Connectome filled with positive associations, and a Republican Brand Connectome filled with negatives.

As discussed, emotional connection results when a brand projects content or messages—visual, verbal, or otherwise—that fit with what consumers already have in their heads; it's like clicking two pieces of a puzzle into place. But as they stand, the Democratic Brand Connectome and Republican Brand Connectome don't "click" together—when one side's positive is another side's negative, the two connectomes repel one another, like the opposite poles of two magnets. When two people's or two groups' connectomes are in such opposition—when they are polar opposites—it's hard to find common ground. But it doesn't have to be that way.

The Brand Connectomes of the Republican and Democratic Parties have their own brand image, personality type, and values, and like any consumer product brand, their own perceived "users"—very often a caricature of the real people who affiliate with each brand. Also, as with commercial brands, the associations the brain has created about these parties may or may not be true. But whether they are true or not does not matter at all. Democrats and Republicans each have a convergent ecosystem of cumulative associations across loyalists' brains, both about their own party and the one they don't favor. Try to *persuade* a Republican to vote Democratic or a Democrat to vote Republican, and you're not going to get far. It's hard to persuade members of the two parties to even talk with one another these days, let alone agree on policy. When they do end up in a room together at a family celebration, or on national TV to discuss politics, the extreme contrast of their connectomes creates a firestorm. Hearts begins to race. A fight-or-flight response kicks in. Faces turn red.

When Wharton neuroscience professor Michael Platt studied brain activity related to brand loyalty, he found something truly amazing. During the study, when a brand's users were told critical news about their product, their brains' pain centers lit up. Imagine that. An insult about a brand you're passionate about could cause the same physical reaction in the brain as if you were in pain. This is what's happening in cases of political brand loyalty as well. In fact, the physiological response in such cases is likely even stronger. What's behind that response is the confrontation of two opposing connectomes, one a mirror reflection of the other.

Some scientists have argued that a Republican brain is functionally different from a Democratic brain. In one study from 2011, Darren Schreiber, of the University of Exeter, and his colleagues found that by looking at people's brain function, they could correctly predict their political party 82.9 percent of the time. But obviously there is no genetic disposition to a particular party. No one is *born* leaning left or leaning right. People's political propensity is different not because they have biologically different brains but because of the vast web of memories that have accumulated in their minds, the result of their environment, upbringing, friends and influencers, media, and personal experiences. When it comes to politics, it's nurture not nature. And in a world where social media algorithms have created echo chambers, continually reinforcing people's current point of view rather than exposing them to other perspectives, political connectomes have become increasingly polarized.

What can we do about this polarization? How do we take the temperature down? The key to finding common ground is to introduce new positive associations to each group's connectomes. To start, we need to defy the social media algorithms that divide us. Democrats need to seek out balanced sources of information about the Republican Party, and Republicans need to do the same to balance out their Democratic Party Connectome. And that is the personal responsibility of each individual.

If instead of yelling at each other about the culture-war topic du jour, the two sides were repeatedly exposed to the more moderate ideas from the other side of the aisle, headway would be possible. Look at any angry soul attacking someone on social media and we will show you a skewed Brand Connectome. It doesn't come from diverse political influences; it comes from constant exposure to only one. And it's downright unhealthy, for them personally and for our society. We are in this together! If members of both parties learned more about each side, they would be surprised to find that more unites than divides us, creating positive associations in the process. New neural pathways would form, balancing out the connectomes in both party members' minds. In the process, personal growth would occur, their biases would be reduced, and everyone's blood pressure would go down.

Once we understand that instinctive preference for one position over another is simply the result of a positively or negatively biased connectome, we can make progress on any divisive issue. Knowing what lies underneath our biases is freeing because it enables us not only to understand one another better but also to influence others in a more productive way. Because the rules for influencing what appear to be entrenched biases are exactly the same as the rules you use to change someone's go-to brand preference. No position on an issue, brand, or political affiliation is truly fixed. All you have to do is replace negative associations with positive ones. It's not about vilifying people. It's not about telling them they're stupid. It's not about criticizing. It's about connecting with them based on shared ideals, using stimuli with powerful cognitive shortcuts they're drawn to, and adding positive associations that cause new neural pathways to form and flourish. Essentially, if you want a less polarized, thriving society, brains on both sides of the aisle need to grow.

When a brand has an abundance of negative associations, the traditional bag of tricks won't help you. That's because the brain is literally "switched off" to the brand. When that happens, all the promotion in the world won't incentivize prospects to convert. Moreover, when a brand is laden with negative associations, it's vulnerable. Then, if an external issue of some kind were to happen (such as a contaminated product or a social media blunder), the already weak business would take a further downturn. But the good news is that almost every business, no matter how much market share has been lost, can usually be revitalized. The only exceptions are brands that have been in decline for so many decades that they're too far gone. But such situations are few and far between. (Sears might have been one.) Most downturns are reversible by overwhelming the negatives with positives.

McDonald's revenue in 2022 was $23.18 billion, and it remains the largest fast-food company in the world. Obviously, many of the negative associations consumers may have, or may have had, with the chain's food have been drowned out by positive associations. But that of course doesn't mean negative associations can't creep back in. The same is true of your own brand, personal, professional, or otherwise. That's why you need to continuously monitor and tend to your connectome, increasing positive associations on your journey toward higher growth. When you do that, you stay one step ahead, in control of your brand, instead of a victim of circumstance.

Chapter 5

THE SNOW-CAPPED MOUNTAIN EFFECT

INSTINCT RULE: Familiarity is more powerful than uniqueness, but distinctiveness is strongest of all.

W alking through the supermarket, you don't give a second thought to the bottled water you grab from the shelf. There's no contemplation. No premeditation. No pondering. If you're a Poland Spring drinker, you instinctively reach for the green-and-blue package with pine trees and a babbling brook. Or if Aquafina is your go-to, you zero in on the blue bottle with the snow-capped mountain. Your brain uses cognitive shortcuts to enable such snap decisions. It's one of the ways it helps you make sense of the world. Today's average grocery store has over thirty thousand items in it. If your brain didn't have this ability, you'd be confused and overwhelmed—it would take you weeks to do your shopping.

No matter which brand of bottled water you instinctively reach for most often, chances are its dominant color scheme is blue and white, the colors of water and ice, and it features iconic symbols of sparkling streams, mountains, or gushing geysers. Those colors and graphic images are a match with positive memories and associations in your mind—the cold serenity and refreshing wonders of nature, all bottled up, ready to enjoy. Such similar colors and images are used across the most successful bottled water brands for an important reason: they indicate to your brain that this water is the *best* you can buy, in its ideal state, whether purified, filtered, or untouched by human hands.

But the traditional conscious rule of marketing would say that if you run a bottled water company, you'd better *not* use sparkling streams, snow-capped mountains, or the colors white and blue in your packaging. These are all clichés. Been there, done that. Generic. One of the most enduring principles marketers are trained on—and that has infiltrated the mindsets of armchair marketers worldwide—is the belief that uniqueness is core to success in building brands and businesses. For decades, the business world has heard exhortations like "Stand out," "Be the purple cow," "Differentiate or die."

When considered closely, however, the rule of uniqueness just doesn't make sense. And it doesn't bear out. The brain science is clear. As humans, we are hardwired to connect with the *familiar*, not the unique. We crave it. Take a baby out of its mother's arms and it will wail until it's returned. This was perhaps never more clear than during the early days of the COVID pandemic panic-buying, when our survival instincts were at an all-time high. Consumers didn't seek out the unfamiliar; they reached for legacy brands like Campbell's, Smucker's, Huggies, Cottonelle, and Scott (the latter three made by Kimberly-Clark) that made them feel comfortable and secure. They bought what they knew best.

Contrary to what we've all been taught, uniqueness doesn't draw people to your brand; it pushes them away. Still, many design firms become so focused on coming up with work that's different, hoping to stand out, they totally miss what truly connects with consumers.

Look at the top name brands in the bottled water market, with combined sales in the billions: Aquafina, Evian, Glaceau, Poland Spring, Crystal Geyser, Deer Park. They all utilize similar colors and iconographic imagery.

In the midst of the bottled water aisle is Fiji (you'll notice their name missing from the list of top sellers). An image of a brightly colored pink hibiscus flower practically reaches out, 3D-like, to potential buyers. The graphic of the flower, and its square-shaped bottle, makes the package highly differentiated in the bottled water market. And, hey, it looks great! Unfortunately, it *has little to do with bottled water.* It certainly is unique, but it's not familiar, it feels unrelated, and it doesn't have the associations that elevate one brand of bottled water over another.

Sure, it could be argued the flower summons the natural beauty of the three-hundred-plus-island archipelago, purity, and the South Pacific Ocean glimmering in the sun. But no one is drinking bottled ocean water. And though Fiji is gorgeous, everyday buyers don't necessarily know much about it, let alone that the water comes from an artesian aquifer in the island of Viti Levu. So, though the package design may be appealing or unique, it's not nearly as relevant to customers' connectomes as its competitors', and its focus on standing out will always limit the brand's potential. Standing out has little to do with the choices a person makes. Familiarity does.

Which brings us back to the snow-capped mountain. The snow-capped mountain is a marvel of marketing because of the place it holds in the unconscious mind. The mountain is not unique—not by a long shot—but it has a plethora of inherent positive associations that are unmatched in meaning and significance: pure, pristine, natural, cold, eco-friendly. You can even imagine people climbing to the top of the mountain to fill buckets with pure glacier water, then taking them back down the mountain to have their contents bottled and delivered to a nearby store. Why wouldn't you want all those associations connected to your bottled water brand?

But it's not as simple as finding an iconic image and using it "as is." There's more to it. The image needs to carry positive associations and be used in a way that it becomes inseparable from your brand. That's why though familiarity trumps uniqueness, *distinctiveness* is best of all. Distinctiveness enables you to leverage those familiar, positive pathways, memories, and associations that already exist in the unconscious mind, but associate them with *your* brand, driving your target's decision to choose your brand instinctively.

Distinctiveness is different from uniqueness. Uniqueness is about standing out, being the black package in a red tomato sauce category. The pursuit of uniqueness can actually push people away, whereas distinctiveness pulls them in. Aquafina, the leading brand name in the bottled water category, did this beautifully, designing a stylized, abstract snow-capped mountain range with an orange sunrise and placing it prominently on its packaging. This image plays on the positive associations of the icy mountaintop, but by making it stylized and abstract, it became distinctive—their own version of that iconic image. Therein lies your goal: leverage the familiar while creating something distinctive to your brand.

LEVERAGE FAMILIAR CONCEPTS AND IMAGES

If a company can bring a brand to market and get it to stand out, especially in a crowded field, the thinking is the brand will do well. Ads that capture attention, even briefly, cut through the noise and get noticed for their creative achievements. They're often the ones that win the Cannes Lions Awards, the Oscars of the advertising world, the CLIO Awards, the D&AD Awards, and the One Show. And rightfully so. They're the ones that make us take notice. Laugh. The most creative, intriguing. They're the commercials we talk about after the Super Bowl or maybe even watch again online. They're the ones that stand out. But standing out doesn't necessarily translate into sales.

"Breakthrough" is actually an extremely important key metric in the advertising industry, used to track the success of its work across channels, whether digital, print, TV, or any other. It could be a thirty-second commercial on TV or a seven-second video on You-Tube. When breakthrough occurs, it means viewers of the ad can remember both the ad itself and the product or service it is selling. The problem is that the majority of the marketing and advertising industry believes the key to achieving a breakthrough ad is *uniqueness*. The more novel, the better; something from the planet Mars, never seen before. Many ad agencies and marketing departments are still steeped in the old conscious rules of marketing.

In fact, this predisposition to the unique has rubbed off on all of us. We are all stuck believing we must stand out, following in lockstep with marketers' continuous pursuit of creative, new products and communications no one has ever seen before. And therein lies the problem—*breaking through doesn't come from standing out, it comes from pulling people in*, creating a match between people's memories and what the brand projects. When our brain recognizes something familiar in a new context, it is drawn to it like a moth to a flame. When that happens, instead of creative that simply wins awards, you have creative that truly builds your business. It doesn't matter if you're a Fortune 500 CMO, an entrepreneur launching a leadership coaching consultancy, or the CEO of a tech start-up, the question is not whether your advertising is unique; it's whether it has the stickiness to get your audience to buy into your brand.

Take a look at the strongest-performing TV ads and you will find that they consistently heed this approach. For example, in PopCorners' *Breaking Bad*–inspired commercial shown during the 2023 Super Bowl, actors Bryan Cranston and Aaron Paul reprise their roles as Walter White, the high school science teacher turned drug kingpin, and Jesse Pinkman, his meth-cooking sidekick, that earned the TV show sixteen Primetime Emmys, two Golden Globe Awards, and a slew of other accolades. In the PopCorners commercial, the unlikely duo cooks up a whole new batch, but instead of Blue Sky—their signature drug—they create an unstoppable chip and implicitly establish its delicious addictiveness. PopCorners' "Breaking Good" ad is a perfectly executed example of a creative twist on the familiar—one of the most effective techniques in our playbook. The ad's Creative Effect Index score of 216 from Ipsos's Creative|Spark shows just how effective the ad was. The average rating is between 70 and 130. According to the market research firm, ads with a high Creative Effect Index score deliver a 44 percent sales lift over poorer performers.

During that same Super Bowl, Disney and Google both ran ads that received high Creative Effect Index scores, 184 and 130 respectively. Disney's called to mind the company's hundred-year history, with iconic scenes from its many franchises, from *Sleeping Beauty* and *Mary Poppins* to *Frozen* and *Encanto*. It even included a voice-over from Walt Disney himself. Almost everyone has a childhood connection to Disney, a connection that lasts well into adulthood for some of us, full of positive associations. By placing these nostalgic clips in a new context, viewers' brains were captivated. Google did something even more noteworthy. Their "Fixed on Pixel" ad showed Pixel users "erasing" portions of, or people from, their photos. By repeating the same visual device of circling part of the photo and rubbing it like an eraser over and over again (a familiar gesture), Google created breakthrough engagement and conversion without relying on celebrity. No small feat.

Standing out too much isn't all it's cracked up to be. You wouldn't wear a Halloween costume to a black-tie event. If you did, you'd certainly stand out, but you probably wouldn't be invited to the next one. If you interview for a job at a multinational bank in a Hawaiian shirt, board shorts, and sandals, your interviewer will certainly remember you, but you won't make it past the first round of interviews—you may not even make it beyond the moment you turn on your camera in the Zoom call. Which takes us to another change in the rules. Instead of standing out, your messaging needs to create a cognitive shortcut between the brand and the audience's brain, like how Ana's white pantsuit signaled intention and follow-through while invoking the power of early twentieth-century suffragettes. By leveraging the familiar through cognitive shortcuts, your brand seeps into your audience's memory structure.

When it comes to innovation, we don't want something we've never seen before either. We want something we recognize, that we can easily place in a context, even perceive as safe, albeit with a fresh twist. For example, the Swiffer mop was heralded as a huge innovation in the household cleaning category, but it still looks, pushes, and cleans like a mop. It's iterating around the same core offering the unconscious mind recognizes and expects: a long handle and a mop head. By leveraging the familiar, we work with the brain, playing into existing neural pathways, as opposed to introducing something entirely new. This concept drives success in every arena, from the products we buy to the movies and TV shows we watch and beyond.

LINE EXTENSIONS, SEQUELS, AND PREQUELS

Every year, hundreds of brands launch product line extensions, expanding their existing line of products with a slight change. It's a fresh take on an existing product. Maybe that's a low-cal version of a cracker, a smartphone upgrade that has a third camera lens, a new cut of pants, a mascara with a wand that boosts lashes two times more, a new season of a streaming series, or a self-help book based on the authors' previous ones. All of these can be seen as line extensions, and companies build a whole pipeline of them years in advance to send out into the world. That's why a company like Doritos ends up having a hundred different flavors, from the classic Nacho Cheese and Cool Ranch, Spicy Sweet Chili, and Flamin' Hot Nacho to Simply Organic White Cheddar and Mountain Dew. They're all still the signature tortilla chip but topped with a different flavor.

There's a fairly obvious reason why brands create line extensions instead of launching new products—it's much harder to develop and launch a brand-new product from scratch. And that's not just because it's expensive. Line extensions ride the brand's existing associations, leveraging its connectome. By creating a line extension, the brand utilizes the same positive associations, drafting off the years of brand development they've already done. And the closer the line extension is to that product, the better that line extension will do in the market. Doritos has developed some wild flavors consumers never dreamed of (Late Night Cheeseburger anyone?), but the original line extension after Nacho Cheese, Cool Ranch, is the most popular.

Sequels and prequels are the entertainment equivalent. Though there's plenty to choose from, consider *Wednesday*, the 2022 hit Netflix series, which was streamed for almost six billion minutes the week it was released, and was one of the top three most-watched Netflix shows of all time. The show is based on the popular Addams Family characters, who first appeared in a 1938 cartoon, followed by a TV show in the 1960s that would eventually be syndicated worldwide. Three movies in the '90s, the first of which had the second-largest non-opening weekend ever, and the twelfth-largest opening weekend ever at the time, and two feature-length cartoons in 2019 and 2021 kept the family in the public's mind, while introducing them to a new generation. The enduring Addams equity lent itself to a reimagining for contemporary audiences.

Wednesday still features the same main characters that made up the horror-inspired, gothic family of macabre misfits. But here, instead of Morticia and Gomez, we find their daughter, Wednesday, the star of the show—a perfect evolution for an era in which strong female heroines have become the stuff successful series are made of, from Daenerys Targaryen in *Game of Thrones* to Miriam Maisel and Susie Myerson in *The Marvelous Mrs. Maisel* to June Osborne in *The Handmaid's Tale*. In *Wednesday*, the Addams daughter is plopped down in Nevermore boarding school, having been kicked out of her last school for a stunt involving the male swimming team and two plastic bags full of piranhas.

Boomers remember the '60s black-and-white TV show. Millennials recall the movies. And Gen Zers have been taken with a particular dance Wednesday performs, a sensation that made its rounds as a viral TikTok video with everyone, and their mothers, performing Wednesday's moves to the Cramps song "Goo Goo Muck." The Addams Family Connectome had been growing for almost eighty-five years when *Wednesday* was released, and the new iteration of the character only served to grow it further.

Since familiarity breeds comfort in our brain, the more recognizable a product, streaming show, or idea, the more likely people are to choose it over another. The Addams Family was already kicking around in our neural networks, so their revival played to the associations and memories we held there. But then there's the twist. The show doesn't take place in the '30s, '60s, or '90s. It's contemporary, with outfits to match, smartphones in hand—but only for the characters *around* the Addams Family. Morticia, Gomez, Pugsley, Lurch, and Wednesday still remain clad in black and gray turn-of-the-twentieth-century attire. Wednesday sports her signature black braids, as she always has, and remains cold and emotionless. If the revamped version were to arrive onscreen smiling, with a blond bob and a daisy-print summer dress, it would be as if the character didn't compute. Our brains would reject it, and the show would not be nearly as successful (or would never have been made).

The power of familiarity can be seen across the entertainment industry. The same year *Wednesday* came out, *Top Gun: Maverick*, the long-awaited sequel to 1986's *Top Gun*, was the highest-grossing theatrical release, raking in $719 million in the US and Canada alone, and a total of $1.4 billion worldwide. The *Top Gun* Connectome was so big, forty years after the first movie, its only line extension still blew the competition away. There were, of course, merchandise, parodies, and cultural references in the interim that kept the movie and its characters active in our minds, allowing that familiarity to further take hold. No one can hear Kenny Loggins's "Danger Zone" or the "Top Gun Anthem" and think of anything else but the movie. And Tom Cruise has been a constant in almost any moviegoer's life since that time. His *Mission: Impossible* movies are another great example. Originally based on a TV show from the 1960s, the eight movies, which started coming out in 1996, have been a massive success.

Line extensions are how franchises are built: James Bond, Indiana Jones, Star Wars, the Marvel Universe, Batman, Sherlock Holmes, and the list goes on. But beware—the success of a line extension is not guaranteed. If a Brand Connectome is weak or has a lot of negative associations, the line extension will likely have little success because it's extending off a weak base. Before you consider a line extension, ask yourself two questions. First, are you launching an extension just to fill a revenue gap, as a result of a decline in your base brand? Second, are you bringing new customers into the master brand? If you say yes to the first and no to the second, chances are your line extension isn't going to reach its full potential. But a healthy, thriving Brand Connectome can create years of successful line extensions to round out its offering. Over time, a single brand in one category can develop into a cross-category mega-brand.

Some will argue that by only leveraging familiar associations from an existing brand, the results are likely to be generic, boring, or stale. How many times do we need to reboot the Addams Family? Hasn't it run its course? Obviously not. And here's why: When you ride on familiar associations already in people's memories, you have a much greater chance of success. But make no mistake—copying exactly what has been done before will not work. You have to create a new and fresh take on the familiar. There needs to be something distinctive.

THE POWER OF DISTINCTIVENESS

Picture the perfect orange. Vibrant. Round. The smell of citrus, a slight acidity paired with a deep sweetness. Natural. Fresh from the grove. Florida's finest. Add this image to a bottle of orange juice and it becomes an Image Trigger. But Tropicana, the best-selling orange juice on the market, has one small detail added to its orange that creates a powerful distinction: the red-and-white-striped straw. Sticking out, ready for drinking the juice straight from the source, you can almost feel the action of the straw being plunged into the fruit, as if someone was so anxious to drink from that perfectly ripe orange, they just couldn't wait. It's more than just an orange. But not much more. Yet it speaks volumes.

Positive associations come pouring out of that image, but now they are not just associated with the perfect orange, they are associated with the perfect orange juice: peak flavor, undeniably fresh, real fruit, straight from the grove, picked at its prime, and unprocessed. Like all effective Growth Triggers, this cognitive shortcut creates the impression of superiority, playing off a wealth of positive associations. Again, this is just a minor creative twist on the familiar orange. But that tiny difference not only makes the image distinct, it makes it distinctive *to Tropicana*. It's just a piece of fruit and a straw. But that orange with a red-and-white-striped straw has become part of our brains' memory structure making up the Tropicana Brand Connectome and contributing to its vast web of positive associations. And that's why Tropicana remains the leading orange juice in the US, with nearly a billion dollars in sales in the "refrigerated orange juice" category alone. Now, that's real breakthrough.

Distinctiveness is often the result of distinctive brand assets (DBAs). DBAs are familiar elements a brand owns, whether purposely or by association. These are powerful identifiers that seep into memory structure and become intimately connected with a brand. The beauty of DBAs is that they help accelerate the growth of salience, increasing the size of the connectome; create relevance, especially if they have meaning for the audience; and add distinctiveness, otherwise known as differentiation or clarity. Logos are the original distinctive brand asset. The Amazon arrow, Mercedes-Benz's star, the Olympics' interlocking rings, Instagram's camera, the CVS squared-off heart, the *New York Times*' T, or Apple's half-bitten apple are all shorthand cues for their respective brands, instantly recognizable. But logos are not enough. To build salience today, you need a whole portfolio of distinctive brand assets, used repeatedly across and within consumer touchpoints, to tell your brand story and build a healthy, large Brand Connectome. These DBAs include:

- Brand World. This is where the brand exists, a world that stays consistent no matter what channel you're using. If you produce and sell hiking boots, your brand world might be a beautiful trail through the woods or up a mountain.

- Expertise. Here you would present a graphic or visual that quickly communicates a product or company's approach to create superior results. Colgate's multicolored oval swoosh, for example, symbolizes its comprehensiveness— that it creates a protective barrier around the whole mouth, not just keeping cavities away, but killing germs on your gums, cheeks, and tongue. Used both on the package and around individuals' heads as a universal signal of protection in Colgate advertising, the swoosh conveys superior oral care expertise.

- Consumer Benefit. Another important one, these are visual assets that convey how the user will be impacted or will benefit from using your product or service. An example is Red Bull's wings—the visual manifestation of how the drink's energy will make the consumer feel.

- Symbols. Symbols are the most succinct and simplified shorthand cue packed with positive associations. Examples include a leaf in a round seal that says "100%" natural or the triangular recycle symbol on packaging. Note that a seal itself is a mark of authority and prestige, and therefore a powerful shortcut, but it only becomes a DBA once a designer turns it into something distinctive for a particular brand.

In an Ipsos study of over two thousand pieces of US creative advertising that includes visual or audio, nonverbal distinctive brand assets are 34 percent more likely to be high performing (high recognition and correct brand attribution) than ads that don't use such assets.

Though DBAs may sound similar to Growth Triggers, they are not necessarily one and the same. In the case of Tropicana, the straw in the orange is a distinctive brand asset, but it is also a Growth Trigger because of all the inherent positive associations mentioned. A brand's mascot, however, may be a DBA but not a Growth Trigger. Tony the Tiger will forever be connected with Kellogg's Frosted Flakes, but a cartoon tiger on its own would not provide any positive associations (or likely any associations at all) related to cereal. The same goes for the Aflac goose or GEICO's gecko—on their own, a goose and a gecko are not imbued with positive associations relevant to the insurance category and are therefore not Growth Triggers.

The real win is when you find a mental shortcut imbued with powerful associations that you can then co-opt as a DBA for your brand, like Tropicana's orange and straw or Aquafina's snow-capped mountain. These two logo marks are more than Growth Triggers; they are what I call a *Distinctive* Brand Trigger® (DBT), both a power-packed cue in its own right and a DBA. With that in mind, the best way to start developing DBTs is to take an image or symbol that is meaningful in your category and associate it with your brand but render it in a way that is distinctive. Doing so is paramount because it gives you the best chance that the asset will get stored in memory structure—which is essential for rapidly scaling your Brand Connectome and accelerating revenue growth. For example, the logo for Herophilus, a biotech start-up focused on discovering new medications to treat and cure neurological disorders—also known as neurologic, or "neuro," drugs—is a simple graphic of a two-sided brain. Seems apt, considering the space they're working in, but it's far from generic. On the left side, there are a number of circles, distinct synapses or neurons representing the inner workings of the brain, and on the right, a more typical rendering of the outer cerebrum.

Together, it's a striking image that instinctively conveys expertise, simplification of the complex, and scientific rigor. We instantly believe that Herophilus has the ingredients for successful neurological breakthroughs. The name itself is another DBT, referencing the ancient Greek physician (335–280 BC) remembered as one of the first anatomists. This provides positive historical associations while equating the brand with originality and the start of something new and revolutionary. Packed with positive associations, the logo mark and name become distinctive brand assets for Herophilus, creating perceived superiority.

Distinctive brand assets are so effective, the legal community has questioned whether using assets similar to those of another brand could constitute intellectual property infringement. Aren't they "stealing" the positive associations that have been built up over time through the use of a company's DBAs? The case could certainly be made. Think of Johnson's signature teardrop found on their baby shampoo and related baby products. That teardrop has been associated with Johnson's "No More Tears" formula for more than half a century, but private label or store brands—the most prevalent borrowers of large-brand assets—often use a similar one on their packaging. They change the teardrop ever so slightly, and the retailers then place the product right next to Johnson's. The result? By leveraging positive associations the original brand took decades to build in people's minds, these brands pick up a significant percentage of market share. Though private and store label market share is below 10 percent in some categories, in others it can range as high as 30 percent or greater, all because they are riding on existing associations from established DBAs.

DBAs are so strong that even if you show a portion of one, the consumer's brain fills in the rest of the blanks. Try it with any well-known brand's DBA. If you see just the D or e in Dove's signature cleansing bar, for example, you still immediately recognize the brand. The same goes with any of the brands mentioned throughout the chapter thus far: The D in Doritos, the point of the Amazon arrow or bite mark in Apple's apple, the summit of Aquafina's snow-capped mountain, a portion of Tom Cruise's face in aviator sunglasses in *Top Gun*.

Showing just a portion of the DBA actually creates further engagement—it's like a fun puzzle for the brain. Essentially, our brains are able to predict the rest of the DBA based on previous exposure. Instead of just processing the information our brains take in, our brains are actively predicting the stimuli and inputs they are presented with. When your DBA becomes so well known, used throughout all of your marketing, that it becomes almost ubiquitous, our brains can better predict the missing parts, completing the picture without seeing it in its entirety. If your DBAs are powerful enough for your audience to recognize them even when they are incomplete, they are obviously doing their job.

Unfortunately, many companies don't necessarily recognize the power of their distinctive brand assets. They don't know their value. In the name of modernization or innovation, or simply from a lack of understanding their importance, some willingly drop these DBAs. They change a name, update packaging, get rid of a mascot, remodel their store's environment. But in doing so, they inadvertently strip out elements that have meaning. Think of the brain as having its own GPS. When a company removes a distinctive brand asset, it is as if they are removing the guideposts consumers' brains use to find their product *and* judge its quality. Remove too much from a brand, and there's nothing to feed the brain or direct it toward your product or idea. To truly understand the tremendous power of distinctiveness and DBAs, it's useful to consider what happens when DBAs are taken away.

THE RED-AND-WHITE STRAW

In 2008, Tropicana decided to freshen up its brand, leading to what is considered one of the most famous package design blunders in marketing history. "Blunder" doesn't really do the mistake justice. It was a full-on disaster, costing the company roughly $55 million. After hiring Arnell Group, a design and communications firm, the decision was made to remove not just the straw from the orange, but the orange itself from the juice's packaging. The iconic image and distinctive brand asset were replaced with a large stemmed glass of orange juice, freshly poured, bubbles still floating near the top of the rim. Though they also added a new cap to the cartons, resembling an orange itself, it wasn't enough for customers' brains to connect to. Where was the straw? Where was the *orange*?

It seemed that the Arnell Group persuaded Tropicana to move the focus from the real orange to the juice inside it. But there are so many positive associations that are leveraged when a food or beverage is perceived as being close to its natural source. Instead, Arnell and Tropicana changed direction, so the imagery was further from the source and closer to consumption. Goodbye, orange; hello, glass.

But pouring a glass of orange juice out of a carton and into a glass, then drinking it, is much different than sticking a straw straight into an orange and sucking the juice out the way you would drink water straight from a fresh spring. The straw and orange speak to the source of the juice and therefore its quality. A glass of juice, however, could be from concentrate. It could be watered down. It could easily be low quality. In one brief moment, all of the positive associations the brand had accrued as a result of that powerful cue were wiped away. Instead of having a positive effect on the brand, the package redesign was an example of *value destruction*.

This type of value destruction was anything but nominal. When the new packaging appeared in early January 2009, the financial impact was almost immediate. The company hemorrhaged cash, with sales dropping 20 percent ($30 million) within two months, while competitors raked in former customers. How could something like this happen? The answer is simple, and it happens all the time. Companies don't always understand the precious assets they own and therefore underestimate their importance in the instinctive decision-making process. Before changing one hair on a DBA, you need to find out the associations that consumers have with it.

We're not talking about attributes. We're not talking about whether consumers like it or dislike it. For example, in traditional research, you might show two package designs, in this case the Tropicana orange and straw versus the glass of juice, to a focus group. If you ask which is most "appealing," the traditional research question, consumers might choose the packaging with the glass, giving the reason that it's more modern. But that's their conscious mind speaking. Instead, you must ask for the associations the two designs conjure. When you do that, you will find that the orange with the straw has an avalanche of positive associations that elevate the product, in quality, naturalness, and freshness, relative to the glass, which only has a few. If you learn that your asset has this kind of power, and particularly if it's a cue consumers use to find their brand online or on the shelf, you want to tread carefully and avoid any material changes to it.

Very simply, Tropicana's design firm didn't realize the power of the DBA they were working with. They were cavalier about it, removing a highly familiar asset that was not only a precious signpost consumers used to find their go-to brand on the shelf but also a cognitive shortcut carrying a wealth of positive associations that created perceived superiority of their orange juice. They changed the font too, but that change paled in comparison to dropping the orange. Most consumers looked for the striped straw and orange more than the name itself. Though a font can be a DBA, in this case, it was certainly overshadowed by the change in imagery—the brand became unrecognizable.

Understanding how the brain works, it's no wonder why this package design change was such a failure. By taking away the distinctive element that had become a physical part of consumers' memory structure, Tropicana was essentially excising itself from customers' brains, not unlike how memories are removed from characters' brains in the 2004 movie *Eternal Sunshine of the Spotless Mind*. (If you've seen the movie, however, you'll recall the strongest, most positive memories are never fully lost.) When shoppers found the new Tropicana label peering back at them from the shelves, the first thought they likely had was "You changed my juice. Where is the one I know and love and buy every week?" Since what's on the outside of the packaging communicates what resides on the inside, when you take away that powerful cue, you're also signaling the juice itself has changed.

In fact, package design updates can easily result in a 10 to 15 percent reduction in sales because even a minor change can give customers the impression that the product itself has been altered. And that's even when the product inside is *exactly the same*. The projected gain in new customers from the so-called improved packaging is rarely enough to make up for the loss of existing customers who were turned off by the change. With Tropicana, that strong visual cue was no longer there for *new* customers either, meaning potential buyers coming into the category weren't experiencing the Image Trigger that had pulled in so many customers in the first place. Without this DBT communicating superior orange juice, Tropicana not only lost existing customers but potential ones as well.

This happens all the time. Someone likely convinced the powers that be that the orange and straw were played out. Every orange juice brand uses an orange; let's try something different. Something—you guessed it—unique. But you don't want unique. You want familiar and you want meaning, with a distinctive twist. In 2008, there was also a tiny green leaf connected to the underside of the orange, further leveraging the idea that the orange was freshly picked. Without the straw, it was a familiar category cue; with the straw, it was a distinctive brand asset. Without either of these items, it was a flop. And as soon as Tropicana saw what was happening, they announced the old package design would be coming back. Though it was still sans leaf, the straw and orange returned, and Tropicana regained its position, remaining the leader in the category to this day.

MADGE VS. THE DUCK

A major change in package design in which a critical cue or DBA is taken away or significantly modified is just one form of value destruction. There are many more. Let's take another look at mascots. For beloved mascots that implicitly convey overwhelmingly positive associations, dropping them can be the difference between leading a category and getting pushed out of the number-one slot.

In the 1960s, Palmolive dishwashing detergent introduced Madge, a lovable middle-aged manicurist played by actress Jan Miner. Featured in both US commercials and print ads for nearly thirty years, Madge often joked about the state of her customers' hands—"Call the police! These hands are a crime!" or "When I see your hands, I wish I was a nurse"—and time and again offered a surprising solution. That's right: Palmolive. The customers would respond in disbelief, only to realize that the liquid Madge had already placed their hands in was, indeed, the dishwashing liquid. "You're soaking in it!" she'd say. The customer would reflexively pull their hands out of the liquid. "Mild?" one unsuspecting salon customer asks, taken aback. "Oh, more than just mild," Madge replies. But with the refrain "Palmolive softens hands while you do the dishes," she convinced even the most skeptical patrons, typically housewives, of the wonders of Palmolive.

Dishwashing liquid needs to provide two benefits to the consumer: it must be effective and gentle on the hands. The idea that Palmolive not only gets dishes clean but could also do wonders for dry, cracked skin may have been an attractive proposition on its own, but Madge was the star of the show. People loved her. She was funny, irreverent, and down-to-earth, willing to share her best-kept secret. Viewers, especially those the ads were targeting in the '60s, '70s, and '80s, felt a bond with her, similar to one they may have developed—or wished they could develop—with their own manicurist at the local salon. Or better yet, they didn't have to go to the salon at all—they had Madge, and they could always buy the Palmolive.

This was a time period in which many women were staying home, taking care of their children and running their household. A trip to the manicurist or salon could serve as a social and even emotional outlet. Most moms in the US were not going to therapy in the 1960s, but they could speak openly and honestly with someone like Madge. In the Palmolive commercials, Madge was there to care for them; she'd never do anything to harm her clients or their hands. She looked out for them, and in return, they trusted her.

And then, one day, after decades helping to build the brand, Madge was gone. The marketing team in the '90s decided she had run her course. She was no longer relevant, or so they thought, especially to Gen Xers. It was time to move on. But Palmolive didn't recognize how many associations had been built up through the use of Madge over the years: caring, trusted adviser and friend, effective, says it like it is, and funny, among them. They tried a number of different ads in Madge's place, diverging from the manicurist as friend and confidante.

Though her removal was abrupt, the fallout was somewhat slow, at least compared with Tropicana's. At first, Palmolive didn't see any major shifts in their brand attribute tracking, which looks at a brand's equity, or its total value. Then, seemingly out of the blue, after a few years, the brand's overall health attributes took a nosedive—a sharp double-digit decline. They didn't know what hit them. That's because companies don't monitor people's memories. As discussed, they only track attributes, which can be misleading, not associations.

What happened here? A DBA like Madge is so unforgettable, her memory stuck around in consumers' brains long enough to positively influence brand perceptions for a time. During those years, it was likely that company leadership felt buoyed by the fact its business was rolling along and brand health attributes were stable. But after several years of level results, memories wane, and brand health declines precipitously along with it. Management is caught off guard because they aren't monitoring the implicit mind.

Like medications or caffeine, memories have a half-life in our system. They linger for a while. But without reinforcement, memories start to fade over time, getting crowded out by new memories and associations, and physically decreasing the size of your Brand Connectome in the audience's brain. This happens all the time across categories and brands. After several years of either DBA removal, inconsistent campaigns, or advertising budget cuts, the brand stays stable for a few years and then suddenly free-falls. Remember, the human brain is constantly changing due to input and stimuli. Removing a strong asset is like getting out of line for a movie on opening night. Once you're gone, getting your spot back is nearly impossible.

And that's what happened with Palmolive. As they lost memory structure in people's minds, a major competitor was slowly moving in, taking their place in line in consumers' minds, thanks in part to their own mascot: a cute little yellow duckling. In 1978, after years of testing different methods of cleaning off birds in the aftermath of oil spills, the International Bird Rescue Research Center (IBRRC), now known as International Bird Rescue, found that the best cleaning solution for the job, out of all the other dish detergents they tried, was Dawn. According to IBRRC director Jay Holcomb, Dawn cut grease, removed oil quickly, could be ingested by the birds, and was harmless to their skin and eyes, as long as it was flushed out. It is not just an effective way to clean oil off the birds, it is also gentle and safe on their delicate feathers, readily available—even in the farthest reaches of Alaska, as Holcomb pointed out—and still works best. You couldn't pay for such press.

But it wasn't until 1989, in the aftermath of the *Exxon Valdez* spill, that Dawn's connection to cleaning and saving these birds really came to the public's attention. Volunteers were shown using the dish soap on the water's shore, gently and carefully removing the oil from the ducks' feathers. And if it could effectively and carefully clean oil from a little duckling, Dawn could certainly get the grease out of dishes while protecting your hands. When the company saw the huge success of the PR they received, they made the bold move to put little yellow ducklings right on the package.

Usually advertising drives PR strategy; this time PR drove their packaging and advertising direction. Taking a symbol that came out of a PR campaign and placing it on your package as the overall symbol of the brand had never been done before. Like all Growth Triggers, the duckling is packed with powerful positive associations that become transferred to Dawn: gentle, soft, precious, environmentally conscious. And let's not forget superior cleaning power. This cognitive shortcut communicates that not only is Dawn gentle on the most fragile living things, but it's also effective enough to remove oil, one of the most toxic and dirty elements in existence. In one of the most spectacular PR campaigns in marketing history, the yellow duckling became Dawn's mascot and a powerful DBT associated directly with the brand. Thirty-five years later, younger generations that don't even remember the *Exxon Valdez* oil spill still find the ducklings relevant, transcending the symbol's origins. The perfect balance of gentleness and efficacy, Dawn's new mascot was more powerful even than Madge. By communicating the two most important benefits of a dishwashing liquid (effectiveness and gentleness), Dawn was able to tremendously increase share, leaving Palmolive in the dust.

Uniqueness is overrated. That's the reason nine out of ten brands fail: They try to attract customers through something that is too cutting edge, something customers have *never* seen before. And that's simply not what people want. People crave the familiar, not the unique. We like a distinctive twist, something our brains still recognize and can easily latch on to. We don't want new ideas as much as those that add value to something we already know and understand. By developing a range of distinctive brand assets, particularly ones built on powerful preexisting touchstones, you establish multiple footholds for your brand in people's minds. To eliminate those DBAs is a form of value destruction that can be hard to bounce back from. When you wipe out distinctive brand assets, you wipe out the memory structure you've built in your audience's brains. And when you walk away from years of positive associations, you not only hurt the health of your brand, you hurt your business.

In fact, dropping a DBA or DBT is like axing off a branch of your tree or digging up its roots. DBAs and DBTs have the strongest root system in the mind, going deeper into the brain than any other assets. When you start chopping them up, they no longer have the opportunity to grow in your target's memory structure. Every time you make a change to your DBAs, you decrease your connectome, making it harder for your consumers to connect the dots as they lose positive associations. Instead, you must protect DBAs like a mother protecting her cubs. You cannot be cavalier about these assets; you must have reverence for them and their power. And if you drop them, don't be surprised when revenue declines inevitably kick in. You want to be in the business of building a portfolio of distinctive brand assets, not destroying them. And if you don't understand the importance of the distinctive brand assets in the brain, you are making it harder to scale your business.

Chapter 6

WHY LAYERING
BEATS FOCUSING

INSTINCT RULE: A single brand message stifles growth; multiple messages fuel it.

CeraVe skin care launched in 2006, offering consumers just three products: moisturizing cream, moisturizing lotion, and hydrating cleanser. Over the following decade, the brand quietly grew its market share, when in 2017 it was purchased from its parent brand, Valeant, by L'Oréal. Over the next four years, to the shock of most companies in the skin care category, the brand rocketed to the top, expanding to over seventy products and taking the category by storm. By 2021, CeraVe's hand and body lotion was the US category leader, with approximately $200 million in sales, reigning over some of the best-known legacy brands, including Gold Bond, Nivea, Cetaphil, Jergens, Eucerin, and Aveeno. CeraVe also beat out the competition in the facial cleanser category, pulling in millions more than Cetaphil and almost $70 million more than Neutrogena in the same category. And if that wasn't enough, they had the number-one facial moisturizer that year, outpacing Olay, the original queen of the facial skin care market.

If you're familiar with the brand, you likely know CeraVe products are developed with dermatologists, as clearly stated on their predominantly white-and-blue packaging. But the secret to CeraVe's success goes well beyond that fact. If CeraVe were to focus solely on its dermatologist approval and development, there would of course be some immediate positive associations there: tried and tested, scientific, and made by experts. But that would not be enough to catapult CeraVe to the top of the food chain, eating up profits from so many long-standing skin care giants. Instead, CeraVe did the very thing most marketing and agency professionals say not to.

Business school, ad agency, and marketing training programs all teach that communications should be distilled to a single, powerful, big theme, focusing on one singular message. Some marketing professionals call this "your strategic one thing." Others refer to it as "your point of difference." Volvo equals safety. Tylenol stands for caring. Apple for creativity. This cardinal rule of traditional marketing is steeped in the misinformed belief that if companies present multiple benefits simultaneously, they will dilute their message. Their reasoning: the brain can only focus on one idea at a time. But that's neither here nor there when it comes to connecting with your audience. Though the brain does indeed covet simplicity, to achieve instinctive brand preference, the brain must become immersed in multiple messages and cues at the same time—not just one. These layers provide more for the brain to latch on to. They add dynamism and flavor. Think of a lasagna. Without the layers of ricotta, tomato sauce, sweet Italian sausage, and ground beef, all that's left is a bunch of limp dry noodles.

A multiplicity of themes or ideas helps grow your brand's connectome, making it more salient. When CeraVe first hit the market, the messaging was all about *dermatologists*. And for as much as consumers may trust doctors with their health-care decisions, a guy in a lab coat, staring into a microscope, is one-dimensional and bland on its own. But if you look at the CeraVe package, watch one of their ads, or check out their website and social media, you'll see something different today. Though their rating as "the #1 dermatologist recommended skincare brand" is mentioned, and their packaging reflects that highly clinical image, there's so much more going on. Multiple messages intertwine. Take one of their most viewed commercials online: Beautiful imagery of the skin on a woman's shoulder, face, or body is contrasted with a clean white background. The model could just as easily be in an ad for a high-end cosmetic product. Undulating graphic blue and white waves emanate from the jar of cream moisturizer, lightly caressing the woman's skin as they float across the screen.

Viewers soon learn these wavy lines symbolize *ceramides*, molecules found naturally in the skin, whose presence is necessary to stave off dry skin, acne, and eczema. The translation in consumers' brains is clear: by using ceramides in its products, CeraVe is supplementing and protecting the skin's natural rejuvenation process without harmful chemicals. Then there's a cutaway to a "demo" sequence, in which the same blue and white waves, paired with digitized droplets, sink into a cross-section of skin, with copy explaining how ceramides restore your skin's natural moisture barrier, sealing in moisture while protecting it from harm.

Close-ups of beautiful skin, juxtaposed with how the product works inside skin, provide a complete story, fully engaging consumers' brains. The original scientific, doctor-backed premise of CeraVe is still there, but the audience now receives *a more comprehensive, well-rounded picture* of the brand. Like the character of Evelyn Wang in *Everything Everywhere All at Once* or the classic *Cinderella* coming out of her shell, it turns out there's a lot more presence, style, and pizzazz when that dermatologist's lab coat is tossed aside. In a perfect blending of beauty, science, nature, and expertise, CeraVe emerges as much more than just a clinical, doctor-recommended brand. The previous owner, Valeant, had discovered an advanced technology, ceramides—lipids found in skin cells that help maintain a healthy skin barrier. With this special ingredient, CeraVe could keep common skin issues such as eczema, acne, and dryness at bay. It was L'Oreal who linked the technology story with the beautiful, pristine, smooth skin everyone wants. When the brand relied solely on the clinical, sure, it grew, but when it was positioned around multiple themes, it exploded in the brain, and sales followed.

Though both science and beauty are important to the skin care category and its customers, true to the old rule of single-minded marketing messages, many brands tend to focus on one at the cost of the other. Some brands overemphasize the cosmetic feel in their communications with little to no evidence of the efficacy or functionality of their products. Others focus solely on product technology and ingredients. CeraVe brilliantly marries the two while incorporating a host of other positive associations that bloom in consumers' brains, quickly growing CeraVe's connectome.

Traditional marketing will claim that all of these additional themes layered on top of "skincare developed with dermatologists" are frivolous, unnecessary, and harmful to the brand. Many marketing and advertising leaders will push back, asking how you could ever possibly cram five different themes—moisture, advanced science, natural, health, beauty—into one communication. But, as with many of the old rules of marketing, they don't hold up. Just look at any CeraVe ad and you'll see that these five themes come together in glorious harmony. As long as you tie all the messages together, they won't fight each other at all—they will work in concert, contributing to and reinforcing a multidimensional yet united brand story.

For CeraVe, the use of one continuous visual Image Trigger— the blue and white waves simultaneously symbolizing smooth skin, moisture, and ceramides—throughout their communications doesn't hurt either. Like a beautifully wrapped package, the continuously undulating ribbon helps tie the themes together in a perfect bow. And that bow is crucial. Vectors of associations need to be complementary, coming together to create an overarching cohesive perception, not just a bunch of disconnected or contradictory associations thrown at the wall. When done right, layered messaging helps develop the type of all-encompassing brand world necessary to grow your connectome and take over physical real estate in your target audience's mind.

Not only did CeraVe top the skin care category in 2021, it hit a billion dollars in sales that year. When L'Oréal purchased the brand in 2017, they immediately started layering messages consistent with the company's beauty and fashion background and flagship brands, such as Lancome, Garnier, Shu Uemura, Armani, and YSL. Managing this portfolio of upscale department store and designer brand equities, L'Oréal knew how to create aspirational imagery, and that's exactly what they brought to CeraVe.

When L'Oréal purchased CeraVe, it was already considered a fast-growth brand in the US skin care category. L'Oréal acquired it along with two other skin care brands (AcneFree and Ambi), whose combined revenue was approximately $170 million. To buy such a business and turn it into a billion-dollar brand in less than four years is no small feat. Most people would venture the reasons for this success were simply the increased marketing support and L'Oréal's vast distribution muscle, launching the formerly domestic brand to global markets. By 2022, sales were up more than 40 percent year-to-date in the US. There was also a tremendous push by TikTok influencer Hyram Yarbro, who has over six million followers, mostly Gen Z.

This distribution advantage and viral social media exposure undoubtedly played a major role in the brand's growth, but these factors are not the only ones driving its success. Big companies buy smaller companies all the time, providing greater funding and distribution, but they rarely receive such an extraordinary return. And while influencers can be a major growth driver for brands, they rarely catapult a brand to the top of its category completely. One of the biggest changes between the ownership by Valeant and L'Oréal is that L'Oréal's beauty expertise and sensibility added dimensions CeraVe did not previously have. These new layers created an unstoppable overall brand story.

Between 2017 and 2021, CeraVe's sales grew aggressively year over year in the US market, thanks to the layers of associations it planted across consumers' minds: moisture, advanced science, natural, health, beauty. This type of diversity of themes is not just nice to have, it's imperative. Though it flies in the face of traditional conscious marketing rules, multilayered messaging leads to greater mental availability, expanding the Brand Connectome. Like many spokes, each one of these positive associations comes together to create a stable wheel. If it were just one spoke, the wheel would never make it out of the garage.

NO ADVANTAGE TO A SINGULAR FOCUS

The idea of presenting only one potent message about your brand was pushed and supported by advertising executives Jack Trout and Al Ries's seminal book, *Positioning: The Battle for Your Mind*. In the book, first published in 1981, the authors describe positioning as working with what's in people's minds already, retying existing connections without having to create something "new and different." Trout and Ries didn't know just how right they were, long before behavioral economics and neuroscience emerged in the marketing sphere. Where they fell short, however, was on how to actually connect with consumers' minds.

Positioning supported the premise of one simple idea per brand. "The best approach to take in our overcommunicated society," they claimed, "is the oversimplified message." So Miller should just stick to being the light beer. 7UP, the Uncola. And Avis should only pitch that because it's number two, it tries harder. The authors write about "filling a hole in the mind." But filling a single pothole won't work. Rather, you have to create a whole network of highways from your brand to other preexisting memories in people's minds to grow your connectome.

Contrary to what Trout and Ries argued, there is no advantage to a singular focus. In fact, distilling your communications down to

one brand dimension is a recipe for *shrinking* your brand and its connectome. A connectome with only one message takes up few neural
pathways. Instead of the giant Thimmamma Marrimanu banyan,
with its sprawling root system and massive canopy, it's a twig. Such
a connectome will own very little space in the mind. Remember, as
in Monopoly, the most effective connectomes take up the most real
estate and have the largest physical footprint. Having a brand that
has just one message or positive association is like owning just one
home in a neighborhood. But if your brand has multiple messages,
creating numerous positive associations, it's like owning real estate
across an entire city. Since abundant positive associations create a
more salient and resilient network within the brain, consumers will
instinctively choose the brand with the largest positive connectome
and a myriad of themes. In fact, the more the merrier.

In the United States, Volvo was long known for the safety of its
vehicles, in part due to the design of its boxy station wagons. They
also pioneered car safety features like the three-point seatbelt, designed by Volvo engineer Nils Bohlin in 1959, and the rear-facing
child seat. Further, they have had a dedicated accident research
team since the early 1970s that analyzes accidents in which a Volvo
has been involved to study what happened and extract data to help
improve the safety of the vehicles in the future.

The Volvo station wagon was once the belle of the suburban family ball due to its safety and size. But those two associations weren't
enough to keep up with changes in consumer taste, especially with
the growing popularity of hatchbacks and SUVs, the modern-day
equivalents of the family station wagon. So though Volvo ditched
the square frame in time, they kept the positive association with
safety, and pulled in others like advanced technology, comfort, innovation, affordability, and luxury. In fact, in 2021, the *New York
Times* even ran an article claiming Volvo was now winning buyers
over with a "sleek new look"—something no one would have said
about the Volvo 900 series of the 1990s. Volvo recognized that to
grow, they needed more than just an emphasis on safety. Keeping

that message core to their positioning was still necessary to holding on to their original brand identity, but by adding new layers, they increased their relevance in prospective car buyers' minds.

The brain craves stimulation. When it has multiple positive associations coming its way, it becomes swept up in the story those associations help develop. By engaging on multiple associations, the brain stays attentive and alert, as opposed to bored and uninterested. Singular messaging has what can be called "low brain utilization." More simply, if you only focus on one message, say, "purpose" or "health," then you're only going to connect with one part of your audience's brain. Multiple messages, similar to multidimensional cues, target multiple parts of the brain. The higher the "brain utilization," or the more parts of the brain that connect with the messaging, the more engaged the brain will become. By providing multiple messages for the brain to latch on to, more positive associations are embedded in your audience's neural pathways.

Nowhere is this principle more evident than in the sphere of college admissions. Steven, a recent applicant, and his parents thought he was a shoo-in for Yale. Top of his class, editor in chief of the school newspaper, soccer star, exceptional SAT scores, and on top of all that, he volunteered at the local hospital on weekends. But Steven did not get into Yale; in fact, he wasn't admitted to a single Ivy League school. Nicolas, another student from the same senior class, with lower scores and some might say fewer credentials, is now living on Old Campus and cheering for the Bulldogs. How did this happen?

The answer is simple. Steven took the conscious approach. He described his passion for software development and its benefits to society, working in the accomplishments he was most proud of. The rational reasons for why he made a great candidate could not have been clearer. In contrast, Nicolas, who had a passionate love of history, which he shared with his grandmother, wove a rich tapestry of layered associations into his common app essay that brought him to life. In a captivating story about his special relationship with his grandma and his first trip abroad, Nicolas transported readers to

Europe's grand historical sites, where he walked among the greats. The hallowed halls echoed as luminaries came to life, providing inspirational mottoes and advice to the young man. Nicolas ended the essay with a FaceTime session with his grandmother where, transformed by his experience, he projects greater resolve about the path he must take.

Why was Nicolas admitted? His essay was operating on a completely different level than Steven's—an instinctive level. Instead of telling, he focused on showing. Instead of promoting past accomplishments, he focused on the future. Instead of *proclaiming* that he was passionate, he proved it through the story. In a cross between historical fiction and fantasy, Nicolas's 650-word essay connected with multiple facets of admissions officers' minds. After all, they make decisions just like everyone else. As the admissions committee contemplated each candidate in their weekly meeting, Nicolas appeared a whole living, breathing human they would want to get to know— with passions, philosophies, quirks, and a sense of humor. Steven remained a one-dimensional list of stats, lifeless on the page. Contrary to popular belief, as long as you're in the ballpark, the admissions decision is rarely about the numbers. It's about rapidly growing a richly layered, multidimensional personal Brand Connectome.

THE ALLURE OF PURPOSE

In 2010, under the leadership of CEO Paul Polman, Unilever began a new Purposeful Brands strategy through their Unilever Sustainable Living Plan. Polman was determined to create a long-term strategy that placed sustainability at the core of the multinational personal care and consumer goods company. But over the years, this myopic emphasis quietly took its toll. As of 2023, the company's profits had been declining for five years, and shares in Unilever dropped almost 18 percent between 2022 and 2023. Investors were, not surprisingly, unhappy.

Terry Smith, founder and manager of Fundsmith Equity Fund, Unilever's fifteenth-largest shareholder, called out Unilever for its purpose-oriented strategy, highlighting the importance of the utility of Unilever's products over the purpose behind them. In one example, he stated that "a company which feels it has to define the purpose of Hellmann's mayonnaise has, in our view, clearly lost the plot." He also called into question the company's Lux brand soap messaging, which was based around "inspiring women to rise above everyday sexist judgements and express their beauty and femininity unapologetically." Smith claimed that the last time he checked, soap was for washing.

Though Smith's statements may seem glib, he was not alone in recognizing how an overemphasis on purpose may have actually been harming the company's brands. Paul Matthews, Unilever's head of communications and corporate affairs, openly admitted that Unilever had "perhaps overstepped...talking about brand purpose in isolation to everything else you need for a brand to grow and be successful." It was unclear to some consumers and investors what the brand stood for, as an overfocus on purpose had overwhelmed all other messaging and wreaked havoc on the P&L. After recognizing the drawback of a singular focus on brand purpose, Matthews expressed his epiphany: "You need great innovation, you need the right pricing point, you need it to be available." The company learned an important lesson. Your brand's purpose, and the values it embraces, are critical, especially in a time when environmental, social, and governance (ESG) frameworks have become central to business practices, and rightfully so. But they are only one piece, not the primary driver of a brand's growth, and shouldn't be given an outsized place in your strategy.

Unilever is not alone in this misstep. Starting around 2009, many brands decided to focus on purpose above all else. Pinpointing exactly why may be difficult, but there was one voice that made a particularly large impression, a message that was reinforced by many others. That year, author and inspirational speaker Simon Sinek gave his now famous TED Talk, "Start with Why: How Great Leaders Inspire Action," which was accompanied by his book on the same topic that year. In the presentation, which has to date been viewed nearly sixty-two million times, he espoused a new vision of how to do business. Instead of focusing on what you sell, how you make it, and why you sell it, Sinek proposed turning that hierarchy upside down, focusing on the "why" first and foremost.

Fortune 500 companies bought the idea hook, line, and sinker. They spent hundreds of thousands of dollars defining their brand purpose and began promoting it in communications backed by millions of dollars of marketing support. Survey companies began tracking how much consumers cared about a brand's purpose, along with important initiatives such as the company's track record on sustainability, diversity, and other ESG. And, as you might expect, the percentage of millennials and Gen Zers who cared about purpose was higher than that of other cohorts, giving those eager to pull in younger consumers even more reason to take notice. Over the next decade, that trend continued, and may have been even further influenced by the COVID-19 pandemic. In COVID's aftermath, consumers seemed more attuned to social issues, whether equity and inclusion or the environment. From 2019 to 2021 alone, the percentage of people who wanted brands to reflect their values rose by six points.

There's only one problem. As you should know by now, what consumers say they want and what they ultimately choose bear little relationship to each other, since their behavior is dominated by their unconscious mind. While 65 percent of consumers claim to want purpose-driven brands, only 26 percent actually buy them. That's because there are a host of other drivers that cause people to choose their brands. These "business drivers," as compared with "purpose drivers," include elements such as consumer benefit, deep expertise, advanced technology, cultural relevance, and the brand's image. Without these, the brand is stuck with one-dimensional messaging that won't contribute to salience.

That's not to say purpose cannot, or even should not, be one of the messages in your multilayered approach. But you need to get the balance right—there is a direct correlation between messaging the right amount of purpose and growing your brand. And it's probably not as much as you think. For example, some purpose-focused brands spend up to 90 percent of their communication on purpose drivers—such as social causes, charitable contributions, or sustainability—reserving only 10 percent for business drivers. They've got the weighting upside down. They should actually be spending only 10 percent of their messaging on purpose; it should be a side dish, not the main course. Further, messaging that you're "doing good" is not the same as actually *doing good* while providing a benefit to your customer.

Communicating purpose has become a new trend in marketing, and industry professionals have swarmed it like bees, with little evidence that it actually works. Because there has been so little understanding of what really drives preference and growth, these types of trends come up every decade or so—whether emotional positioning, hyper-segmentation, or brand love—and are seen as a silver bullet to success. But as is inherent in all trends, they are temporary. So while on the surface, focusing on purpose may seem noble, if your growth contracts and your business plummets, you won't be doing a whole lot of good for anyone.

MULTIPLE TOUCHPOINTS LEAD TO RELEVANCE

As discussed, relevance only occurs when your brand is connected to multiple everyday touchpoints in people's minds. This works not only in advertising but also if you're applying for a job or pitching your services to a potential client. But multiple touchpoints can only be achieved if you layer your messaging. By having multiple brand associations work in concert, you create more paths in the mind and greater salience, better affecting a person's instinctive decision.

By no means should you be focusing on three, four, or five *disconnected* messages or layers that *contradict* one another. Creating a well-balanced Brand Connectome requires being thoughtful in your creation of diversified drivers that, when taken together, tell a cohesive story and create perceived superiority. There still needs to be one overarching brand identity with multiple drivers and supporting pillars underneath. That's what layering is all about.

One famous, storied sneaker brand realized the power in layering after losing market share for over twenty years. Once a leader in the athletic footwear category, its market share slowly declined over two decades, from a peak of 50 percent to 25 percent. Every top ad agency had taken a crack at it, but none of them had been able to move the needle. Enough was enough. The CMO, looking down at his feet in the brand's latest model, picked up the phone and called his business school buddy who worked for one of the top-shelf management consulting firms. After two years of work, and ten million dollars, this group of consultants told him the answer to turning around the business was to change their brand positioning to a sole message: "achieve more."

It seemed like a reasonable enough solution; the brand was, after all, an athletic brand where achievement is paramount. The company went to market with the new strategy, hiring a celebrity basketball player, and spent millions developing digital and TV advertising, and a couple million more to run those ads. Unfortunately, it failed to drive growth. Achievement, on its own, was not the answer to the company's woes. The CMO, now beside himself, decided to try an unconventional approach—conduct strategy work and research at the implicit level. To his surprise, it revealed that multiple themes were critical for bringing in prospective consumers, particularly millennials, where they had a severe shortage of users: themes like advanced footwear technology, style, and the history of the company as an early pioneer in the rise of the running and jogging movement, as well as achievement. The winning scenario that converted the growth target was combining all four drivers. Any one of those individual themes did not work.

Armed with the growth formula for bringing millennials into the business, the company created a 360-degree marketing campaign based on the new strategy—and something amazing happened.

Revenue went from declining to double-digit growth in a matter of weeks. When the marketplace results came in, the astounded CMO remarked: "It's funny, we tried each of those themes separately over the years but we never used all of them at the same time." The results were so extraordinary it seemed like some kind of magic, but it wasn't; it was science. The brand had physically grown in people's minds from a single driver with few associations to a multiplicity of drivers with many associations, creating greater salience and resulting in a fresh wave of growth after decades of decline.

This notion of multiplicity isn't just about breadth, it's about meaning and knowledge. Multiple drivers yield higher conversion because the more we understand about a brand, the more our brains connect with it. For example, if you know the founder's story about a brand, or the so-called backstory, you will be more loyal to it than if you don't. Unfortunately, companies often try to ignore their past and their heritage because they believe it's old-fashioned or going to make the brand appear dated. But when the founder's story is just one layer of the messaging, supported by others, it can do wonders. Not only was this true with the turnaround of the sneaker brand, but it's easy to see in many others. And the history doesn't need to be in the distant past.

Consider California-based Josh Cellars wine, founded in 2007 by sommelier, vintner, and former wine executive Joe Carr, who was still selling cases of Josh Cellars out of his truck as of 2009. As a California winemaker, he was up against a tough legacy market, with the first wine vineyard in California established literally hundreds of years earlier. But Carr had his own history he decided to rely on, that of his father, for whom the wine was named. Even though the wine was new, he infused the brand with a tradition of hard work, detail, and passion, qualities he explains were passed down from his dad. The way he tells his founder's story across his marketing is based around Josh Carr's experience as a craftsperson and family man. When the brand presents its history timeline, it even starts with Josh Carr's birth. They highlight his time spent in service in the military, his marriage, and his work as a lumberjack and volunteer firefighter in his hometown of Berlin in upstate New York.

Now remember, they're talking about the winemaker's dad, not even the winemaker himself. And admittedly, none of this has anything to do with the wine Carr makes, but the brand piggybacks on associations of family, persistence, and even the American Dream. Though some connoisseurs may turn up their nose at the brand, the wine market tells a different story. Josh Cellars showed an unparalleled double-digit growth year over year from 2018 through 2023. In 2014, they sold just three hundred thousand cases. In 2018, over two million. As of 2023? Five million cases in one year. Now the number-one brand in the premium US table wines category, its history and founder's story are imbued with tradition.

But it's not enough to stop at the history. Come up with just one big idea about your brand and it will remain hidden in the mind, a lone road, off the beaten track, isolated from the connections to important associations and memories in your brain. Layering multiple messages on top of that one provides a robust ecosystem of positive associations for your brain to get lost in. Think of each key message as a gear. For example, gear one: What benefit does your brand provide to its target audience? Gear two: How does the product or service work to deliver that benefit? Gear three: What advances or innovations has the brand pioneered? When the gears connect and turn together, they power your brand's engine. They still need to fit together, otherwise you won't get anywhere. But when they do, that engine can become an engine of growth for years to come.

APPLYING MULTIPLE MESSAGES

Multiple messages build an engaging story in which the consumer almost becomes a character. They become part of the story and brand. But that's not what most advertisers and their ad agencies do today. If you advocate for this multidimensional approach in executing your communications, be prepared to get pushback. Many will say it is impossible to get all those messages into one piece of creative. They are therefore forever compartmentalizing. Tell your ad agency your research shows your brand has three business drivers and they will take the traditional approach—dividing them up, placing each one in a different media vehicle.

For example, they might put the product or consumer benefit in TV advertising, the reason to believe in digital ads, and the purpose on their website. But that won't work. The brain can't piece together disparate sources of information into one cohesive, intelligible story about a brand. One well-known cereal brand tried to find the *best* positioning for years. It fluctuated its messaging, at times emphasizing taste, then health, then all-natural, and back again. These efforts went nowhere. Only when they combined three qualities—good taste, healthy, and less processed—into one campaign did the brand finally start growing again.

Each theme or layer in your messaging should be seen as a potential driver of conversion for your growth target. Since that's the case, all of them are important. When deciding which to focus on, consider three to four layers to begin. Imagine, for example, you own a small furniture store, selling handmade pieces from committed craftspeople who live within a fifty-mile radius of the store. The traditional marketing model would say that you should create a single-minded message about local craftsmanship. But consumers may also need to know that the furniture is stylish, which will make their home more chic and inviting. Right there, you have multiple messages to drive someone's choice—local craftmanship can't do that all on its own. Or if you run a coffee shop, you might highlight that all of your coffee is certified fair trade, served in a welcoming environment by professional baristas, and that you support the neighborhood soccer and baseball teams. Here you have messages of coffee expertise, purpose, and community. Note that none of these messages contradict one another, and each one joins with the others to help grow the brand's connectome.

Once you've chosen the messages you want to convey, you need to put them to work. Don't forget your Growth Triggers. A sixty-second commercial about something being fresh, natural, and ripe isn't necessary if you have a few of the right cues or distinctive brand assets that can convey these messages in a few seconds flat. Your brain does the rest. Both category and Brand Triggers® are effective here. And though anyone in the category can own a specific Growth Trigger, as discussed, you want *your* brand to own it. The waves in the CeraVe ad, for example, could be used to symbolize smooth skin by any skincare brand out there. But by rendering them in blue and white (the dominant shades in CeraVe's color palette), having them emanate from the jar of CeraVe cream, and linking them with both ceramide technology and smooth skin, the brand now owns them. When these waves flow and undulate across clean, clear skin, the brain processes the built-in meaning of moisture (water) and health. Just as the product in the demo is shown penetrating the skin, communicating efficacy, this messaging seeps into consumers' memory structure.

Again, the point is to immerse your audience's brains in your brand's story. A useful example of this can be found in Expedia's Vrbo, originally "vacation rentals by owner," which offers homes in the most scenic, beautiful locations around the world. But they combine this message with associations of family, friends, vacation, and getting away from it all. Blended together, these messages create the perfect vacation we all want to have—putting your brain, and you, at the center of the brand narrative. You become immersed, picturing yourself there, surrounded by the people you love, without a care in the world, enjoying each other's company in that beautiful environment. Vrbo also stresses that, unlike Airbnb or a hotel, when you rent with Vrbo, it will be a "whole vacation home," just you and yours, no "strangers" down the hall.

If they just focused on one of these messages, the brain would not get the full story. Bringing family and friends together is great, but if it's in a stuffy, one-bedroom apartment in a congested area of town with few amenities, you're not going to have any takers. That's why Vrbo uses three key themes to drive instinctive brand preference for Vrbo: beautiful homes in breathtaking environments, family and friends, and a full place to call your own while you're there. Further, Vrbo provides us with a great example of how to portray multiple messages through multiple mediums or senses. In their ads, the scenic locations of the homes are not mentioned in any dialogue or copy, they are shown. The imagery does much of the heavy lifting so the burden is not solely on copy points.

When it comes to building your personal brand, the same layering principles hold true. If you were to only give one "message" about yourself, you'd likely seem dull. Think of that one person at a dinner party who tells the same story over and over again every time you get together. After a while, it's easy to lose interest, and your brain checks out. That's also why résumés include more than just how your skills align with a position. Equally important are some statistics showing your results, your education, your volunteer work, and some personal hobbies and details. Employers want to hire well-rounded individuals who will not only know how to do their jobs, but who will also be an overall positive addition to a team.

In a job interview, layering multiple messages is particularly helpful. Think of your strengths, skills, and achievements to date as your brand expertise, how you can help the company as the benefits you provide, and your understanding of and enthusiasm for what the company does as your values, such as teamwork or a strong work ethic. You also have a backstory—the unique narrative that makes you who you are and brought you to this point. While much of that story is going to remain the same from interview to interview, it absolutely must be tailored to each opportunity you apply for. Just as a brand needs to match what is stored in consumers' memories in order to be their go-to, a candidate's dimensions must match the ideal employee the executive recruiter or hiring manager has stored in theirs. That's when you'll get the job offer. Also as with brands, you can't simply *tell* people you're caring, smart, and funny. You have to share stories that communicate those traits, so the interviewer comes to these conclusions about you on their own.

Interestingly, research shows that 70 percent of employers rank a job applicant's personality among the top three hiring factors, whereas only 7 percent include appearance and 18 percent education. Since our brains operate on instinct, the tremendous role an intangible factor plays in the interview process should come as no surprise. The person sitting across the table from you asking you questions is, after all, human. Their brain works like everyone else's, and the same way any consumer's does when choosing a product.

In this case, "personality" is a catch-all, a word employers use to describe the gut feeling they get when the candidate in front of them matches the idealized candidate they hold in their mind. Are they actually judging your personality? Not really. If they like your "personality," that actually means there is a match between the two connectomes—the candidate's and the employer's—based on the messages you're transmitting. Remember, you *are* a brand. And all of the messaging cues work together to build your Brand Connectome. Together, they create a multiplicity of implicit associations that elevate your brand's perception, causing your interviewer to instinctively connect with you—pushing your candidacy away from the "no" bucket and into the "go-to" hire.

For an industry that has been reared on the singularity approach to building brands, this whole notion of multiple messages sounds like absolute heresy. And if you talk to anyone following the traditional marketing playbook and old rules of conscious marketing, they will likely hurl objections your way: You can't fit more than one message in an ad (untrue). The brain can't process more than one message at a time (the opposite is true—it thrives on abundance). Your approach is unfocused and undisciplined (multiple messages can certainly be focused and work to your advantage).

But take a step back and consider: What would the physical earth be without layers? What would our culture be without complexity? What would a story look like without characters, plot, subplots, tension? What would the world look like if we were all the same? Human beings are multifaceted, so it stands to reason that your messaging to them should be multifaceted as well. In some ways, it's just that simple. By connecting with people on multiple levels, you essentially meet them where they are, lighting up their brain with your connectome. Your brand can only expand across all the nooks and crannies of consumers' minds if you fill up as many of their neural pathways as possible, connecting with their positive associations while also creating new ones. One path just won't do the trick.

Chapter 7

THE UNCONSCIOUS NEED FOR FANTASY

INSTINCT RULE: People say they want reality but they instinctively choose fantasy every time.

Conjure a wonderful Thanksgiving dinner. You might recall the turkey as it came out of the oven, the smell nearly intoxicating as it went on a serving plate and was set out on the table. Surrounded by friends and family, home for the holidays, everyone admired the perfectly cooked bird in all its golden, crisp glory with a chorus of oohs and aahs. Looking around at your loved ones—all smiles—you felt embraced by familial warmth and gratitude. This scene is seared into your memory. What you probably don't think of is the hacked-up, half-eaten carcass that was picked over and left out on the counter for too long, its fat congealing as your dog stalked nearby. Nor do you remember the argument that erupted when your uncle joked, once again, that your mother's corn bread was too dry. That's because your brain stores memories in their idealized form, no matter what actually happened.

These less-fond memories are part of the ugly, messy truth that people want no part of. But many advertisers have got it in their heads that this is what the consumers want—reality. They couldn't be more mistaken. Our unconscious minds want *fantasy*. That's why your brain stores the memory of the turkey fresh out of the oven and the joy you felt in the presence of your loved ones long before Fido gnawed the leftovers into oblivion and your mother blew a gasket. Our most aspirational fantasies and innermost desires all come from our unconscious mind, where our memories are stored. Success doesn't come from dramatizing reality; it comes from matching your brand to people's fantasies. By tapping into these positive associations, your brand can ride the same neural pathways as people's fantasies, bonding them together in their minds. Maybe those fantasies include happiness and health, retirement on a megayacht, popularity, or the ability to rout your opponent in a basketball game.

Whole industries are built on fantasy. Take the fragrance industry. There is no better example than Revlon's Charlie ads from the 1970s. Charlie was, in many ways, the original modern fantasy fragrance. With $10 million in sales in its first year (1973), the highest-grossing fragrance launch in history at that point, its ads featured actress Shelley Hack as a stylish, independent, and confidently charismatic woman. In one, as the "Charlie" character, she drives up to an elegant restaurant in her white Rolls-Royce, sprays on some perfume, and hops out in an outfit to match the car—a shiny gold jumpsuit. She floats past the bar as Bobby Short sings, "Kind of young, kind of now…kind of free, kind of wow," spinning around with her date and landing in their private booth with a flick of her hair. In another, she arrives by boat to a party already in full swing on a glamorous yacht, this time in a sequined black blazer and a pair of black slacks, turning heads as she enters yet another bustling restaurant, Mel Tormé now singing the loungy Charlie jingle. A spray of perfume on her neck, and she's off through the crowd, the life of the party.

At the time, these ads captured a fantasy many women of the '70s wanted, a mix of glitz and pizazz with female independence and strength—a new fantasy for a new generation, empowering, sexy, and sleek. Pitched as a "most original fragrance," Charlie was the number-one selling perfume for years. It also played a key role in a major shift in fragrance sales. Before Charlie was released in 1973, most sales of perfume took place around the holidays, typically men purchasing it as gifts for their wives and partners. But with Charlie, Revlon sold the fantasy not to the men, but to women directly, any time of year. Today, some viewers may think of these ads as corny or cheesy, but the famous image of the Charlie woman striding confidently across the room, and across the page in print ads, became synonymous with "women's liberation."

Another obvious industry built on fantasy is automotive. Look no further than Mercedes-Benz. Their 2013 commercial for their CLA model flooded viewers' minds—especially those of men—with fantasy. The short ad begins with Satan (masterfully played by a devilish-looking Willem Dafoe) tempting a potential young buyer to sell his soul in exchange for the all-new CLA. The devil conjures up images of the man's future if he signs the contract: partying all night with Usher, model Kate Upton on his arm on the red carpet, his face on the cover of magazines, and a gaggle of female fans chasing him through the streets as if he were a rock star. Nothing captures the male sports car fantasy more effectively.

It doesn't matter whether viewers really believe this will happen if they buy this luxury vehicle; from the moment Mercedes implants those sticky associations into the audience's mind, they are now forever connected with the car. Better yet, at the end of the commercial, the man realizes he can have it all even without selling his soul—the CLA turns out to be reasonably priced. In that moment, the fantasy becomes attainable. It's the same glitz, glamour, and independence as Charlie, but the fantasy is updated and packaged for a new, contemporary audience.

And of course, there's fashion. The clothes we wear tell people about who we are, or at least who we want others to perceive us to be, and the most successful brands recognize this. For example, today's most valuable fashion brands include Louis Vuitton ($32.3 billion), Hermès ($18.3 billion), and Gucci ($18.2 billion). Similar to cosmetics and cars, each one builds a particular type of fantasy for its audience's minds to latch on to, becoming part of the brand's story. Gucci is both eclectic and high-end, connecting with a desire to be one's true self, while also being glamorous and desired. One ad for their Guilty fragrance line is a perfect example, with actor Elliot Page, actress Julia Garner, and rapper and producer A$AP Rocky spending an evening together full of intrigue and romance.

When it comes to selling fantasy, cosmetics, luxury cars, and designer fashion come as no surprise. Traditional marketers would even tell you these are the "fantasy categories." But contrary to popular belief, fantasy is not reserved for these industries alone. Fantasy drives virtually *all* great brands, speaking to our desire for an elevated, better self, and creating instinctive brand preference across categories. It doesn't matter if that's Bounty's "quicker picker upper" magically absorbing a terrible spill or Otezla's psoriasis medication allowing you to confidently bare your arms. Whether it is paper towels and cleaning supplies, health care and pharmaceuticals, social causes and fundraising, or political campaigns—fantasy rules above all else.

But that's not what people say. They *say* they want reality every time. "I want people who look like me. Who are realistic, whose bodies aren't perfect. Whose homes are a little messy. Whose kids don't listen, just like mine." But that's their conscious mind speaking. As discussed, what we say and what we do are two entirely different things. Still, that doesn't stop traditional marketers and ad agency creatives from trying to appease this supposed desire for reality. After all, they're listening to the consumer. But when it comes down to it, reality doesn't pan out. The creative content that consistently performs best in the marketplace—whether featured on TV, in social media, or in digital ads—is all about nearly unattainable perfection: the clean-cut family eating on an outdoor terrace under a string of vintage-looking lights, the stylish home ripped from the pages of *Better Homes and Gardens*, the elegantly dressed couple getting out of the sports car for an evening out with friends, a father and son falling down with laughter during an impromptu game of football. These are the images that get stuck in our mind, because whether we realize it or not, all of us are influenced by fantasy. We can't help it—our brains crave it.

YOUR BRAIN ON FANTASY

Like layered messaging, fantasies have high brain utilization. They light up our minds, employing multiple parts of our brains, while connecting to idealized ideas and visuals stored in our memories. In doing so, they tap into our positive associations, consuming our attention and closing out the world around us. It's like when you're stuck in a meeting that has run long over schedule and your brain starts wandering, caught in a fantasy about the weekend ahead. You become so focused on that perfect weekend, it may take a moment for you to recognize you haven't answered your boss's question and your colleague is nudging you to speak up and reply.

Fantasies—in which our minds create original fictional stories connected to our future goals and dreams—are constructed using an extended brain network. This network includes the hippocampus, which plays a major role in our memory, learning, and mood, but that's not all. To make fantasy work, other regions in the brain must be involved, encoding and retrieving memories, generating coherent and complex scenes, and regulating our emotions. So fantasies require a lot of brain activity, which is why they can dominate the mind for a time, closing out everything else. They utilize our five senses and fully absorb our attention, allowing us to safely access and develop narratives in our minds that may or may not be out of reach in our real lives.

Fantasies are also universal. While each of us might have different specific goals, large groups of people have the *same* fantasy. If you're an amateur athlete aspiring to the majors or a middle-aged guy who plays a pickup game every other weekend, you still want to win. Everyone, no matter their background, wants a retirement where they can enjoy a life of leisure and freedom from financial concerns, whether picturing themselves on the beach in Bali or relaxing at home without a care. And let's not forget love, the universal desire for romance and intimacy.

When you project your audience's ideal experience, whatever that may be, you create a neural connection between their fantasy, which is stored in their memories, and your brand. Just like connecting with the familiar versus the unique, or the nostalgic memory of the brands your mother used while you were growing up, by matching your audience's deeply held aspiration, you once again tap into existing positive associations, growing your Brand Connectome. When the brand projects the fantasy, the brain not only becomes mesmerized, shutting everything else out, it also shuts out the competition.

LINKING TO HIDDEN ASPIRATIONS AND DESIRES

Fantasies revolve around what we want most, whether hopes for the future or ambitious goals, a more fit body or quality family time, unattainable wealth, a healthy environment, or just a good night's sleep. They represent the ideal state we hope to achieve or the ideal experience we would like to have. Fantasies enable brands to connect with consumers at an unconscious level. When you identify the convergent fantasy your target audience shares, there is a match between their brain and your brand, leaving them mesmerized by the promise of fulfilling their dreams.

Take the consumer obsession with Zillow, the real-estate hunting website. Even people who aren't necessarily planning to move find themselves scrolling through the listings, regularly seeking out homes they can't afford. In a survey from 2021, 55 percent of respondents, out of the one thousand surveyed, said they browse Zillow from one to four hours *per day*, and at least once a week 80 percent fantasize about a home they came across on the site. According to the same survey, 49 percent claimed they would rather be ogling Zillow's listings than having sex. Zillow speaks to the elevated selves of its hundreds of millions of visitors—who they *want* to be, how they *want* to live. They want to picture their home as their castle, not the cramped one-room apartment or messy house overflowing with junk accumulated over the years.

There's a reason home makeover TV shows remain so popular, and HGTV ranks as the ninth most-watched network, with ninety-five million American households tuning in each month. These shows are so successful at promoting a fantasy, they have actually begun to dictate how people buy, sell, and renovate their homes, a phenomenon dubbed the "HGTV effect." Research has shown that homeowners will actually sacrifice their own taste to make sure their homes align with those they see on TV and in magazines such as *Better Homes and Gardens*.

Fantasy sports—a nearly $9.5 billion industry in the US—functions the same way. The world of professional sports is an elite group most of us will never be talented enough to join in our wildest dreams. With fantasy sports, however, we can realize those dreams, even if only virtually. The players we pick become part of our "team," and their real-world success affects our fantasy scores and stats. As we become interlinked with these pros, the fantasy spreads in our minds as we take on the role of coach, owner, and manager. Here, fantasy is not just part of the industry's marketing or communication; it's literally the offering. With more than fifty million people playing fantasy sports in the US alone—33 percent of whom are women—the industry continues to see growth year after year, its players desperate to live out their childhood dreams.

But marketers and advertising creatives of the conscious variety argue that consumers desire products, services, and communications that are accessible—not aspirational. They don't want to scare away potential buyers with something that seems too far out of reach, too glamorous. For example, they would claim a discount department store like Kohl's should signal that it's a bargain, showing ordinary people dressed in everyday, run-of-the-mill clothes. As you can tell from the results, that business model doesn't work. People want the best of both worlds: they want to attain that aspirational style worn by celebrities *and* for less. That's why a company like Target does over $100 billion in annual revenue, promising quality fashion at reasonable prices. Today, consumers at all income levels are more educated than ever because they're exposed to, and intimately familiar with, what fashion, quality, and craftsmanship look like. They know the names of the designer brands celebrities wear, notice special details like fine stitching on designer clothing and shoes, appreciate precision chronographs on watches. Target focuses on the quality and style to make the fantasy achievable.

THE JUXTAPOSITION OF FANTASY AND REALITY

Even when you think fantasy is not at play, if you take a deeper look, you'll find it always beating out reality. And when the two coexist side by side, the results can be powerful. Twenty years ago, concern about climate change was limited to a small niche group—basically "tree huggers" and Greenpeace employees. But in 2006, the percentage of people who agreed with the statement "The seriousness of global warming is generally underestimated" reached an all-time high of 38 percent for that era, and 43 percent of the population worried "a great deal" about the environment. This increase in concern was in large part due to one major event—not a tsunami, an earthquake, a drought, or the disappearance of a species, but a movie that would eventually be seen by millions.

An Inconvenient Truth, released in 2006 and starring former vice president Al Gore, was both a commercial and critical success, winning the Oscar for Best Documentary and grossing almost $50 million. According to one study on the movie's impact, "research and data show that unlike any work or event before it, the film was a turning point for shifting America to think and act more consciously about the warming climate." But what could have made a single documentary—a genre not necessarily known for its wide viewership—so incredibly popular as to spark a mainstream environmental movement?

That's the power of fantasy. For years, other climate advocates had provided research, data, facts, and figures. But these all target the conscious brain, so they did little to change people's minds or affect their decisions. The effectiveness of Gore's film came from his presentation of the ideal natural world, of what once was, a near Garden of Eden. That's our inner desire, and where he implied we could, and must, return. He projected this fantasy through a wide range of majestic images of the world's most iconic, well-known natural treasures. In addition, he contrasted that fantasy with reality in vivid juxtaposition.

Contrast is like steroids for the brain. When an Italian sauce brand showed a side-by-side comparison between its jar of sauce with a wooden spoon standing up straight in the middle of it (labeled with its brand name) next to a jar of sauce with a spoon slumping to the side (labeled "Other Italian Sauces"), the fantasy was immediate: the thick richness of the full-bodied tomato sauce was more vivid because it was contrasted against the reality of the competitor's runny, watery, grade-B product. By showing aerial photos of glaciers and frozen tundra in the Alps, Peru, Argentina, Mount Kilimanjaro, and Patagonia, then showing how that ice has retreated over time, Gore's movie accomplished the same effect. One photo with abundant ice and snow gives way to another of barren brown land. Viewers don't need to consciously think about what's going on—they instinctually grasp the magnitude of the crisis. Had he just shown the fantasy, or just shown the reality, the brain would not have latched onto the idea, and the point would not have been nearly as effective.

Like the snow-capped mountain, glaciers acted as a fantastical Growth Trigger: these majestic, natural formations embody purity, fresh air, the beauty of nature, cleanliness. To see all of that literally melting away before one's eyes was extremely moving. Similarly, Gore showed a grid of various animals with each box fading away, a visual metaphor for the species' decline and ultimate extinction. Then there's the animated polar bear, like something straight out of Pixar. The image of a polar bear swimming to an ever-decreasing ice patch is a negative Growth Trigger—a dose of reality that stuck with viewers and left an inevitable impact on their Climate Change Connectome. The fantasy there is for that lone, weak patch of ice to grow back into the strong glacier it had been in its former glory, prior to climate change. By showing people the gap between what once was and what is now, they were inspired to preserve the natural world. The fantasy was pure air, clear skies, healthy living, and unadulterated beauty. People got on board.

However, when you stop reinforcing the fantasy, you no longer have that same level of brain utilization, meaning the memory fades and you lose mind share. Less utilization, less progress, causing growth to halt or entirely cease. This stalling-out effect can be seen in how US climate concerns have stagnated since at least 2016. Even though over 70 percent of US citizens believe global warming is taking place, that doesn't translate into the concern that might be expected. A Gallup poll found that only 43 percent of Americans are "highly worried" about global warming today (the same as in 2006), and views have been about the same every year since 2016. (According to the Pew Research Center, as of 2022, only 54 percent of adults in the US think climate change is a major threat to the country.)

The movement seems to have lost momentum when they stopped pushing the fantasy of what was possible contrasted with the reality of what was being lost. Instead of moving forward with Gore's tried-and-true formula, advocates for the movement shifted to referring to climate change as an existential crisis, portraying it as almost inevitable. In Greta Thunberg's now famous 2019 address to the UN, for example, the young activist, barely holding back tears, emotionally chastised the members of the UN, and indirectly the viewers at home: "You have stolen my dreams and my childhood with your empty words...We are in the beginning of a mass extinction, and all you can talk about is money and fairy tales of eternal economic growth. How dare you!" Her rage was palpable before she shifted into a litany of facts and figures.

Thunberg had a lot to be upset about, and her speech made headlines. But its portrayal of the grim realities was a classic attempt at conscious persuasion, a confrontational approach that is not only less likely to resonate, it can be downright alienating. Without a message of hope, of what we could do together, how we could save the world and reach an environmental utopia, the speech failed to have the behavior-changing impact it could have had. Research shows that the "Greta Effect" empowered young people who were already climate conscious to feel that their individual actions could make a difference, which is admirable. However, the problem is that she was speaking to her existing customers. It seems that her speech did not have an impact on changing the narrative around climate change, nor did it win the movement any converts. Despite what the traditional marketing rule claims, we don't want reality, we want fantasy—and, in this case, the fantasy is a clean future. If Thunberg and the environmental movement want to succeed going forward, they must tap into people's universal aspirations and desires, not reprimand them.

TOP OF MIND, TOP OF MARKET

In the marketplace, every category has a dominant fantasy. For the outdoors, it's adventure, excitement, reflection, and connection with nature. In skin care, it's that perfect skin, the outward signal of inner health and happiness. In home goods and furniture, it's the stylish, comfortable home of your dreams. In sports drinks it's unmatched performance. Dominant fantasies exist in politics and social causes too, whether safe, clean streets and affordable homes where you can raise a family or a world in which everyone is treated equally. Any brand can tap into their audience's aspirations and desires, connecting with their fantasies at an unconscious level, but within each category, the brand that owns the fantasy dominates.

When you own your category's fantasy, you create barriers to entry. If that ownership is strong enough, you define the category, creating a connection between your brand and the fantasy over others. It's as if all the competitors in a category are climbing up a mountain, jockeying for the top. But only one brand can sit at the peak, forcing the rest off, down the steep side of the mountain. To own the fantasy is to be top of mind. And when you're top of mind, you become the top of the market, and that tends to be a lasting instinctive advantage.

For example, Gatorade has led the sports drink category since its inception in 1965. In 2023, its annual sales reached $6.25 billion, nearly four times those of competitor BodyArmor ($1.65 billion) and five times those of Powerade ($1.26 billion). It's true that Gatorade was the first sports drink on the market, but its continued success is the result of how it pushed the fantasy of unmatched performance, as represented by its 1980s–1990s celebrity spokesperson Michael Jordan, with neon-orange droplets coming out of his pores, symbolizing his superior athleticism, his inner drive fueled by Gatorade. By owning this fantasy, Gatorade is physically more dominant in viewers' brains. But you don't need to be first to market to own a fantasy; you just need to recognize what that particular fantasy might be and associate your brand with it.

For example, in 1984 Folgers coffee started a new ad campaign that would become legendary in advertising circles and marketing history, while producing one of the most effective distinctive brand assets: the iconic slogan and accompanying jingle "The best part of waking up is Folgers in your cup." (If you know the song, you can't help but hear it as you read those words.) Throughout the 1970s and early 1980s, Folgers and Maxwell House were two of the largest coffee brands in the US, with essentially equivalent share and parity performance in blind taste tests, and were neck and neck in the marketplace. Both long-standing companies, Folgers got its start in the 1850s, amid the California gold rush, serving miners, and Maxwell House was established forty years later in Nashville in 1892, its name a homage to the founder's first customer, Maxwell House Hotel.

When the "Best Part of Waking Up" ad was released, however, Folgers quickly overtook Maxwell House, and in a few short years it emerged as the number-one coffee brand in the US. Why? Because the campaign allowed Folgers to own the fantasy of the perfect morning. Believe it or not, no coffee company had yet zeroed in on that crucial part of the day. Until then, coffee companies feared that if they focused solely on morning, they would be putting all their eggs in one basket, missing out on other times and occasions when people wanted a hot cup of fresh joe, like the 3 p.m. afternoon pick-me-up or the post-dinner cup. What they didn't understand is what brand strategist and managing director of Triggers Morgan Seamark explains so well: "What you market and what you sell are two different things." Folgers may have been selling coffee, but they were marketing so much more.

The creative team at DDB Needham working on the assignment for Folgers kept hitting a wall while trying to develop the ad. The creative director reviewed idea after idea from the team and kept shaking his head. After one such occasion, he poked around the team's office, pointed to a bunch of sketches on the floor, and asked, "What's that?" The copywriter said it was nothing good, more or less cast-offs meant for the trash. But something caught the creative director's eye. He asked the team to walk him through the campaign that showed a person smelling—*not drinking*—the coffee in the cup, eyes closed, a developing smile, inhaling its rich fragrance. The creative director could *feel* this idea had promise. The ad romanticized the moment in which the coffee drinker starts a new day full of possibility, transformed not by the caffeine in the coffee, but by the coffee's aroma. It turned out that, in the brain, aroma is code for superior rich taste—one of the most powerful Growth Triggers in the coffee category.

Any concerns of losing afternoon and evening coffee drinkers quickly dissipated. Folgers discovered that the fantasy of that first transformative cup in the morning was one that users wanted *all the time*. It wouldn't stop Folgers from being chosen at other times of the day. That's because the first cup is the "torture test"—the one that counts the most. Waking up to a bad cup of coffee could ruin your entire day. The strength of the morning fantasy increased the Folgers Connectome, and rather than limiting usage, it caused the brand to become the go-to no matter what time of day. Folgers' market share skyrocketed, and the brand continued to enjoy a significant instinctive advantage on "rich taste and aroma" (perceived versus actual), eclipsing Maxwell House and creating barriers to entry for other coffee brands for years to come.

THE UPSIDE AND DOWNSIDE OF CELEBRITIES AND INFLUENCERS

Fantasy and celebrity go hand in hand. Whether online or news personalities, professional athletes, popular actors and musicians, successful entrepreneurs, or anyone who may embody the current cultural zeitgeist, these figures can be an effective Growth Trigger when used correctly. Celebrities are one type of influencer. Other types of influencers may also hold sway over your decisions—the alpha in your social set, that charismatic coworker who's always one step ahead of everyone else, your cool neighbor who seems to lead a charmed life, or your friend from the gym with great abs—but none are able to leverage fantasy quite like celebrities.

When a brand uses a well-known, well-liked celebrity in their messaging and marketing, they connect with the audience unconsciously because of our instinctive belief that celebrities lead magical lives. They are rich, attend better parties, hobnob with other important people, meet with presidents, own multiple homes, go on glamorous vacations. These people have an elevated status in society, causing us to look up to them and place them on a pedestal. The more cynical among us may deny it, but we all have celebrities we admire—it's part of how our brain functions.

This has been the case throughout human evolution—we are hardwired to look up to the people with the most prestige. According to Harvard University's Joseph Henrich, a professor of human evolutionary biology, and political anthropologist Francisco Jose Gil-White, natural selection favored those of us with the ability to copy the behavior of the most successful people in our orbit. This also included ingratiating ourselves to these people, looking to interact with them as much as possible. In time, as humans dispersed and people's circles of influence grew larger, this desire remained and developed into an instinctive preference to imitate and revere the most popular figures in society overall.

Look no further than the Taylor Swift frenzy of 2023 for one of the most intriguing celebrity phenomena. Her Eras tour earned over $590 million in ticket sales alone, the highest-grossing tour by a female artist of all time. More than 3.5 million people registered for presale tickets, and even after "breaking" Ticketmaster due to the overwhelming volume of traffic on the site, two million tickets were sold in one day. Wall-to-wall fans with outstretched arms hoped some of her magic would wear off on them. This was 1960s Beatlemania all over again.

Part of her success comes from reinforcing the different "eras" of her music, feeding on the nostalgic impulse of current fans and constantly introducing new ones to her material. But more importantly, Swift manages her stardom in a unique way that allows her Swifties entrée into her fantasy life while being open and real about its ups and downs. While most celebrities might act aloof, Swifties get an unparalleled mix of aspiration and accessibility—they feel that she's their friend. They even make friendship bracelets to commemorate their deep connection.

Remember, a brand is known by the associations it keeps. When a brand receives a celebrity endorsement, we unconsciously believe that the product, service, investment, or cause must be good, as the positive associations we have with that celebrity are now conferred to the brand. Their status elevates the brand it is associated with.

According to Temple University professor and psychologist Frank Farley, when we learn about celebrities or other famous figures in the media, we "often live some of our lives through them." This gives new meaning to the term "starstruck." It's not that we're necessarily running out to take a tour of Hollywood celebrities' homes. Rather, it's that we unconsciously want to connect with their status. Farley explains, "We all have dreams of wealth and fame and happiness and style and social influence and so on, which starts early with fairy tales and the way we raise our kids."

As a result, if a famous person were to tell you about a product, concept, or idea, it would be more likely to stick in your Brand Connectome because you already know the celebrity. Celebrities already have large connectomes, so your brand rides the coattails of their established associations. As the celebrity's connectome and your brand's connectome merge, your brand experiences greater salience and share of mind. In essence, you're gluing them together: the celebrity and the fantasy they represent, and your brand. A study by the University of Leicester showed this "gluing" effect in action. They first showed participants an image of Jennifer Aniston at the Eiffel Tower and watched as a particular neuron fired. They then showed Aniston and the tower separately in two different images. The same neurons fired in both cases. The Eiffel Tower had become inextricably linked to Aniston in the participants' minds.

Audience's brains already have a physical Aniston Connectome, built up from her many roles over her thirty-year career in movies and television, especially as Rachel in the hit sitcom *Friends*. Aniston is the girl next door, America's sweetheart. When we see Aniston connected with Aveeno skin care or Smartwater, new messages about those brands are added to the neural pathways we already have for Aniston, making the brands stickier in our memories and causing their connectomes to sprout and grow faster. It doesn't hurt that Aniston looks phenomenal in her fifties and brings healthy, fit, and confident associations to both brands. If you leverage a well-known celebrity and add new information or visuals to them, you create a new association faster and more effectively than if you just provide something new by itself.

Of course, the Jennifer Aniston neuron can equally be applied to other Hollywood actors, professional athletes, socialites, and the ever-growing landscape of social media influencers who have captivated millennial and Gen Z audiences. The modern-day use of the word "influencer" was not officially added to Merriam-Webster's dictionary until 2019. That same year, the market research firm Morning Consult found that 54 percent of young Americans surveyed would become social media influencers if given the opportunity, and 86 percent were willing to be paid to post sponsored content. Pew Research Center found that 54 percent of social media users, age eighteen to twenty-nine, report online influencers as impacting what they decide to buy. Social media influencers are also big business, with an estimated $16.4 billion spent on global influencer marketing in 2022.

A-list celebrities are expensive; they can cost a brand millions of dollars a year. But internet influencers provide some of that celebrity power at a much more reasonable price. What some of them lack in fame they often make up in expertise and audience engagement. Influencers' audiences can range from a few thousand to a million-plus. No matter their number of followers, if they are speaking to a niche audience or connected with a specific community, their voices can have a huge impact. Such influencers have their own network of enthusiasts who are obsessively interested in their advice—which amplifies their voice. For example, they might not be world-renowned household names, but influencers like the "millennial parenting whisperer" Dr. Becky and makeup artist and beauty blogger Huda Kattan have millions of devoted followers. They're not alone—other influencers focus on healthy kid-friendly recipes, carpentry, skin care, and investing. And that doesn't include social media personalities like the Italian "silent comedian" Khabane "Khaby" Lame (who as of 2024 had 161.5 million followers on TikTok) and the dancer Charli D'Amelio, the highest-paid TikTok influencer in

2022. Still, audience size is not the most important factor in the influencer world; rather it's the level of audience engagement.

A highly engaged audience of ten thousand that buys everything an influencer recommends is more valuable than an unengaged audience of a million. Influencers are like a celebrity endorsement but on a smaller, targeted scale. And you don't need to work for a massive company or run a multimillion-dollar corporation to hire such an influencer. If you're an entrepreneur or run a small business, take the time to learn about the influencers in your sector—a voice people trust and respect. They may not be a celebrity, but if your audience connects with them on a deep level, they could be an efficient way to quickly expand your Brand Connectome.

But be careful. Many brands over-rely on celebrities and influencers to the detriment of their business. If you are too dependent on them to make your brand stick in consumers' minds, they can become a crutch. Worse yet, they can overwhelm your brand. Advertising testing often reveals that people remember the celebrity better than the brand they are promoting. A celebrity should be a catalyst for dramatizing the brand's benefits, not become the story. If your advertising becomes more about the celebrity than the benefits and expertise of your business or cause, consumers will never get a solid understanding of what you're selling. Further, what if that celebrity falls out of favor? Gets canceled? If your brand becomes too dependent on that celebrity, with the two connectomes merging, any negative associations the celebrity takes on will negatively impact your brand too. Celebrities come and go—you don't want them to take your brand with them if they disappear from the public eye.

According to market research company Ipsos, the average likelihood of an ad being high performing, versus low performing, is 6.01 times more with a branded character, and only 2.84 times more with a celebrity. So celebrities can give you a lift for sure, but their connection to the brand can't possibly be as strong as a distinctive character created especially for the brand. There are so many other ways, aside from celebrity, to build memory structure and go-to brand salience. Distinctive brand assets go way beyond characters, colors, and package shape. From distinctive brand worlds to symbols, this area of marketing is an untapped treasure trove of possibilities. Many businesses would be better off developing distinctive brand assets and Growth Triggers to create consistent brand recognition, rather than making a huge spend on a celebrity.

THE MADOFF EFFECT
AND THE NEGATIVE USE OF FANTASY

Overall, fantasies are good for us. As American psychiatrist Ethel S. Person explains, "We are really infused by our fantasies, they can help establish goals and provide motivation to strive for them." But our fantasies can also be exploited. People can exert undue influence on us through the power of fantasy. If they have our best interest at heart, then no problem—a mutually beneficial transaction can take place. But when our best interest is not taken to heart, things can go awry quickly. Therefore, understanding how fantasy works can also help us recognize when something might be too good to be true.

Our instinctive attraction to aspirations like celebrity and fame, or notoriety and social currency, can cause us to overlook red flags. Even when the truth is right in front of us, hero worship and desire can displace common sense, and we'll do just about anything to get a slice of that fantasy. We fail to look further into the matter, or perform the proper due diligence, because we're blinded to the reality. It's called the "Madoff Effect," named after the disgraced investment manager Bernie Madoff and his nearly thirty-year Ponzi scheme.

There are three elements that constitute the Madoff Effect. The first is a nearly impenetrable goodwill buffer. Madoff had developed such a buffer over the years, a result of the positive associations he accumulated over a stellar career spanning decades. After getting his start in finance in the 1960s, developing relationships with high rollers and influential businesspeople in New York City and Palm Beach, Florida, he built a name for himself helping launch the Nasdaq market and acting as its director for three terms in the early '90s. Known as reliable and trustworthy, he was chummy with financial regulators, even sitting on Securities and Exchange Commission (SEC) advisory committees. Madoff solidified his reputation in the late 1980s when his brokerage business was one of the few to answer the phone when hundreds of clients wanted their money during the 1987 stock market crash, a day that became known as Black Monday. But Madoff came out looking like a knight in shining armor—pristine. On that day alone, he created such a large goodwill buffer, no one would ever suspect he was secretly running the world's biggest Ponzi scheme.

The second element of the Madoff Effect is the combined promise of wealth *and* celebrity. Madoff wasn't just a Wall Street darling. He developed a client base that had the air of exclusivity, made up of A-list celebrities and top-rated banking institutions: Steven Spielberg's Wunderkinder Foundation, Elie Wiesel's foundation, Mets owner Fred Wilpon, billionaire media mogul Mortimer Zuckerman, the UK's HSBC Holdings, the Royal Bank of Scotland, Nomura Holdings in Japan, and BNP Paribas in France. In time, everyone wanted in, and recognizing the power of fantasy and prestige, Madoff stoked the flames of interest. By using the names of celebrities and respected financial institutions that invested with him, people assumed it must be a smart, safe investment. All Madoff had to do was say "Spielberg put money in my fund" (an obvious verbal Growth Trigger) and investors practically *begged* him to take their money. And if not every investor in Madoff's fund could mingle with his celebrity clientele, then at least their money could.

Just like any successful brand, the third element of the Madoff Effect incorporates distinctive brand assets and Growth Triggers. Consistent with his brand, he leveraged DBAs that held associations of wealth, prestige, exclusivity, and success. He moved his offices into the glamorous, iconic Lipstick Building on Third Avenue in Midtown Manhattan and took a seaplane into work from his home in Rye. Elite money managers started telling people they had to invest with Madoff—he's magic. He was creating extraordinary returns for his clients, only further solidifying his reputation as the wizard of Wall Street.

An outcome of these three elements is that the Madoff Effect targets our inherent FOMO. As Rabbi Leonid Feldman of Temple Emmanuel in Palm Beach explained, "If someone said, 'I want to invest five million in your fund,' he would say 'no no no.' You had to know somebody who knew somebody who knew somebody to get to invest with him." People were clamoring to do so. In other words, the Madoff Effect relies in part on the scarcity effect, a cognitive bias that causes us to value something that is in short supply. If something sells out or if somebody tells you someone else wants it, you want it more. There is nothing better than empty shelves to stoke interest.

Although they had received multiple reports implicating Madoff, even the SEC was fooled, thinking he could do no wrong. Meanwhile, $50 billion in assets was going straight into Madoff's pocket. Perhaps the most tragic part of the Madoff Effect is its ability to hurt innocent people who are caught up in its swirl. Everyday folks who had the "privilege" of investing with Madoff were completely wiped out. For example, seventy-six-year-old former carpet salesperson Arnold Sinkin had invested all of his and his wife's money with Madoff, around $1 million after fifty-four years on the job. Within forty-eight hours of Madoff's arrest, the Sinkins' entire life savings and retirement fund vanished.

It seems that every few years another shocking report of investors getting ripped off comes to light. From Enron in the mid-2000s to the 2022 collapse of the FTX crypto exchange under CEO Sam Bankman-Fried, there are unfortunately too many examples out there. They all say a lot about how our brains work and how the Madoff Effect preys on our unconscious desire for both fame *and* wealth, a lethal combination. These opportunities are so elevated, they seem like a no-brainer. Our brains instinctively brush aside the need to conduct research and investigation on decisions that really require it. Our fantasies cause us to put people on pedestals, overstate upside, understate downside, and forever lure us into the possibility of easy money. So though fantasy can be helpful in creating a large connectome and building your brand, you also need to be aware of its pitfalls.

Like a moth to a flame, we are drawn to aspirational brands and ideas, even if so many of us consciously claim we want reality. Fantasies come in many forms, and our brains welcome them with open arms. Some we look forward to achieving; others may never come to fruition. But that doesn't stop us from dreaming. Some are as small as having a fresh-smelling home; others as large as becoming unimaginably wealthy. But rest assured, fantasy is not a technique limited to a handful of industries like cosmetics and fashion; it works effectively across all industries, from health care and financial services to television and entertainment. Though the details of aspirations and desires may vary from person to person, our fantasies are remarkably convergent—family togetherness, being appreciated at work, going on an exotic vacation. They all speak to who we want to be, what we want out of life, or what it might be like to do something totally outside our ordinary, everyday experiences.

Because of their high brain utilization and multidimensional connections, fantasies dominate our minds, shutting out everything else. Similarly, by connecting your brand to a fantasy, your connectome grows, shutting competitors out and contributing to an instinctive advantage. But fantasies can also blind us if we're not careful. They tend to close us off from information we should seek out, such as hard data, proof of performance, and downside risks. By understanding this fact, and how these concepts work, you can recognize when due diligence is necessary, and protect yourself from people who might use fantasy to take advantage of you.

Chapter 8

BRING IN THE NEW

INSTINCT RULE: Relying on existing customers is a trap. You get more growth out of people who don't buy your brand.

I n 1997, Chip Wilson took his first yoga class. The onetime Alaska oil-pipeline worker turned skateboard, surf, and snowboard clothing designer and manufacturer had been hearing more and more about yoga in the preceding months: he'd seen an ad for classes posted on a telephone pole, read an article in the newspaper, and found himself eavesdropping on a conversation at the coffee shop when the topic came up. He decided to see what the chatter was all about and take a class himself. Over the following four weeks, Wilson was amazed as the class ballooned from five participants to thirty, all women, aside from himself. He sensed a change was afoot. Whereas gym clothes had been confined to crummy old T-shirts and worn-out shorts—nothing you'd wear in public anywhere outside the gym—Wilson decided to develop a new type of more technical clothing for an emerging market: young, professional, successful, athletic women. In 1998, Lululemon Athletica was born.

What started as a design studio during the day and yoga studio at night turned into a dedicated store in 2000, focusing on Lycra yoga pants for women. Fast-forward to 2023 and the company had expanded to 650 retail locations around the world, with 350 of them in the US. Lululemon's 2022 revenue was $8.1 billion, an astonishing 29 percent increase over the prior year, with online sales approximately 52 percent of total revenue. Chip Wilson had revolutionized "gym clothes" into a whole new breed of athletic clothing—athleisure.

Still, what's most impressive about the brand is not its past but how it is positioning itself to create sustainable growth into the future. Though Lululemon may have gotten its start with yoga pants for women, as they moved forward, they kept something in mind many brands lose sight of—their nonusers. Most brands that follow the traditional, conscious marketing model rules don't think big enough. They have a shortsighted notion that new customers are either not worth pursuing or are impossible to win over. But that raises the obvious question: What are you going to do to keep generating growth? Though incremental revenue can be achieved through acquisitions, most brands cannot just acquire their way to the top. Further, organic growth is by far the most respected type you can achieve, and it is the key to increasing a company's stock price. You can dally by trying to get "like" customers, those similar to the ones you already have, to choose your brand, but that severely limits the pool of prospective buyers.

Lululemon, on the other hand, has effectively held on to its loyal customers while pulling in an entirely unexpected growth target—men. Any traditional marketer would say that this is virtually impossible. How can a brand that's known for women's yoga pants possibly draw a male audience? Never going to happen, most would say. But they would be wrong. While almost 70 percent of Lulu's revenue comes from women's products, menswear is now 30 percent of sales. And guess what? Men are loving it. In 2020, Lululemon's men's category revenue grew 27 percent on a two-year compound annual growth basis, outpacing the growth of their women's category. In

2022, the *Wall Street Journal* reported on a fervent following of men obsessed with Lululemon pants. That same year, *Esquire* magazine referred to the company's ABC pants (a colorful acronym for how the pants fit men around the most sensitive area of their bodies) as a "cult classic."

Lululemon's most popular men's pants, the ABC pant and the Commission pant, don't look like the baggy, dumpy sweats you might wear around the house on a Saturday. They are formal enough to be dress pants, but the fabric is the type Lululemon has become known for—technical, athletic, stretchy, and comfortable. Dubbed "Lulule-Men," this growing customer segment for the brand is, according to Deb Hyun, the company's SVP of global brand management and operations, becoming a large share of total purchases. Stripped down, without a lot of buttons or zippers, the beauty of these pants lies in how they strike a wonderful balance between three drivers: style, comfort, and advanced technology.

But a great product alone doesn't explain how Lululemon was able to bring in its growth target so successfully. The master brand had to evolve. The traditional thinking that a man would *never* be caught dead walking into a women's yoga pants store—let alone wearing clothes displaying a Lululemon logo, which resembles a woman's hairdo—is based on conscious marketing principles. The influencer effect acted as an unspoken endorsement here. Men seeing other men they respect—whether a friend, coworker, NBA player, someone walking down the street or whom they came across in their feed—in a great pair of Lulus made all the difference. That gave men implicit "permission" to embrace what they may have otherwise dismissed as a "women's brand."

Despite what traditional marketers think, Lululemon's ability to pivot from a female-only to male target proves you are not stuck with your existing customers. The key for Lululemon was creating an extendable expertise, "stretching" their high-tech combo of simple style and comfort from women's to men's across their product portfolio, and letting influencers work their implicit magic. Any brand has the ability to reach new customers if they work at the instinctive level. And it's not just that they *can* bring in their growth target—they *must*. The traditional wisdom states that competitive users will be nearly impossible to convert because of their loyalty to other brands' products and services, so you're better off focusing on your core audience. That couldn't be more incorrect. Our brains are learning machines. They are constantly changing, and it's easier than you think to get a person to create a new habit. Relying on existing customers is a trap, but it's one you can escape from, or avoid entirely, if you consistently prioritize your resources on gaining new customers.

THE CORE CUSTOMER TRAP

Each year, approximately two-thirds of chief marketing officers and marketing leaders report that their focus in the coming year will be on marketing their products and services to *existing* customers. Seems logical. They assume it is easier and less expensive to sell more products to existing customers than to acquire new ones. New customers, they believe, have entrenched, difficult-to-change habits and loyalties that would make pulling them into their franchise nearly impossible. There's only one problem with this way of thinking: businesses that prioritize their marketing efforts toward current customers over new ones stagnate and ultimately shrink over time.

These brands include some mentioned earlier in this book, such as Kohl's and Victoria's Secret, but there are many others, such as Sears, Kmart, JCPenney, Toys"R"Us, Circuit City, Lord & Taylor, Borders Books and Music, Kodak, and Blockbuster. All of them tended to focus their marketing resources, consumer research, and positioning on their current customers. The results speak for themselves: declining market share, lower growth than competitors, and, for some, bankruptcy.

Companies that are laser-focused on existing customers lull themselves into believing their brand is fine as is. I call this the Core Customer Trap. Why a trap? Three reasons: First, there is constant churn in every franchise. So-called loyal customers are not as loyal as you think. Second, if you're not constantly replenishing your franchise with new generations of customers, your business is going to diminish in size. It's your job to introduce your brand to new generations of customers. If you're not scaling, you're dying. And third, core customers give you a false sense of security because they tend to like your brand just the way it is.

Every brand accumulates negative associations over time, but your core customer will rarely reveal those flaws. You can only discover potential issues by monitoring the negative associations that seep into the mind of your growth target. By understanding the nature of those negative associations, you start to understand what you need to do to overwhelm them. That's the key to bringing new users into your fold.

Whether you believe your brand is essentially perfect and doesn't need to change, or you believe that selling to existing customers is simply easier, the end result is the same—you focus mainly on existing users and growth slows down. But most brands don't take any of this into account. And when they find that growth is stalling, they may actually believe it's because they're not catering to their existing customers *enough*. As a result, many double down, hoping the loyalty of their current customers will see them through. But what they need to recognize is that loyalty is only as strong as your connectome.

TRUE VS. INCENTIVIZED LOYALTY

Companies spent $5.6 billion on loyalty programs, rewards, and related incentives in 2022. But if they're spending all that money to, in essence, buy their customers' loyalty, can that really be called loyalty at all? If they have to constantly incentivize their customers with an endless stream of rewards, loyalty programs, and other financial incentives to get them to stay, what does that say about their relationship with their customers in the first place? The connection only lasts as long as the rewards do. If "loyalty" is this fragile, then all signs point to the fact that these companies never created a large enough positive Brand Connectome in people's minds.

Over time, businesses that rely on the supposed loyalty of existing customers derive lower and lower returns from these efforts—it's like making lemonade by continuously squeezing the same lemons. This type of loyalty is tenuous at best. Sure, the hospitality and airline industries are renowned for some of the most elaborate loyalty perks, and reward programs can help keep your existing customers coming back. Loyalty can also help create stability, especially if your brand is in its early stages. But if you are too dependent on such programs to *keep* customers, there's obviously a problem with your connectome. How do you know if this is happening? If you're only able to achieve your sales numbers through aggressive discounting, chances are you're falling prey to such dependency.

Take New Jersey–based Bed Bath & Beyond, which filed for bankruptcy in April 2023. Much like Kohl's, this brand, ubiquitous throughout the 1990s and early 2000s, fell into the Core Customer Trap and couldn't escape. Instead of prioritizing their growth target and pulling in new customers from competitors, they continued giving discounts and coupons to existing customers. Their coupon program became so central to the brand's model, they became better known for their small blue-and-white slips of paper offering 20 percent off than for the wide range of home goods they sold.

As described by *CNN Business*, the program was "iconic" and a "pop culture symbol," with customers throughout the country hoarding the coupons in wallets and purses, cupboards and desks. In fact, the coupons were so prevalent that over time they almost lost their value, as shoppers across the 360 locations, and the 120 dedicated babies' stores, Buybuy Baby, began to expect that 20 percent off no matter what. With layers of coupons, one on top of the other, consumers began to lose sight of what the products Bed Bath & Beyond sold were *actually* worth. And even if some of these customers kept coming back, many others were finding new places to buy their pillows, towels, and curtains.

The rise of online retail and the arrival of Amazon certainly played a part, but it would be willful ignorance to think the internet alone killed the brand. Other brick-and-mortar stores like Costco and Walmart were scooping up customers at the same time that BB&B was declining. Meanwhile, other discount retailers were beating out the chain on price as well. Without their former 20-percent-off competitive edge, from 2012 to 2019 the company found its sales stagnating. Those so-called loyal customers had no issue jumping ship. When the company filed for bankruptcy, it had assets of $4.4 billion against a debt of $5.2 billion.

In 2023, Bed Bath & Beyond was purchased by Overstock at a price of $21.5 million—for a company with $7.9 billion in sales, that's a fire sale. Overstock assumed their name and put the entire operation online, combining the two companies' extensive product lines and giving Bed Bath & Beyond a second chance at life. If they change their strategy and stop discounting every product so deeply, they have a chance at survival. But only time will tell. Though Overstock's CEO has stated that they will use the blue coupon less frequently, their strategy continues to feel overly weighted toward rewards and 20 percent discounts. The success of the reimagined brand remains to be seen.

If your brand is truly healthy, you shouldn't need these types of loyalty incentives at all. Your brand's connectome should be so large and positive that consumers' brains become hooked not on coupons, but on your brand. That's where true *instinctive* loyalty comes into play. In other words, loyalty exists, but it's probably not what you think it is. Loyalty is not some type of conscious devotion to you and your brand. It's not an emotional love of the services you offer or your products. And it's certainly not the result of endless discounts and rewards. True loyalty can't be bought. It can only come from having an enormous physical Brand Connectome, overfilled with positive associations. This is when consumers buy your brand on autopilot over and over again. This type of connection does not need to be incentivized—it's instinctive.

Instinctive loyalty is driven by a large, healthy, 90-percent-positive Brand Connectome. Bought, conscious loyalty is driven by incentives, promotion, and reward programs. Top management consulting firms have built billion-dollar advisory practices by promising clients they can help them measure and increase conscious customer loyalty with concepts such as Net Promoter Score. But in truth, they can't. Even as customer loyalty is touted as one of the oldest and most trusted marketing concepts, it is based on this faulty premise. Loyalty is vulnerable, it is not entrenched, and it is not the key to growing your business.

THE CUSTOMER ADVOCACY ILLUSION

A 2003 article titled "The One Number You Need to Grow," by Bain fellow and loyalty guru Frederick F. Reichheld, claimed that loyalty drives top-line growth, and that true loyalty is not about repeat purchases, but rather the influence of loyal customers on others as advocates for a brand. In the article, Reichheld introduced readers to the metric he had created to accompany this concept: Net Promoter Score (NPS). Business leaders quickly glommed on to loyalty because they could measure it, and with NPS they finally had a way to make comparisons across brands and companies. Management teams became focused on increasing the metric on existing brands. Investment banks and private equity firms began using it—in addition to the usual financial ratios—when doing their due diligence on acquisition opportunities. The concept became widely adopted in Fortune 500 C-suites. There was only one problem—there is sparse evidence that NPS or loyalty are actually correlated to business growth.

Professors Andrew Ehrenberg and Frank Bass questioned the validity of focusing on the loyalty of existing customers as early as the 1960s. Ehrenberg and Bass—after whom the Ehrenberg-Bass

Institute for Marketing Science at the University of South Australia, founded in 2005, was named—took a mathematical view of marketing and brand growth. Similar to Triggers, they challenged many accepted marketing beliefs, and demonstrated statistically that to grow, brands needed to increase household penetration, the percentage of households that buy a specific product or service.

Though Ehrenberg and Bass saw existing customers as a way to maintain brand stability, they warned that relying on loyalty as a path to growth is ineffective. In fact, they challenged the entire concept of loyalty, explaining that customers don't buy only one brand over and over again. People use an array of brands in the same category, meaning even if yours is the go-to, consumers often supplement with others under certain circumstances. If your toothpaste doesn't happen to be in the aisle that day, your customer will pick a competitor's. Ehrenberg and Bass recognized that the only dependable way to grow is by focusing on expanding your new customers.

Greater penetration leads to higher revenue and profits—as penetration goes up, so does share of market. The same cannot be said for loyalty. Like the Core Customer Trap, Ehrenberg and Bass described three problems with depending on existing customers. First, there is continuous customer churn in every franchise. Even brands with the highest loyalty rates, like Tide and Coca-Cola, suffer from this problem. No matter how great your customer service and experience, a significant amount of defection is going to happen. Second, there are only so many loyal users of each brand. Heavy users typically make up, at most, 20 percent of a business's customers. Moderate users tend to comprise 30 percent, and light users make up the rest. If heavy users are only 20 percent of your franchise (even if they are responsible for 50 percent of your volume), your targeted customer pool is simply too small to create high growth relative to the millions of customers out there in the world. Third and lastly, heavy users are already buying a large amount of your brand—they are saturated. For example, if you sell shampoo, it's unlikely you are going to get your customer to wash their hair more than once a day.

The Ehrenberg-Bass Institute maintains that 50 percent of users leave a franchise every year. Elyse Kane, marketing professor and former VP of insights and analytics for Colgate-Palmolive, describes this situation as the leaky bucket scenario. To keep the bucket full, you need to continuously pour more water in at a faster rate than the water is spilling out. That means companies need to replenish 50 percent of their volume with new users just to keep their business from declining. And they need to add more than 50 percent in order to grow. If 50 percent of your customers are leaving every year, you better get yourself a fire hose of new customers.

New customers also represent a much larger source of volume than current customers. As described above, loyal customers are the smallest portion of your franchise; they make up a tiny population. In contrast, there are millions of customers out there who are your potential market. You want to target the largest pool of customers you can, not the smallest. It's simple math. The more people you address with your marketing outreach, the more you will get back. That is why you can only achieve aggressive growth by recruiting the largest possible audience of new customers. Whether you're running a start-up or a large legacy brand, to get the most growth, your overriding goal needs to be to increase household penetration, not loyalty.

Penetration differs significantly between large brands with higher market share and small ones with lower market share. For example, a brand with 15 to 20 percent market share will have much higher penetration rates than one with only 2 percent share. But there is *minimal* difference in loyalty between high and low market-share brands. This means there is little to no correlation between loyalty and market share growth. If there were, we would see higher loyalty with higher market-share brands. Like a hamster on its wheel, brands go around and around chasing loyalty, but they're chasing the wrong metric. Like brand purpose, loyalty is a marketing distraction; it does not help you improve or scale your business.

Does this mean current customers aren't important? Of course not. You absolutely need to treat your core customers with appreciation and do everything in your power to keep every single one. In fact, when it comes to customer experience, getting high satisfaction scores from core customers is not good enough. Companies need to shoot higher and achieve the "ideal" experience. It's just that even with your best efforts, loyalty will rise ever so slightly. And it certainly won't translate to significant growth.

PRIORITIZING YOUR GROWTH TARGET OVER YOUR CORE

So while you of course need to optimize your customer experience to retain customers, you need to put more of your resources into customer acquisition, which is only possible by targeting people who *aren't* your customers yet. Your growth target will only become your users if they are positively biased toward your brand, meaning they have a robust Brand Connectome, thriving with positive associations. As discussed, the brain is constantly adding and losing associations. It doesn't matter if you're talking about a current customer, a competitive user, a nonuser, a lapsed user, or an occasional user. If you can grow your Brand Connectome in your users' minds, then you can do so in virtually anyone's mind.

That said, competitive users are lower-hanging fruit than nonusers since they are already buying in your category. If competitive users are not buying your brand, then by definition, you have a smaller Brand Connectome in their mind than their go-to brand, and your connectome likely has some negative associations creating barriers. Most people have a go-to brand, but that doesn't mean they're monogamous. Being one of several instinctive choices in a category is the path to increased penetration and greater market share. To accomplish this, you need to constantly look at your brand in your growth target's mind, determining how you're going to create improvements, remove barriers, and make your Brand Connectome larger and more positive.

Take, for example, Tide and Seventh Generation, both known for their laundry detergents and cleaning products but with very different positionings: powerful, efficient cleaning versus environmental responsibility, respectively. Launched in 1946, Tide is one of the largest brands out there, with a household penetration rate of approximately 49.3 percent. Seventh Generation, established forty-two years later in 1988, less than half of that. One of the reasons Tide's penetration rate isn't even higher, though, is because they have either lost millennial and Gen Z heads of household—who are more concerned about the environment than earlier generations—or failed to pull them in at the same rate as they did older heads of households.

Many brands would say that Tide will never pull in the "natural" consumer. Nor will Seventh Generation ever get Tide customers to convert to their brand. Those assumptions are simply not true. In fact, most of Seventh Generation's customers came from mainstream brands such as Tide and others, as these consumers have slowly shifted more of their purchases to "natural" across categories. There's no reason Tide couldn't reach, say, 60 percent penetration if they were to overcome the mental barriers resulting from negative associations in "natural" customers' Tide Connectome. Similarly, if Seventh Generation took time to figure out what was keeping more customers from leaving Tide and other mainstream legacy detergents to come over to their brand, they could create messaging full of positive associations, overwhelming any negatives and growing the salience of their connectome in their growth target's minds.

The Seventh Generation Connectome in Tide users' minds likely contains associations of being too expensive and not efficacious enough. The Tide Connectome in "natural" millennial users' minds is laden with negative associations about being harsh on skin, hard on the planet, and made with chemicals that could seep into your body and harm your family's long-term health. Again, whether these perceptions are accurate doesn't matter; the results are what counts. If Seventh Generation wants to make a concerted effort to pull customers away from Tide, they simply need to overwhelm Tide users' negative associations about Seventh Generation with positive associations and grow its connectome in their minds. With an increasing "green" trend, it's likely that some of Tide's existing customers are going natural in other areas already, shopping at Whole Foods, for example, and eating healthier. That "in transition" consumer is a perfect target for Seventh Generation as they try to increase their household penetration.

To win these competitive users, Seventh Generation would have to overcome each of its mental barriers while being careful not to inadvertently reinforce them. Millennial Tide consumers may be eating more naturally, but they haven't crossed over to natural in laundry detergent because they're concerned Seventh Generation won't get their clothes clean enough. Their whites won't be pristine. Germs will be hiding inside the cuffs of their pants. For Seventh Generation to make headway with these customers, they need to convince them that their brand is just as efficacious as Tide. Currently, the company pushes the tagline "Clean with purpose," but purpose should not be the main, or only, message a brand sells. (Note that Seventh Generation is also owned by Unilever.)

By going after Tide's customer base, Seventh Generation could help solve their leaky bucket problem. With a nearly 50 percent household penetration, Tide has a huge volume of customers, and going after your biggest competitors has the best ROI because they have more users to lose—which means more for you to gain. If Seventh Generation can persuade even 5 percent of those Tide customers to convert, that's a huge win. But to prove their products work just as well as Tide's, they need to build that efficacy and expertise into their communications. For example, the brand is currently clear about what ingredients it leaves out, those that are harmful to the environment, but less clear about which ones they include. To make headway with Tide customers, they could create a mechanism-of-action story to explain how their formula gets clothes clean. Essentially, they have to convey that their cleaning power is equal to or better than Tide's. Note that this messaging is not changing their core business in the slightest; it's just highlighting an aspect of their product that is overlooked.

In the process, Seventh Generation could show their growth target (mainstream detergent users) that they don't have to make a single trade-off: they can get the same cleaning results while also using a more natural product. And if they continue building their connectome in their competitive users' minds, who knows how many they could convert? Remember, it's all about growth. The larger your connectome, the larger your audience; the larger your audience, the higher your penetration; the higher your penetration, the higher your market share and revenue growth.

And though so much of the business world is stuck on loyalty as a path to growth, cracks are beginning to show in the wall of this popular thinking. Based on an analysis by Bain & Company of almost one hundred thousand shoppers from around the globe, trying to create loyal customers that purchase more of a company's products or services over time is a fool's errand. "Instead," they explain, "there's a simple rule that successful brands follow: it's all about increasing household penetration."

THE MOST POWERFUL IDEAS ARE UNIVERSAL

At the end of the day, there are only two customer segments that matter: your core customer and your growth target, the people who buy from you and those who don't (at least not yet). But most marketing people would never agree. They believe in segmenting audiences as finely as possible. This type of market segmentation is one of the most popular research and marketing techniques today. It's also a relic from the past. Still, consulting and research firms continue to sell it to companies year after year for hundreds of thousands of dollars per study, despite little evidence to suggest that more segmentation is more effective.

Assigning different handles to different segments with different characteristics isn't helpful. Building a bunch of profiles, whether

"Knitting Nancy" or "Jogging Joe," doesn't provide useful insight when you're trying to grow your franchise with as large an audience as possible. Besides, if you do segment your audience into smaller and smaller slices, you'll never have enough resources to market to each one separately. Even the largest Fortune 100 companies don't have sufficient resources to carry on separate marketing efforts to more than one or at most two target audiences.

One theory behind segmentation is that in this increasingly divisive world, people are so extremely polarized from one another that the same message would never work for multiple audiences. But when considered through an instinct lens, the picture changes. On an implicit level, people are much more similar than we think. Their memories about brands, and their fantasies about family and future, are remarkably similar. That means the most powerful ideas out there are universal. Your messaging should be too. A strong, healthy brand is a convergent brand, featuring the same associations across vast segments of the population. So if you find yourself tempted to split your audiences up, or fragment your media spend too much, beware. When you over-segment your target audience and give each one a tailored message, little by little, your brand starts to fall apart. When your brand means something different to different people, it stops being a brand. And it costs you a whole lot of money in the process.

The most salient brands bring similar themes and associations to mind for everyone—new customers and existing ones alike. So the question you need to ask is not "How are our customers different?" but "How are our customers alike?" In certain scenarios it makes sense to tailor your message for your audience, but far more often, it is much more efficient and easier to concentrate your limited resources on getting a universal message out to as many people as possible, and through as many different channels as you can.

You can find universally powerful messages even across segments that people believe are totally disparate. On the surface, for example, Democrats and Republicans seem to have diametrically opposed perspectives on everything from military spending to social issues. At least that's what political polls will tell you. But an interesting experiment was run in a blue state. When you put an *R* (for Republican) next to a candidate's name on a ballot, that candidate automatically incurs between a –5-point and –20-point disadvantage, depending on the district. However, place a *D* (for Democrat) by the same name, while keeping the *exact same messaging*, and the opposite occurs—a 5- to 20-point advantage. That means there are universal messages out there everyone can agree on—it's just about creating the right associations so you can get them accepted by both sides.

To maximize growth, brands need to concentrate on trying to win over their growth target, not on creating fragmented audiences and messages. In fact, the messages you use to elevate the brand and bring in the growth target are likely to help maintain your current users as well. If you subscribe to the segmentation approach, however, you'll only be distracted from what you actually need to do: create greater household penetration. Instead, you'll be trying to hold 24/7 conversations with a myriad of different audiences, chopping them up into increasingly finer segments, diverting you from the real prize of gaining the growth target while holding on to your current customers. That, after all, is the fastest, most effective way to maximize growth and scale your brand.

Each year, a vast 75 percent of CMOs say they plan to sell existing products to their existing customers. Clearly, many leaders have an inherent fear that it will be difficult, if not impossible, to bring new customers or even competitive users into their franchise. So they stay in their lane, never deviating, focusing on their core customers, and piling on incentives to keep them in the fold. But you can't draw blood from a stone. Without fail, just like a leaky bucket, over time, customers leave. If you don't refill that bucket, before you know it, it will be bone dry. Growth has to come from somewhere, and the only way to keep that bucket full is to put most of your marketing resources into new-customer acquisition—not your existing customers. To be effective at converting your growth target, you must take down their barriers and address their choice drivers, which can be different than those of current customers. But the alternative—continuously trying to find more customers with the same profile as the ones you have—is a fool's errand. There will never be enough of them. If you have one dollar to spend, you want to put it against the largest pool of prospects you can because it will buy you the greatest return.

And guess what? When you elevate your brand for the growth target, you get a wonderful side effect. Existing customers feel validated, stand a little straighter when using your brand, and churn declines. After all, they were right all along. That's the beauty of operating with an instinctive lens. What's good for the growth target also ends up being good for the core, and the positive effects start to compound, leading to growth from both sources. Like a well-watered plant, your entity grows in multiple directions.

Chapter 9

DITCH THE FUNNEL

INSTINCT RULE: Break free from the funnel, and build your brand overnight.

That is the true genius of America, a faith in the simple dreams of its people, the insistence on small miracles. That we can tuck in our children at night and know they are fed and clothed and safe from harm. That we can say what we think, write what we think, without hearing a sudden knock on the door. That we can have an idea and start our own business without paying a bribe or hiring somebody's son. That we can participate in the political process without fear of retribution, and that our votes will be counted—or at least, most of the time...

Yet even as we speak, there are those who are preparing to divide us, the spin masters and negative ad peddlers who embrace the politics of anything goes. Well, I say to them tonight, there's not a liberal America and a conservative America—there's the United States of America. There's not a Black America and white America and Latino America and Asian America—there's the United States of America.

When Barack Hussein Obama first uttered these memorable words, he was not yet the forty-fourth president of the United States—in fact, he was far from it. On July 27, 2004, a virtually unknown senator from Illinois, Obama walked out onstage to deliver the keynote address at the Democrat National Convention (DNC) in Boston, Massachusetts. His national awareness was slim to none. Unless you lived on the South Side of Chicago, you probably didn't have an Obama Brand Connectome in your mind at all—no roots, no branches, no leaves, no canopy. But when he stepped behind that pulpit, if you watched the speech that followed, that connectome went from barren soil, to the tiniest of seeds, to the largest of trees, all within those sixteen minutes.

Onstage, reading from a teleprompter—a device he had never used before that summer—he began by expressing thanks, saying that "tonight is a particular honor for me because, let's face it, my presence on this stage is pretty unlikely." He went on to tell the story of his heritage—a father who grew up in Kenya, attending school in a tin-roof shack and herding goats as a child; a mother who grew up in Kansas with an "abiding faith in the possibilities of this nation." As he spoke about the greatness of that nation, he invoked the Declaration of Independence's famous line about all men being created equal, a theme he carried throughout.

During his speech, he addressed not just the Democrats sitting in the audience of the FleetCenter that night, but anyone watching from home, no matter their political affiliation. Though he was ostensibly there to stump for John Kerry, much of the speech laid out the young Obama's philosophies and values for all to hear, what would eventually become his presidential platform four years later. But these weren't just the typical Democratic talking points. They weren't Republican messages either. They were specifically designed to appeal to the broadest possible constituency.

Like watching a tennis match, he volleyed back and forth between issues each side cared about: not over-relying on government to solve problems, and ensuring opportunity is open for all, no matter where they are from or the color of their skin; being prepared for war and defeating enemies abroad, and providing health care at home; supporting constitutional freedoms, and seeking energy independence. This approach hit a thematic climax when he said, "The pundits like to slice-and-dice our country into Red States and Blue States; Red States for Republicans, Blue State for Democrats. But I've got news for them, too. We worship an awesome God in the Blue States, and we don't like federal agents poking around our libraries in the Red States. We coach Little League in the Blue States and have gay friends in the Red States. There are patriots who opposed the war in Iraq and patriots who supported it. We are one people, all of us pledging allegiance to the stars and stripes, all of us defending the United States of America."

The idea is that these were *American* messages, full of universal Growth Triggers that worked across genders, ages, ethnicities, states, and districts. He spoke about people he met in small towns and big cities, VFW halls and city streets, middle-class families and working families, veterans and patriots. And it was all underlined by the idea of hope, which would become his political rallying cry in the coming years. The number of positive associations coming at people over that quarter hour were too many to count. And as he left the stage that evening, there were already whispers of Obama's future as a US president.

On NBC's *Hardball* that night, Obama was described by Andrea Mitchell as a "real breakout" and a "rock star," but Chris Matthews called it when he said, "I have seen the first black president." Kevin Lampe, a well-known Democratic political consultant who worked with Obama leading up to and on the night of his DNC speech, echoed that sentiment: "I walked on stage with my state senator from my neighborhood, and I walked off stage with the next Democratic president of the United States." In that one single moment, Obama launched his general presidential campaign, cleverly positioning himself for the moderate middle, independents, and swing states that decide elections.

That speech made Obama. He blasted onto the political scene like the finale of a fireworks show, and his brand dug into the neural networks of every viewer. You couldn't unsee it, you couldn't unhear it; the speech was literally unforgettable. He eclipsed any potential candidate in that moment, his tree growing high above the rest, elevating his brand to become the de facto for the primary four years later. He distinguished himself, not because he was unique, but because he connected his brand with all sorts of issues, values, and ideals people cared about on the right, on the left, and in the center. By doing so, he grew share of mind in *everyone's* mind at the same time. He built his brand overnight, creating relevance and salience in a matter of minutes.

Make no mistake, this is not a political statement. Nor is this an endorsement for or against the policies Obama put forward while he was in office. It doesn't matter whether you love Obama or hate him, whether you voted for him or not, if you're a Republican or a Democrat, left, right, or center. This is a lesson in superior instinct-based marketing. The brilliance of what he and his team were able to accomplish in a matter of minutes, and continued to accomplish after that, is a master lesson in how to grow your Brand Connectome in record time and defy the traditional rules of marketing.

Obama would go on to build his Brand Connectome over the subsequent four years. He appeared on the top television shows multiple times, discussing the problem with modern politics on *The Daily Show with Jon Stewart*, reading the "Top Ten" on *Late Show with David Letterman*, and promoting the idea of empathy on *Oprah*. In all of his appearances, he struck a rare chord—combining levity, humor, and charm with a serious take on the issues facing the country and world.

Equally important was that by appearing on these shows, he was connecting his brand to beloved entertainers people watch every day. Many people thought "these are our shows" and so he is "our" candidate. And thus, his connectome became indelibly intertwined with popular culture. When he went on these shows, he was riding their

Brand Connectomes too, creating an implicit endorsement of his candidacy. *The Daily Show* attracted young audiences, Letterman had been on for nearly twenty-five years, and Oprah's daytime audience was enormous. Not only did people see Obama the candidate, but also Obama the man. His humanity was reinforced further when he was seen playing basketball, having a beer at a local bar on the campaign trail, or even sneaking a cigarette from time to time.

But his success all started with the speech.

In politics, the brain is constantly trying to categorize candidates into the bucket on the left or the right. Based on the candidate's appearance, background, talking points, and visual cues, people make a snap judgment—they're either a Democrat or a Republican, which immediately limits your audience to half the voter population. But though he ran as a Democrat, Obama resisted classification. He might not have ever moved staunch Republicans to his side, but he didn't have to. By speaking about issues that mattered to all sides of the political spectrum, moderate Republicans' and Independents' brains couldn't neatly place him into either bucket, causing him to settle in that rarified air, the fantasy pinnacle so many voters yearn to reach but can never achieve with the candidates they're served up—the moderate middle. It's as though people's brains were following that tennis match, looking from one end of the political spectrum on the left to the other on the right and then back again. They had no choice but to see the candidate as something fresh and different in the "sweet spot" center.

He was inspirational and authentic, calling for unity in a time of division and inspiring hope for the future. This speech caused him to beat the odds. Though it takes most political brands decades to develop their connectomes and become well known, giving them a tremendous advantage at the polls, Obama shot up out of nowhere. He was not part of any political dynasty like the Kennedys or Bushes, who built on the familiarity of their family name one generation after another. He had neither the benefit of being a legacy brand nor the benefit of incumbency. He was a newbie.

By bombarding the audience with the right positive associations at an accelerated pace, you can sprout a giant Brand Connectome overnight. This high-speed pummeling effect breaks through the brain's conscious barriers, putting brand growth on overdrive, as if the brain's memory terrain has been treated with Miracle-Gro. That's exactly what the speech did. Positive associations of hope, equality, liberty, freedom, history, shared success, American strength and pride, safety, peace, persistence, and an immigrant success story all sprouted up. There was no one "big idea," but many simultaneously. And he studiously avoided ideas such as infrastructure projects, economic stimulus (a euphemism for spending), and living constitutionalism, which are notorious for turning Republicans off. Though Obama mentioned Kerry several times, viewers' brains heard all of these positive ideals and connected them with Obama. And those connections lasted for years—some would argue they still exist to this day.

In a way, Obama is the ultimate disruptor brand. The combination of universal Verbal Triggers and his charismatic personality, down-home swagger, and tell-it-straight personal style, atypical of most politicians, broke through the clutter. He created an avalanche of positive associations that connected to familiar touchpoints in people's lives, he leveraged the connectomes of pop-culture figures, and he presented a strong overarching message—the audacity of hope—with a multiplicity of messages that were Growth Triggers underneath. All these positive associations accelerated the expansion of his Brand Connectome overnight. It's possible to do, but it's rare. That's because most candidates don't employ so many of the new rules for gaining the instinctive advantage simultaneously the way Obama did.

Obama defied the classic marketing construct known as the marketing funnel, a step-by-step process conceptualized over one hundred years ago. The funnel claims that to get someone to choose your brand, they must go through a series of set stages during which they consciously decide whether to choose or reject it. But this concept emerged long before anyone had an inkling of how the mind actually makes decisions. It was designed for a world in which people thought the brain worked sequentially, like a data processor.

But connectomes grow organically through cumulative memories, which means you don't need to push your way through a multistage process to get someone to choose your company, cause, or idea. An ecosystem of brand connections can develop in audiences' minds anytime—because the growth process is not sequential, nor does it need to go through stages. Though a Brand Connectome can take years to develop, as Obama shows us, you can sprout a whole highway system of pathways all at once. Which means if you harness instinctive techniques, you don't need the funnel at all.

MARKETING FUNNEL FAILURE

Advertising executive E. St. Elmo Lewis is credited with coming up with the concept of the marketing and sales funnel back in 1898. Considered one of the first formal marketing theories, the funnel has been treated like gospel by nearly every marketing, sales, and media department in the business world. Though there are a number of variations, it essentially consists of five stages: awareness, interest, desire or consideration, action or conversion, and loyalty or advocacy. The funnel is often simplified to awareness, consideration, conversion, and loyalty. Somewhere along the line, most businesspeople are taught they must work their way through this funnel.

The widest part at the top of the funnel is the awareness stage, after which it narrows throughout the customers' journey, as they hopefully go from being aware of your brand to choosing and supporting your brand, the loyalty or advocacy stage at the funnel's narrow end. Each stage calls for a different overt marketing technique meant to help usher the potential user through the funnel, priming them at each stage for the one that follows.

For example, awareness may include broad reach techniques like TV or digital advertising, social media, and search engine optimization; interest may be supported by more direct, detailed communication with users, such as sending emails or newsletters, answering questions through live chats, or providing case studies and success stories to the target; desire and consideration may be established through the use of product or service demonstrations, videos, and competitive comparison charts; and action or conversion, which is also called "trial," may be incentivized through promotional techniques such as discounts, samples, coupons, and free-standing inserts (FSIs). Marketers may then look to create loyalty or advocacy through customer loyalty programs—though, as discussed, over-relying on these can put a brand in a precarious position in the long run.

Marketers think that if consumers have already heard of the brand (the awareness stage), they are more likely to conduct research or listen to specific information in the interest stage. From there, desire and consideration deepen. And so on. But the funnel doesn't take into account what's actually happening on an instinctive level—the growth and expansion of the connectome. As you learn new information about a brand, associations get added to your brand's neural pathways. If you provide enough positive associations simultaneously, these pathways or branches can extend out in different directions, and a robust network can form all at once.

The moment your connectome is fully grown with a larger physical footprint and more positive associations than your competitors' connectomes, the consumer is ready to choose your brand, meaning they take action and make a purchase. When your tree grows so high its canopy blocks out the rest of the forest, your brand becomes the automatic first choice. Stages have nothing to do with it.

The real process that occurs is not linear because that's not how our brains function. People don't make decisions sequentially or based on some rational linear model. But it's easy to understand how the funnel concept became popular. Breaking the process into stages gave marketers a way to manage and, more importantly, measure it. Or so they thought. Measuring the stages of the decision-making process doesn't get your target audience any closer to making a choice. Plus, working your way through the stages of the funnel, if approached in this traditional manner, is like watching a kettle boil, seemingly taking forever. It also causes leaders to spend excessive amounts of money on consumer promotion and other techniques that are hit or miss.

If you're happy with the slow-burn method and pace of acquisition—which can take anywhere from six months to a year or longer—then feel free to carry on. But I suspect most everyone would prefer to get through this funnel as fast as possible, moving from awareness to advocacy in minutes, days, or weeks, as compared to months, years, or decades. Let's face it: you'd likely do anything to speed up the pace of customer acquisition and conversion. When approached through the lens of connecting with the instinctive mind, spreading positive associations across the brain and building the Brand Connectome, the funnel becomes obsolete.

As you know, convincing anyone—consumers or B2B buyers alike—of *anything* is nearly impossible, which is why it takes so long to work through the funnel. The marketing techniques at each stage are designed to push, pull, and pound on the doors until they reluctantly fall open—if they ever do. In short, with a conscious brain that is stubborn to change, you have to use a lot of force to send a potential customer down that funnel and convert them to a loyal user. But with the right cognitive shortcuts, you are able to piggyback on the memories that already exist in your target's mind, adding positive associations and sprouting new roots and branches almost immediately. It's like a time-lapse video of disparate seeds growing into a rainforest in a matter of seconds.

In essence, you can skip the funnel. But you'll never hear anyone in the marketing world admit that out loud. Still, the facts remain. If the marketing funnel were an unavoidable phenomenon, every company would go through that same step-by-step process. But they don't. Digital disruptors from Dollar Shave Club to Casper Sleep have built their businesses practically overnight. That's because brands don't have to go through these decision-making steps in people's brains. By leveraging the brain's native mechanism, you can abandon this outdated funnel strategy and, like Obama, go from completely unknown to global sensation in an unbelievably truncated amount of time.

SHORTCUT TO GROWTH

Direct-to-consumer companies often use Growth Triggers more effectively than many of the top Fortune 500s. That may be because they were never taught the old marketing rules in the first place. Fortune 500 companies' marketing departments are more likely to provide training programs in the classic marketing techniques. The right content paired with the right cues that match consumers' associations and memories is in many ways more valuable than having deep pockets. When filled with Growth Triggers, that content implicitly creates a flood of positive associations. It bypasses rational thought and fabricated emotional benefits and goes straight to the instinctive mind, with multiple themes and rich associations. By tapping into the brain's shortcuts, you eliminate the need for stages and accelerate the customer conversion process. You don't need to spend a lot of money to drive growth; you just need to supercharge your communication with the right content.

One of the best examples of this accelerated process is found in the success of Dollar Shave Club. When Dollar Shave Club (DSC) released a YouTube video in 2012, not even founder and CEO Michael Dubin knew what was about to happen. The video, featuring Dubin as the company's spokesperson, went viral. Their website crashed that day due to all the traffic, and they received twelve thousand orders over the next two days. DSC made $3.5 million in revenue that year; four years later that figure was up $225 million, at which point Unilever bought the company for $1 billion—giving the brand unicorn status. The simple digital video, not even shown on TV, only cost $4,500 to make, and it was filmed over one day by a friend of Dubin's who had done improv with him years before.

Dubin's acting chops shone through. In the video, he remains straight-faced through what could only be called an onslaught of zany, but relevant, humor, while espousing the qualities of the product and getting digs in at their largest competitors. But it wasn't just that the video was "funny" or that the mostly millennial audience is a major direct-to-consumer (DTC) customer. Dubin was throwing out Growth Triggers in rapid succession, tapping into positive associations in the audience's brain and creating a sprawling connectome.

As a DTC company, DSC was always low priced—embodied by the slogan "Shave Time. Shave Money"—but that was only one layer of their messaging. Quality and effectiveness were conveyed with the steel razor and aloe strip, and the claim that the razors were "f!@#ing awesome." Gentleness was communicated by a toddler shaving an adult man's head. They touted the convenience of their home delivery. And a layer of simplicity was ever-present. While major players like Gillette and Schick were incessantly adding more blades and features, DSC focused on getting back to basics. As Dubin queries in the video, "Do you think your razor needs a vibrating handle, a flashlight, a back scratcher, and ten blades?" There was even a layer of familial history when he referenced "your handsome-ass grandfather had one blade...and polio." And let's not overlook the side dish of values and purpose when he showed a worker at the warehouse, pointing out that "we're not just selling razors, we're also making new jobs."

Part of the video was filmed in what looked like Dubin's basement office, before he walks out onto the warehouse floor, a far cry from what most consumers would expect from one of the razor industry's giants—shiny, stale skyscrapers, buildings with no personality. But the DSC video was *all* personality, with Growth Triggers bursting out at the audience a mile a minute. This entrepreneurial bare-bones brand world was the perfect backdrop for their bare-bones approach. DSC created a stark contrast with the competition: low cost, high quality, conveniently delivered straight to your home. And let's not forget the humor, poking fun at the dinosaurs of the industry. By creating this contrast, DSC blew up the funnel and built a dedicated customer base in the one minute, thirty-three seconds it took people to watch this video.

By adding negative associations to dominant competitive connectomes like Gillette, DSC's tree became larger and more robust, causing the competition's to become less healthy. It's as if DSC's smaller canopy eclipsed that of Gillette, stealing its sun; DSC's roots grew so quickly, they sucked up Gillette's water and nutrients. Consumers didn't need all the bells and whistles on their razors, nor should they overpay to keep Gillette's shiny office up and running, but they didn't consciously make that decision. In that moment of extreme contrast, their synapses fired, their brains lit up, and their instincts drove their choice.

In the process, Dollar Shave Club took market share from major players like Gillette and Schick. Note that these are two of the biggest brands in the category. Some outside observers might think it would have been better for DSC to focus on competing with other brands its size. But that's an entirely backward strategy, not to mention a recipe for failure. If you're a start-up or a smaller company, chances are you have limited resources, which means your focus should be on a competitor that has a *huge* volume of consumers, not a small one. Imagine, for a moment, you have only one dollar to spend on marketing. Do you think you're better off betting that dollar against a small competitor with several hundred customers—or against a large competitor with several thousand? The answer, of course, is the larger one. It's simple math. You will get a higher ROI on your efforts by going after a large player than by focusing your limited dollars on a smaller brand.

The largest dominant competitor has the most customers for you to gain. And particularly when your company is small or you're just starting out, you need to deposition your competitors and get your growth target coming in quickly. If done right, this strategy will enable you to make tremendous inroads overnight. Dollar Shave Club's success shows how you can simultaneously create awareness and persuade people to switch brands from a major competitor. Further, if this approach can be adopted by small start-ups, it can be adopted by established household names as well, enabling them to harness their untapped growth potential.

ACCELERATING RESISTANT BEHAVIORS THROUGH METAPHOR AND HUMOR

One of the biggest myths in marketing is that existing behaviors are nearly impossible to change. But that's only because people typically try to effect these behaviors through conscious techniques, like persuasion or promotion. Even brands with high loyalty, such as Facebook or Tide, can be unseated. That's why, more often than you might expect, tiny DTC brands are able to take share from large legacy brands that would otherwise be thought of as invulnerable. When you know how to change the Brand Connectome, you can shift the most resistant behaviors—whether smoking, political partisanship, or brand loyalty—in a short period of time. Again, instead of forcing people through the marketing funnel, you can play to their existing associations and memories, breaking down resistance at an accelerated pace. Metaphors and humor are powerful devices that are particularly effective in this process.

METAPHORS

Metaphors are the Michael Jordan of instinctive devices, quickly shifting entrenched perceptions and behaviors in the ultimate slam dunk. By incorporating metaphors in your messaging, you can bombard your audience with positive associations and rapidly grow your connectome. As super-effective Growth Triggers, metaphors indirectly influence people's minds, leveraging what already exists in their memories. They help change perceptions quickly, reframing an idea almost instantaneously, riding on current neural pathways or creating new ones that become part of the interconnected vectors in the brain.

Metaphors work so well because they are easy for the brain to understand, helping it make sense of a concept that might be rather complex. Remember, our brains are lazy, and they don't want to work hard. Metaphors ensure they don't have to, allowing them to understand one idea in terms of another one they are already familiar with. In doing so, new connections are created between the reference in your mind and the brand you're selling.

The most effective metaphors are those that are common or incorporate well known examples, making them easier for the brain to grasp on to. Though some might argue this approach reeks of cliché, remember, familiarity is a *good* thing. Using common metaphors is better than using obscure ones. For example, if I were to say a company's growth has the trajectory of the *Titanic*, you would easily understand what is meant. If I were to say a company's growth has the trajectory of the *Barge 129* whaleback—a sunken ship discovered in Lake Superior in 2022—it's not going to have the same impact. Similarly, the start of this section referred to arguably the greatest NBA player of all time, Michael Jordan, and his world-famous dunking capabilities. If this section had begun with "Metaphors are the Kevin Martin of instinctive devices, quickly shifting entrenched perceptions and behaviors in the ultimate shot rock closest to the button," unless you're a huge curling fan, you'd likely be at a loss. (No offense intended to the "Old Bear," Kevin Martin, the all-time greatest Canadian male curler.)

Metaphors are particularly powerful because they elicit cognitive processes beyond language, tapping into the audience's mental map that includes imagery, sounds, sensations, and smells. For example, the image of a blooming flower may be a metaphor for personal growth and reaching your full potential. The sound of the wind whipping in a boat's sail could be a metaphor for freedom or travel.

The smell of mulled cider for fall. This power can be seen across industries, not just in consumer products.

A significant level of illness in the United States, at a great cost to its health-care system, is a result of patients' lack of compliance with therapeutic treatments. In other words, not everyone takes their health-improving medication when, how, and to the extent they're supposed to, nor do they always follow advice from their doctors. Every year in the United States, nonadherence to medications constitutes up to 25 percent of hospitalizations, and can account for up to 125,000 deaths and 50 percent of treatment failures. Among patients with chronic diseases, only approximately 50 percent of medications are taken as prescribed. Medication compliance in patients with asthma or COPD—chronic obstructive pulmonary disease—ranges from a high of 78 percent to a low of just 22 percent. As hard as it is to believe, compliance is not where it should be even in categories such as cancer, where the use of medication can be a matter of life and death.

Let's face it. People don't like taking medicine. Pill burden is a real issue. And in a world where people are eating more naturally and kicking products with chemicals out of their pantry, it's no wonder patients are reluctant to take their medicine. But there are two issues. First, there are many conditions where compliance with medications is critical to health. Second, medication nonadherence is expensive, costing taxpayers and the overall health-care system $548.4 billion per year.

The medical community, health-care industry, and large consulting firms have tried nearly everything to change this behavior. Instructional videos and education from nurse practitioners and doctors, warnings, reminder alarms, stickers and messaging on pill packaging—the list goes on. In over 115 risk communication intervention research studies, which involved more than thirty-four thousand participants, very few moved the needle; the overall assessment of these compliance interventions was mixed at best. It's easy to understand why. Every single one of those approaches is trying to persuade the conscious brain to do something it's resistant to.

These techniques simply do not work at changing instinctive behavior. But metaphors can help.

A separate study, conducted in 2008, stands out from all the rest. It found a marked difference in patient behavior through the use of a metaphor, not in regard to medication compliance, but in regard to an even more resistant behavioral health problem: smoking. The traditional techniques used to change smokers' behavior included the usual fare you would expect—images of corroded lungs and the effects of cancer, and explanations of how many years smokers' lives would be shortened if they continued to puff away. These typical confrontational techniques had not made headway in the past. Nor had conducting spirometry breathing tests that reported how well smokers performed on lung capacity and respiratory function, or other tests that measured the speed at which they could breathe. The science felt obscure, irrelevant, the scary photos of black lungs alienating. Without anything familiar for the brain to latch on to, the point was entirely lost on the participants.

But in the 2008 study, smokers were shown their "lung age." Lung age is a simple metaphor for how well the participants' lungs function. Instead of focusing on the science, the clinicians running the study told participants the age of the person their lungs belonged to. For example, a twenty-year-old learned he had the lung age of a forty-year-old. A sixty-year-old participant's lungs were more like those of a seventy-five-year-old. And guess what? It worked. It was one of the few studies to show a significant difference in smoking cessation. But here's the important question: Why did this happen?

Turns out, learning one's lung age is more powerful than learning the lungs' actual condition. Think about it. What twenty-year-old wants to be told they look like they are forty? The symbolic characterization of a smoker's lungs was more powerful than the literal one because it rode on existing, established neural pathways about aging. Instead of introducing and explaining the spirometry breathing test or breathing speed, or images of some other person's lungs, the explanation was immediate and personal. Smoking cessation rates literally doubled from 6.4 percent to 13.6 percent as a result of this approach. Participants didn't need to learn any new jargon or try to picture themselves in the place of another person. Instead, the road was already paved in the mind, enabling it to blast through one of the most resistant, self-destructive behaviors on earth. To that end, metaphors may be the ultimate Growth Triggers—they can literally save lives.

HUMOR

In addition to metaphor, humor is another device that can help break through resistance and quickly build a connectome. But not any old humor will do, as shown with Quiznos and Skittles in their 2023 Super Bowl ads. Much of the humor seen in marketing communications today is superfluous: unrelated silly humor, humor for humor's sake, humor that tries to leverage a cultural trend but is disconnected from the brand itself. All of these go in one ear and out the other. Similar to how marketing and advertising professionals can sometimes conflate creativity with effectiveness, humor is sometimes undertaken simply to get a laugh. And though the result can be funny, it is often forgettable or irrelevant. Instead, the humor presented must be connected to the benefit you're providing to your target audience or highlight a contrast between you and your competitors. Otherwise, you won't create a sticky enough association to get glued to the brain and grow the Brand Connectome.

One of the best ways to use humor is to deposition your competition. Just as Dollar Shave Club's Michael Dubin got a laugh out of the audience at his competitors' expense by showing them as overengineered, expensive, and frivolous (an effective use of humor), humor is regularly used to great effect during political debates. For example, in the first Republican primary debate of 2023, all of the eight candidates came out swinging. But one of the most memorable performances came from former governor of South Carolina Nikki Haley. Though being outnumbered seven to one by men on the stage could seem like a disadvantage, Haley managed to turn it into a positive. At one point during the debate, nearly all of the other seven candidates were raising their voices over one another, and among all the yelling and chaotic cross talk, it was almost impossible to discern who was saying what. When moderator Bret Baier directed the next question to Haley, she replied with a perfectly timed quip: "So, Bret, what I would like to say is the fact that this is exactly why Margaret Thatcher said if you want something said, ask a man; if you want something done, ask a woman." The audience roared.

In the 1984 presidential debate between then president Ronald Reagan, who was seventy-four years old at the time, and former vice president Walter Mondale, Reagan was questioned on whether he might be too old to be president. The Gipper's reply? "I will not make age an issue of this campaign. I am not going to exploit, for political purposes, my opponent's youth and inexperience." Even Mondale couldn't keep himself from laughing. But he wouldn't be laughing for long—Reagan won that year's election in a landslide.

As a rhetorical device, humor can have a similar impact as metaphor. It stimulates your brain, draws you in, and can leave a lasting impression on your connectome that facts or figures alone cannot. Where it's different from a metaphor is that when we "get" a joke, we feel part of the crowd and closer and more aligned with the person telling it. That's why it's particularly powerful in politics. The point the politician is making becomes more memorable because of the humor, and we side with them in the process. But humor that is just used to get a laugh, without making a point, is a useless endeavor. By using humor as a shortcut to deposition your competition or accentuate a benefit or expertise, your message becomes stickier and seeps into the memory structure faster, creating nearly immediate salience—and that's no joke.

The marketing funnel's one-hundred-plus-year reign proves how ingrained it has become. And much like many of the other conscious marketing approaches, the concept of the funnel distracts marketers from what they really need to be focused on: building the physical footprint of your brand. The stages of the funnel are unnecessary. If you use the right codes and cues, build enough positive associations, and succinctly connect with the audience on an instinctive level, you can drive brand choice in one fell swoop. The proof is in the pudding, whether with direct-to-consumer companies, successful politicians, or even health care: disruption can build a Brand Connectome in a shorter period of time than you would ever expect. Metaphor and humor can certainly help in the process, but it all comes back to layering positive associations and connecting to touchpoints in people's lives that they care about. Don't plod your way through the stages of the funnel—when done right, salience can be just a few minutes away.

Chapter 10

THE IMMORTAL BRAND

INSTINCT RULE: There's no such thing as a finite brand life cycle. If you care for your brand properly, it can live forever.

n March 2020, the tenor of reports on the COVID-19 pandemic began to shift. What was initially thought of in the US that winter as a distant virus in Wuhan, a city most Americans had never heard of, began to come into focus as a serious threat to the country's health and safety. In time, calls for sheltering in place, mask mandates, and vaccines would all be introduced, but early that spring, most people were just getting their footing, trying to understand what this all meant on a greater scale. Schools, offices, and restaurants began to close. But essential businesses, like grocery stores, remained open, forced to balance the safety of their employees with the needs of their customers.

Walmart, the nation's largest grocer—with 25 percent market share—and largest retailer, was one such business. With nearly 4,700 stores in the US, and another almost 5,300 abroad (not to mention their almost 600 Sam's Club locations), they were vital to providing people with what they most needed in uncertain times, from groceries to toilet paper, soap and shampoo to cleaning products, and an ongoing supply of hand sanitizer. When the White House announced new social distancing guidelines on March 16, Walmart sprang into action.

During a period when their sales could have taken a terrible downturn, the company's performance during the pandemic will go down in history as a best practice. They changed their hours and began closing locations early to perform deep cleans throughout the store at night, with special "clean teams" for additional sanitizing, and they added hand-sanitizer dispensers and wipes for customers and workers. They were also one of the first large retailers to add plexiglass sneeze guards at their checkouts, and they created a seniors-only hour to help keep the at-risk population away from crowds. Further, they limited the number of customers at a time, added floor markers to encourage social distancing, and gave employees free telehealth doctor appointments.

Meanwhile, their e-commerce business exploded. In April 2020, in the US, when retail had overall plummeted 16.4 percent, and 2.1 million people had lost their jobs, Walmart's e-commerce sales went up *74 percent* as customers took advantage of the chain's grocery delivery and curbside pickup options. With that immense uptick in sales, they hired 235,000 new associates. Their e-commerce sales have continued to grow since the pandemic subsided, posting a 27 percent year-over-year increase in online sales for the first quarter of 2023.

What might be most impressive, though, is that Walmart figured out what no other company could during the pandemic—how to strike the perfect tone. While most advertisers were repeating platitudes around "the new normal," focusing on "unprecedented times" and uncertainty, Walmart communicated the perfect combination of messages—safety plus progress. The idea of safety, along with the precautions they'd taken, reassured people they could come into their stores without contracting COVID, while an equal emphasis on progress encouraged shoppers to move ahead with their lives. This dual message, launched in May 2020, was reflected in the strongest campaign of the pandemic: "Let's keep America moving. Safely."

The positive associations that grew Walmart's connectome during the pandemic were an extension of its already giant presence. Fifty years of growth, since its founding in Arkansas in 1962, have led to it becoming the largest private employer in the US, with approximately 1.6 million associates (or in-store workers). With a revenue of $611.3 billion in 2023 (a nearly 7 percent increase from the prior year), the company continued its reign as the number-one Fortune 500 company for eleven consecutive years. But the retail and grocer crown has been anything but a foregone conclusion.

Walmart had its share of setbacks over the years, especially in the early 2000s, including criticisms for low wages, a lack of affordable health care for workers, and the environmental impacts of its sprawling supercenters and greenhouse gas footprint. But the company met these well-founded criticisms head on, trimming off these negative associations by overwhelming them with positives. Their 2011 Global Responsibility Report, for example, pointed out that the company had increased locally grown produce in its stores by 97 percent and managed to stop 80.9 percent of its waste from ending up in landfills. The company also increased its minimum wage over time, including a sizable bump from $12 to $14 in 2023. Further, they found ways to decrease health-care costs through programs such as their Centers of Excellence, in which they connect employees with health-care facilities to treat a wide range of conditions, including back pain, infertility, and cancer. Many treatments are free for employees with most of Walmart's medical plans.

Like the Rocky Balboa of retail, Walmart has taken enough punches to the face to frankly suggest it should be long dead. Throughout the company's existence, it has weathered legal troubles and multiple recessions, but it has come out unscathed. How has it done this? Much like Procter & Gamble, Walmart has an "evolution" mindset. They proactively adjust to trends by creating continuous improvements and operationalizing quick solutions to customer desires or problems. "Operationalize" is the operative word. To make a major consumer-facing change throughout nearly eleven thousand stores during the pandemic, and do so without a hitch, is no easy feat. The company's growth, and its resilience through hard times, is not a random stroke of luck.

If your branding is strong, people will come into your franchise. But if the operations don't deliver, they will leave. If your branding is weak and operations strong, you have a superior offering, but you don't get credit for it. That creates a growth problem, in which it's hard to attract new users. The world's top brands, such as Walmart, have strong brand perceptions *and* their operations deliver on those perceptions. One feeds the other, and everything clicks.

Brands like Walmart entirely dispel what is known as the "brand and product life cycle," a classic marketing concept immortalized in 1967 in *Marketing Management: Analysis, Planning, and Control* and still taught in undergraduate and graduate business programs at top universities and in major corporations. The four stages of the life cycle—introduction, growth, maturity, and decline—have become an accepted business principle, or what some might call dogma. The life cycle theory states that brands increase their market share the most at their introduction, or birth, when they gain rapid distribution and early adopters catch on, and during their growth stage, when brands can afford to spend more money and expand. Brands are at the height of their strength and health during these first two stages, but as they mature, the life cycle claims a slowdown in growth is inevitable: a sales peak, followed by a descent into decline, with brands ultimately being put out to pasture. With time on the x-axis and sales on the y-axis, the cycle is regularly portrayed as a bell curve; introduction is on the bottom left-hand side, growth on the upward ascent, maturity near the top as growth slows and flattens, and decline as the curve dips back down on the right-hand side.

But like so many theories on which the old rules of marketing were based, it turns out this one is a myth as well. The life cycle concept is not only scientifically inaccurate, it also causes missed opportunities, as so-called mature brands lose out on potential investment and continued growth. There's no reason growth can't continue its upward trajectory after the maturity stage. Brands are not human. They don't have finite life spans. They don't go gray. They don't get osteoporosis or suffer from arthritis or Alzheimer's. Yes, brands can experience a decline in sales if they don't receive the right care, but that's not a foregone conclusion. If they are nurtured properly, brands can live forever.

Just think of all of the brands that have been around for one hundred years or longer: Kraft Foods, Ford, Crayola, Aqua Velva, Harley-Davidson, L.L.Bean, Nikon, Target, Coca-Cola, JCPenney, Whirlpool, Carhartt, Boeing, John Deere, GE, Equifax, UPS, Kellogg's, Johnson & Johnson, Filson, GMC, Dodge, Red Wing Boots, Laird & Company, Cadillac, Schott, Chevrolet, Lincoln, Pabst Brewing Company, Chivas Regal, Budweiser, and Buick. That's not to mention the brands that have been around for at least *two hundred* years, including Colgate, Brooks Brothers, Jameson, D.G. Yuengling & Son, Harper, Jim Beam, Ames, DuPont, and Dixon Ticonderoga. These centennial and bicentennial brands deserve to be celebrated. But what they've accomplished does not have to be unique to them alone. *Any* company can stave off decline and become a centennial or bicentennial brand. That's because a decline in sales has nothing to do with a brand's age. It has everything to do with the accumulation of negative associations, weighing brands down and holding them back from growth.

How did the life cycle theory get it so wrong? It's easy to understand how traditional marketers came to this conclusion. Like all the other conscious marketing principles, it was based on surface observations. Sure, if you track brand and product growth rates over time, you will find a slowdown, which is what life-cycle proponents saw as brands became older. But that's not the whole story. What they observed was a *correlation* not causation. Slow growth is not due to a brand's age; it is a result of a loss of salience. Unbeknownst to business leaders, negative associations accumulate in competitive and nonusers' minds, making them unreceptive to marketing efforts. Leaders are unaware that these negative associations are eating away at brand growth because they're simply not tracking them. Though some marketing professionals believe a brand can extend its life cycle by adding new usages or launching line extensions, they do not recognize the impact of the negative associations that weigh brands down. When you know about these negative cumulative memories, you have the power to change the shape of your life cycle.

Centennial and bicentennial brands continue to grow because, like Walmart, they remove negative associations the minute they show up. They don't just hope they'll go away. They add new positive associations to overwhelm the negatives, and continuously adjust to ever-changing social and cultural environments, all while holding on to their roots. Sound tough? It's only difficult if you aren't monitoring the unconscious mind. As discussed, when negative associations accumulate in the brain's pathways, the connectome becomes more negative than positive. It is then harder to convert new customers, and growth slows down. As you know by now, negative associations have to be removed as soon as they become part of your brand; if they aren't, they become increasingly burdensome and difficult to excise, like dead leaves consuming a tree.

Just as the funnel doesn't reflect how brands grow in the mind, the life cycle curve doesn't reflect how they mature over time. Your brand can live on, continuously growing and maturing, gaining new customers and creating continuous penetration. With such a life span and growth, you truly gain the instinctive advantage. But if you fail to get rid of negative associations, you will find yourself sliding down the steep side of the life cycle curve. The good news is you can avoid this untimely fate. People can't live forever, but your brand can.

REVOLUTIONISTS VS. TRADITIONALISTS

Without continually adjusting your brand to match the changing environment and customer needs, your brand will lose relevance and salience. But knowing how much to change (or what to change and what not to) is the difference between success and failure. The basic rule of thumb is that you should change as little as possible. For example, instead of dropping a distinctive brand asset when it gets old, imbue it with additional associations and new meaning. Hold on to the key drivers for your current users while adding new positive associations the growth target needs to convert to your brand. And certainly don't change things just for the sake of changing them. Changes should only be made based on what's turning off your growth target; removal allows them to convert to your brand. In short, the brand needs to stay the same brand. If you change its core positioning, people won't recognize you. Worse yet, you will start to lose authenticity, something consumers can sniff out a mile away.

Unfortunately, many companies tend to be too cavalier about altering their brand's positioning, messaging, DBAs, and logos, and as a result, they often lose brand meaning and, sometimes, their identity. In an effort to intentionally improve the brand and keep it fresh and exciting, they accidentally hurt it instead. We call these types of companies "revolutionists." They suffer from optimism bias. They become overly jazzed by a new look, idea, or trend, often getting sold on what somebody tells them is modern and cutting edge. As a result, they change what their brand stands for with some frequency.

It's these companies that jump headfirst into an ocean of change, without recognizing what's beneath the waves—the undertow that can suck brands into the water, causing them to get lost out at sea and drown. Too much change not only makes it difficult for your existing customers to find your brand—which, as in the case of Tropicana, can become unrecognizable—it can cause them to feel abandoned. Your job as the brand's owner is to protect the implicit meanings and assets residing in your existing customers' memories and preserve their role in driving choice. Without the vital guideposts, you lose your brand's essence, along with your existing customers.

Meta, formerly Facebook, is one such brand that fell prey to this type of change, seemingly overcompensating for a growing interest in all things tech, digital, and VR. In 2021, founder and CEO Mark Zuckerberg announced Facebook would be changing its name to Meta, reflecting how the company planned to focus its attention on the "metaverse" in the coming years. If you were following the news and perplexed by this repositioning, you were not alone. As reported by *Forbes*, Kirsten Martin, professor of technology ethics at the University of Notre Dame's Mendoza College of Business, responded to the name change with a strongly worded critique: "Facebook executives have not proven to be trustworthy with their products in the real world, so it's not clear why we should trust them in a virtual world." Criticisms aside, more likely than not, most people, including Facebook users, were asking, "What's the metaverse?" And many still are.

Though descriptions vary, the basics of the metaverse involve an online digital world augmented by virtual reality, so captivating that users are almost unable to separate it from the real world. Some analysts put a price tag of $5 billion on Meta's investment to develop and enter the metaverse, starting with a social VR platform. Come 2023, those billions had been spent, but the metaverse was no closer to reality. Time will tell, of course, but as ChatGPT and interest in AI exploded that year, the metaverse seemed to be pushed out of mind by a new, much more tangible big tech development.

Though it could be argued that this interest is a result of the "hot new thing" distracting people's attention, what really happened is that Zuckerberg bet on revolution instead of evolution. If he had been able to keep the Facebook brand attached more directly to the metaverse concept, it might have only strengthened the brand's connectome, growing it further and introducing an exciting new dimension. He could have leveraged Facebook's positive associations around friendship, homegrown community, and connection, while adding Meta's high-tech associations, to create a more balanced connectome—the marvels of the virtual tech universe rooted in humanity, with the comfort of friends and family you already know. As it stands, the metaverse could disappear before it ever takes off.

While revolutionizing a brand is one of the fastest ways to destroy it, going to the other extreme is just as dangerous. Such companies—let's call them "traditionalists"—tend to hold on to their past positioning too rigidly, afraid to deviate from it in any way or to add new dimensions. Traditionalists play to their core customers, believing their brand equity is entrenched in people's minds, immutable, so it cannot, and should not, be changed. But while these leaders stress the "true DNA" of their brand, they typically have little proof that it is actually keeping consumers loyal or is effective in bringing new users into the fold.

If you're a traditionalist, you are going to keep your brand exactly the same, afraid to deviate from what it originally stood for. Like a lioness looking after its cubs, traditionalist companies protect what *they* believe is their brand DNA at all costs, often not really knowing what the brand looks like in people's minds. When taken to its extreme, this mentality can create a stagnant brand, because leaders are overly focused on their existing customers and positioning. They feel anything they do to evolve the brand for new customers could hurt them in existing customers' minds, so they refuse to alter the slightest thing, even if the brand has become irrelevant. Traditionalist marketers also think a brand can only stand for one thing, and don't understand how you can layer new messages without losing the brand's current identity. This approach leads to rigidity, akin to a tree standing still in the path of a tornado.

So although you don't want a brand that fluctuates with every cultural whim, you also don't want an immutable brand. Instead of either revolution or inertia, the goal you want to pursue is continuous evolution—a balance between staying true to your brand's core identity and values and evolving with the times. In contrast to traditionalists and revolutionists, we call these brands "evolutionists."

On the change continuum, evolution falls in the "just right" midpoint between revolution and inertia. Change too little and prospective customers with implicit barriers to your brand have no reason to come in. Change too much—pull a 180—and you can seem inauthentic, unrecognizable to existing customers. That almost always causes your current customers to flee. To bring in your growth target, your brand must hold on to the positive associations it's known for, yet gradually and continuously evolve to remove the barriers that stand in the way.

A FORMULA FOR CONTINUOUS EVOLUTION AND GROWTH

Evolution comes down to tending to your connectome so your brand remains fresh, new, and vibrant. While brands don't intrinsically grow old, they can become unhealthy if you're not paying attention. Maintaining your brand's health and wellness therefore requires constant vigilance. If you nurture your brand's health at every turn, it has the opportunity to continue developing, evolving, and thriving, reaching immortality. Luckily, this process is not a guessing game. There is a simple, proven formula to help breathe new life into your brand over the course of every changing era: "Keep, Stop, Add."

KEEP: Reinforce positive associations. Just as you must put your brain and muscles to work so they stay strong, you must keep "working" your brand's memory structure to keep it healthy and fit. You have to *keep* the positive associations your brand already has among current users and nonusers. You can't assume everyone knows your brand or what it stands for. On the contrary, you have to assume nonusers know *nothing* about you. Continually reinforcing the positive associations your brand has (for example, its benefits, expertise, founding story, and DBAs) allows you to grow your connectome with prospective customers, including new generations who did not grow up with your brand. Reinforcing a brand's positive associations is also critical to ensure existing customers stick with you while you're evolving the brand. In short, use it or lose it. If you learned how to play piano as a child, but then didn't practice for twenty years, when you go back to tickle those ivories, you're likely to be all thumbs. The connections in your neural pathways that previously allowed your brain to decipher sheet music and send messages to your fingers on exactly how and where to move will have become weakened or lost entirely. The same is true with a brand's positive associations.

STOP: Root out negative associations. You have to *stop* any negative associations from accumulating, otherwise they will turn into barriers that prevent new customers from converting to your brand. But in order to do this, you need to find out what your negative associations *are*. You won't learn that from traditional research or attribute-based surveys. Sure, you can identify the brand's *conscious* barriers that way (for example, artificiality in food and beverage categories), but you probably already know those. The negative associations that really hold brands back are the ones you *don't know* and that arise organically over time. They are nuanced, often image- or persona-based, and are discoverable only through implicit research. This type of work reveals the often misguided cognitive connections people have made about your brand, a negative narrative you could never have imagined. This knowledge is empowering. After all, how can you create a strategy for a brand without knowing what you're up against? By ceasing any communications that may be inadvertently reinforcing a negative association, and replacing them with positive associations, your audience can focus on what counts: the wonders of your brand. Like cutting out fatty foods or quitting smoking helps improve your physical health, getting rid of negative associations improves brand health. When you weed out negative associations, you set the stage for the positive ones to flourish.

ADD: Build Growth Triggers. But reinforcing existing positive associations, and overwhelming the negative associations with positive ones, gets you only so far. That's where "add" comes in. To continuously evolve your brand, you must *add* new positive associations that the growth target needs to start using your brand. Growth

Triggers are the fastest way to do so. Growth Triggers are like giving your brand a shot of B12, imbuing it with vigor, vitality, and new life. As discussed, these cognitive shortcuts supercharge prospective customers' connectomes with positive associations that make the Brand Connectome grow and become more salient. Like superfoods, shortcuts—such as the snow-capped mountain in the bottled water category, a fresh-cracked egg for a fast-food breakfast, or Dad taking care of an infant for baby shampoo—are packed with nutrients on which the brain thrives. When you add them to your existing Brand Connectome, Growth Triggers cause new pathways to sprout, increasing the physical footprint of your brand in prospective customers' minds at an accelerated pace.

"Keep, Stop, Add" is the new mantra companies must follow to keep their brands healthy, both in the short and long term. By reinforcing the positive associations people already hold in high esteem (Keep), eliminating the negative associations (Stop), and adding new associations that prospective customers need to convert (Add), you can drive penetration while reducing churn—a surefire recipe for high growth. This process—learning how to overcome the mental barriers of new customers while holding on to existing ones—has a marvelous added bonus: It forces you to keep evolving and raise your company's bar. To that end, "Keep, Stop, Add" requires that you strike a balance of old and new associations, just as the most successful centennial brands have been able to.

Procter & Gamble is a good example. Their marketers are highly protective of their brand equities—like Tide, Charmin, and Bounty—but they continually refresh their messages and imagery and constantly innovate to meet changing consumer trends, all while still holding on to the cherished distinctive brand assets that historically built their brands. Though they could do more to pull in certain customer segments, such as millennial heads of household and natural consumers, they keep cultivating their portfolio of cherished Brand Connectomes. For a company founded in 1837 as a soap and candle manufacturer, they have maintained incredible relevance for generations of consumers, contributing to their nearly $81 billion revenue in 2023, up 3.5 percent since 2022.

Brands that stand the test of time keep reinforcing the strong memories and associations embedded in the connectome that exists in consumers' minds, while also adding new positive associations to it. That's why, for example, P&G's toilet paper brand, Charmin, and two of its sub-brands—Charmin Ultra Soft and Charmin Ultra Strong—are still among the top ten best-selling toilet papers in the US, and Bounty remains number one in paper towels. Many consumers might not even know that P&G owns these brands, but they are intimately familiar with their best-sellers due to their size and salience in *all* of our minds, not just some. That universality is not by happenstance; it's a result of continually educating new generations of consumers about the benefits and expertise of their brands and perpetually growing their connectomes so they keep adding years to their lives.

DIGITAL BRAND ATROPHY

Like negative associations, there is another hidden force at work eroding brand health. And it's a product of today's digital world where content has become king. Brands today feel the need to engage in a 24/7 dialogue with their audience on the other side of their screens. Due to the sheer amount of content they push out, and the short amount of time in which they can strategically develop it, brands unfortunately end up straying far from their core messaging and positioning, losing the "keep" component of the formula. In an effort to say something new every day, the brand's benefit and expertise can become diluted or unclear, as audiences often receive tangential information about the brand. Some messages even contradict one another. This digital fragmentation and dispersion of messaging across channels destroys a cohesive brand identity and leads to what I call "digital brand atrophy."

The more dissipated a brand's identity gets in consumers' minds, the more brand mind share gradually wastes away. This is not merely a brand health concern; it's a critical business issue. The dissipation and disintegration of brand associations is directly tied to a decline in revenue growth and market share. Though this phenomenon existed prior to the twenty-first century, it has increased immensely with the advent of Web 2.0, an environment in which audience segmentation and platform fragmentation has people receiving vastly different messages about brands all day long. With so many messages flying around different websites, apps, and social media platforms, brands are losing their ability to create consistent brand communications and effective connections with their consumers.

Of all the issues that can damage brand growth, digital brand atrophy may be the most vital because it holds the greatest threat to longevity. A healthy brand is a convergent brand. When a brand starts meaning different things to different people, it stops being a brand. In 2003, digital advertising revenues were just $7.3 billion. It makes sense. People were getting online, and the digital revolution was upon us. Soon, the internet would change the way we live on an everyday basis, from work to communication to commerce and every area in between. It's no wonder that by 2021 revenue had dramatically shot up—to $189.3 billion. Today, 56 percent of marketing budgets are dedicated to digital channels. There's nothing wrong with that evolution—we live in a technologically advanced world that is becoming ever more digital. But these advancements have also led to fragmentation in how we disseminate, and consume, information.

Thirty years ago, we all sat in our living rooms, watching the same seven channels on TV that the people down the block, across town, or in another city or state were watching. This shared existence led to a common frame of reference and shared values when it came to news, entertainment, and information overall. We all saw the same thirty-second commercials, the same shows, the same nightly broadcasts. It was as if we were holding hands across the US, maybe not quite singing "Kumbaya," but generally in agreement on reality. We lived in a linear world. That's all gone.

With a digital device in every hand, we have become oversaturated by thousands of messages, received at different times, through different vehicles. These days we may even see a personalized message created just for us. Content generation is on an endless loop, so continuous that brands feel compelled to try to engage every day, lest they be left out of the conversation. They have a dire case of marketing FOMO. In an effort to maintain that near-constant dialogue, they grasp at straws, looking to say something—*anything*—to connect, often causing them to get far afield from their brand's actual message. Consumers end up receiving messaging that is only tangentially related, if that, to the brand's benefits and capabilities. The result? Consumers don't understand what the brand stands for or how it works, they struggle to recognize its point of difference, and they lack a clear sense of when to use it.

In the process, creatives are overwhelmed, pushing out whatever they can. Michael Farmer, chairman and CEO of the Farmer & Company strategy consultancy and former Bain partner, explains that in 1992, fifty creatives at one of his ad-agency clients completed 380 creative and strategic deliverables, all of them original pieces of work. That comes out to about 7.6 deliverables per creative per year. Twenty-five years later, in 2017, at a similar office in the same agency, fifty creatives completed 15,000 deliverables, of which 13,000 were "adaptations" of previously developed work. The workload had exploded to 300 deliverables per creative per year across media platforms, including social media posts, digital ads, email blasts, and more.

With this level of project demands, the amount of thought that can go into each piece of content is, by necessity, minimal, forcing creatives and brands to essentially throw as much stuff at the wall as possible and see what sticks. Instead of asking "What do we need to do to move the brand forward?" you are forced to ask "What do we need to do to get all these pieces out the door?" Like Lucille Ball's character in *I Love Lucy*, marketers and creatives are struggling to stay one step ahead of the conveyor belt, shooting posts out, like chocolate candies, a mile a minute. The process has become an assembly line focused on throughput, causing few brand messages to actually stick in consumers' memories.

Obviously, this approach is not going to lead to a cohesive brand identity—it simply can't. When you're trying to come up with the next post ad nauseum, the information you share may have only a tenuous connection to your product or service. Like throwing a pebble in a pond, as the concentric circles spread out, you get further and further away from the brand's center, and you slowly diverge from your brand identity. Key messages, benefits, and "reasons to believe" (the substance behind why customers should trust your brand promises) start to falter or become obscured as you try to keep that assembly line going. Without a unified, clear message entering consumers' memory structure, people create *their own* story about your brand, leading to misperceptions.

The connectome may be forming, but it is more likely to be based on consumers' interpretation of the brand, and much less on the specific positive associations and brand image that the company intends to convey. A meta-analysis of Fortune 500 brands across industries over the past decade shows that Brand Connectomes today are increasingly being overtaken by consumers' own narratives, often false ones, that they have concocted on their own. Since people are not receiving consistent messages about what brands stand for, they connect the dots themselves, often coming to the wrong conclusions. The brand's distinctive brand assets, image, and expertise are less likely to be retained or understood. The reason for this is simple. Because brand leaders are fragmenting their narrative and imagery across channels, their marketing is just not coming through.

Brands need to ensure the messages consumers have in their minds are the ones the brands actually want to get across. To do so, they need more than a brand book—they have to develop a tighter set of guidelines for determining which messages, Growth Triggers, associations, and distinctive brand assets reinforce what the brand stands for and which do not. By creating a portfolio of preapproved messages, Growth Triggers, associations, and DBAs, you will have your whole brand at your fingertips and will be less likely to deviate. Marketers and advertisers often say, "Give me the freedom of a tight brief," and this case is no exception. The more precise you are, the more likely your brand will stay on message while allowing space for creativity within these guidelines. Whether you're a one-person shop or a multinational conglomerate, or if your business is a digital disruptor or a legacy brand, these guidelines support the "Keep, Stop, Add" process of continuous brand evolution and growth. It's never too late. By creating the right guidelines, and sticking to them, you can reinvigorate and increase the longevity of any brand, no matter its age.

THE LEGACY BRAND BOUNCE-BACK EFFECT

Perhaps the best news about the life span of brands is the promise of a second chance—the promise of rehabilitation. Even if a brand has made some mistakes and left their tree untended for a time, they can still reverse the curve and gain that upward trajectory once again. Legacy brands in particular have the ability to rapidly rebound in terms of growth because of their well-established network of cumulative memories. We call this ability the "bounce-back effect." But that's not what you'll hear from a range of business experts who claim legacy brands are old, past their prime, and that you shouldn't invest in them because they're never going to get you much more growth. As a result, even large, cash-cow brands that have been around for ages are deemphasized in company portfolios, and the younger brands are given greater focus and resources. Now, if the smaller brand is in a high-growth category, or if it has a major point of difference, then that strategy might make sense. But if not, a legacy brand does not have to be put out to pasture—nor should it be.

In fact, while all brands can experience comebacks, it's harder for smaller or newer brands because they're not as firmly implanted in people's minds. Legacy brands have a huge advantage. They have decades of accumulated memories and an established Brand Connectome in the public's mind. Remarkably, even if some of those associations are negative, the network is so extensive and established that if enough positive associations are added, the brand can break out of stagnation or decline. Their incredibly thick roots have had years to grow and dig deeper into the brain. It's like when a plant has gone without water for a time and starts to look droopy and lifeless. As soon as you water it, its roots suck up the moisture, the leaves perk up, and the plant springs back to life, rejuvenated.

Take Old Spice deodorant and men's grooming products. In 1937, William Lightfoot Schultz, founder of the Shulton Company, released Early American Old Spice, a fragrance for women inspired by his mother's potpourri. The following year welcomed an Old Spice line for men, including aftershave and shaving soap, and featuring the same original scent still used today. Both the men's and women's branding included colonial sailing imagery that would become a signature motif and well-recognized DBA, even as the men's line cannibalized the women's and solidified the brand's identity.

In the 1970s, its marketing approach was focused on traditional themes of masculinity, and they had the characters to match. In a commercial from 1972, a handsome and somewhat rugged sailor hops off a ship at port with his rucksack in hand and walks through the streets of San Francisco, throwing a buoy-shaped bottle of aftershave up to a shirtless man in a window who seems to have just come out of the shower. His female partner approves as he dabs it on his face. "Wake up with Old Spice and feel the freshness of the open sea," states the voice-over, before the screen cuts to the same sailor now walking down a country road toward a farm, a twangy western tune playing in the background. Crossing the path of a cowboy, he passes on another bottle: "Wake up with Old Spice. Feel the spray on your face and the wind at your back."

The rugged masculine associations remained as the brand introduced new products, including deodorant, cologne, and body wash (one of the first for men), until Old Spice was purchased by P&G in

1990. With the support of P&G, the brand thrived for a time, but there was a target that simply wasn't coming in: young men. By the 2000s, this began to hurt, as Old Spice started losing market share, specifically to younger brands like Axe. It was obvious why: younger consumers thought of Old Spice as something their dads and grandfathers used. The brand felt dated, *old* (it was even in the name!), while companies like Axe—introduced to the US in 2002—had a young, fresh, twenty-first-century feel. Old-school cowboys and sailors were not just from a bygone era, but another millennium; by extension, so was Old Spice. This negative association was indirect, and it likely sneaked in without much fanfare, until it was too late.

Or so it seemed.

Enter the brand's saving grace: Old Spice Guy. Portrayed by actor and former football player Isaiah Mustafa, the Old Spice Guy was featured in a 2010 commercial—"The Man Your Man Could Smell Like"—that first appeared during the Super Bowl that year. It was an instant success. Though it contained some of the masculine swagger of the Old Spice sailor commercial from almost forty years earlier, the commercial was anything but dated. It was an irreverent thirty-second spot that not only poked a little fun at the brand's outdated image, but also spoke to a new audience: women.

The producers of the campaign, ad agency Wieden+Kennedy, recognized that 60 percent of body wash was purchased by women, ostensibly for the men in their lives. "The Man Your Man Could Smell Like" asked female viewers to look from the chiseled, shirtless Isaiah Mustafa on the screen—getting out of the shower, on a giant sailboat, riding a white horse on a beach—to their man sitting next to them. Mustafa's character points out that their man isn't him, but could at least smell like him, instead of like "lady's body wash," if he switched to Old Spice.

The ad struck a chord with viewers and reinvigorated the brand. In fact, it went viral, with forty million views after the first week. The Old Spice Twitter account had a 2,700 percent increase in followers, their YouTube channel briefly turned into the all-time most viewed, and their website traffic went up by 300 percent. Though the company had set a goal to increase their body wash sales by 15 percent, between February, when the ad first aired, and May, Old Spice Red Zone body wash had increased sales 60 percent versus the prior year. Sales doubled by July, and it became the best-selling men's body wash on the market.

The commercial used humor not to get a quick laugh but rather to reinforce the benefit of smelling good for your partner, while pulling in imagery related to their long-standing sea motif. But it also kept with the times, creating cultural relevance. The ad moved away from stilted characters who took themselves too seriously—as shown in the commercial from 1972—replacing them with a sexy, tongue-in-cheek spokesperson who pushed smelling good for your partner, not just after you come off the docks. Everything about the commercial felt fun, even exciting, and it still spoke to the effectiveness of the product. With a nearly seventy-five-year-old connectome at the time, Old Spice was able to shed its old image and negative associations, while including new positive ones that would stick in the audience's mind. A classic example of the "Keep, Stop, Add" process that led to the brand's revitalization and continued successful growth.

But even with that success, Old Spice can't stand still. The same messaging that worked in 2010 would seem dated in 2024. While the core positioning of your brand should remain the same, the particular message must evolve to stay culturally relevant. Today, Old Spice has created a new twist. The "Men Have Skin Too" ads show Deon Cole reprimanding his romantic partner, played by Gabrielle Dennis, for using up his Old Spice body wash because she likes the smooth skin and fragrance it provides. Why shouldn't she use it? The implicit association is that women can do anything men can, and the body wash's scent, and comfort it provides, is for everyone.

Don't let anyone tell you decline is inevitable. It's a defeatist attitude based on an inaccurate assumption. As proven by centennial and bicentennial brands, and those that are well on their way to reaching those milestones, maturity is not the end. It's simply a matter of monitoring the unconscious mind of your prospects and getting ahead of any false narratives; when you do that, you can gain the instinctive advantage. If you tend to your connectome—keeping existing positive associations, stopping negative associations, and adding new positives—no one can hold your brand back from growing high above the rest, and for many years to come. Keep in mind, the oldest trees out in the wild are over four thousand years old. If you treat your brand right, and keep nurturing its growth, there's no reason it can't live forever.

CONCLUSION

A Fortune 500 CMO recently came to Triggers to discuss their healthy snack bar brand, which had been underperforming over the past decade—a 6 percent decline during those ten years. The CMO had been brought in from another top company in an effort to revitalize the brand and push their growth out of the red and into the black. Known as having a "King Midas touch," everything he worked on at previous companies had turned to gold. But this business was proving more difficult than he had ever expected.

He explained they had undergone a full rebranding campaign, based on the recommendations of a major management consulting firm. The campaign pushed the "wholesome goodness" aspect of the snack. In his mind, it was perfect. With a seemingly ever-growing trend for all things natural and organic—cleaning products and soaps, personal care, food and drinks—wholesome was a superior claim they could make, in line with today's tastes and preferences. Before launching, the advertising had been tested quantitatively and with a number of focus groups, resulting in a "green light" recommendation that had been shared with the CMO and other company executives. But the campaign had been underway for months, and the business was still losing share.

We saw the problem right away, and now that you've read this book, I'll bet you see it too. This single driver was not strong enough on its own, and prospects were likely carrying some implicit negative associations that the consulting firm hadn't recognized. That's precisely what our work revealed. Implicit barriers had been brewing in prospective users' minds for years: inauthentic,

uninspiring, bland, unadventurous, and perceived limited usage occasions. We also uncovered three drivers that, working in concert,
removed these barriers: naturally delicious, a proprietary milling
method for their whole grain, and the farmer's market roots of the
brand. "Naturally delicious" combined with "poppy," colorful fruit
imagery created taste excitement, which addressed their uninspired,
bland personality. The proprietary milling method that maintained
more of the germ (the nutritional powerhouse of the whole grain)
provided superior expertise and took down inauthentic barriers.
And the third driver, their humble beginnings in the bustling farmer's markets of the Pacific Northwest, gave the brand a distinctive
personality it had been lacking, creating an inspiring face for the
brand.

When the CMO's team and their ad agencies began incorporating all
three of these drivers in their messaging across channels, the change
in sales was almost immediate. The CMO was thrilled. But he couldn't
help but ask, why had a top consulting firm—that also performed significant consumer research to back up their recommendations—come
to a completely different conclusion than we had at Triggers? It was a
great question, and I could see why it was vexing.

The studies were worlds apart, with differences in philosophy,
methodology, and outcome. The previous strategic direction overlooked three critical principles for sustainable growth. First, the
recommendation assumed that a single benefit could drive brand
growth. But the science shows that you need a myriad of benefits
and positive associations to build salience. Second, the management
consulting firm's work was developed based on traditional survey
research, where conscious questions were answered by the conscious
mind. It's easy to get high marks in answer to a list of attributes,
benefits, or even concepts in such studies, but those results are often
not predictive of purchase. The same is true of advertising testing.
The Triggers work not only captured the traditional quantitative
metrics, it also identified the positive and negative associations of
every positioning and advertising message we tested.

Turns out, while "wholesome goodness" works in many situations, in this particular case it actually had negative associations. Since one of their implicit barriers was blandness, "wholesome goodness" actually reinforced that the snack bar didn't taste very good. The consulting firm would have only known this by monitoring consumers' unconscious associations. But they were focused on attributes. Attributes are one-dimensional, rearview-mirror metrics. Associations are the ever-changing organic story that will affect your business tomorrow. Adding new positive associations builds memory structure and expands your brand's mind share. Attributes do not. Without understanding the associations your prospects' unconscious minds are making about your brand, you only have the first half of the story. The second half is the hidden connections the brain is making—and that's the half that matters most.

Third and finally, their testing had been performed with existing loyal consumers of the brand who were already heavy users. Triggers identified the barriers that prevented *prospective* users from switching and built the positioning to break down those barriers. By tailoring the positioning to prospects—a much larger pool of users, including light and moderate, not just heavy—the client was able to effectively source more volume.

When you tap into latent positive associations in the unconscious mind, sever detrimental connections, and employ cognitive shortcuts that prompt the mind to form new connections, you can change people's behavior. By physically growing mind share, you can increase your market share, win elections, convert people to your cause, and create continuous growth.

We are all trying to sell something—a business, a product, a cause, a candidate, an idea. Every single one of us is a marketer in our own way. And if you're like most people, you're frustrated that you're not making progress as fast as you would like to be. There is a litany of excuses: we're not spending enough on marketing, the economy isn't good, the marketplace is too crowded, or competition is too fierce. But the truth is, none of these issues are the actual stumbling blocks. The real reason is that most of us are using an old playbook, full of rules created at a time when we didn't know how our minds function or how we make choices.

Choice is not the result of a conscious push or pull, or of overt persuasion. Decisions are not made on facts and figures, nor are they influenced by an appeal to logic or emotion. They are instinctive, the result of the countless memories and associations stored in our minds, affecting what we do every single day. By understanding the rules that govern this instinctive approach to decision-making, you can throw out the traditional playbook and approach every challenge and opportunity with the right formula.

WINNING THROUGH THE POWER OF INSTINCT

There are no people, no political candidates, no brands competing for your money or your vote. There are just floating connectomes fighting for dominance in your brain. The battle doesn't take place on shelves or in the voting booth, it takes place in the memory structure of our minds. Throughout this book, we have seen stories of tremendous success, like Harry Potter, M&M's, and CeraVe. You now know those successes were neither aberrations, a matter of luck, nor happenstance. They came from having gained the instinctive advantage, effectively scaling a vast network of memories in the universal unconscious. Each created a myriad of connections comprised of diversified, relevant touchpoints in people's lives. But these successful initiatives demonstrate that you can't grow your brand in the marketplace until you grow your brand's physical footprint in people's minds. To gain market share, you need to gain mind share.

We've seen tales of decline from companies such as Kohl's, Bed Bath & Beyond, and Victoria's Secret, whose business performance seemed to plummet out of nowhere. But a closer look reveals that negative associations had been accumulating over the last two decades—a virus growing in the unconscious mind they just weren't monitoring. These companies' leaders were caught by surprise. Activist groups and Wall Street investors attribute these situations to poor management, which may be partially true. But that's a superficial analysis. Every one of these businesses fell into the Core Customer Trap. They could have been fixed if only they had prioritized prospective customers over existing ones and overwhelmed negative associations with positive ones.

None of these business issues were inevitable. As shown in the self-aware leadership of Ana at the cosmetics company and the leaders at McDonald's—whose brands were also losing mind share and gaining negative associations—redemption and revitalization are possible if you leap into action. They didn't do it by magic or luck. They diagnosed what was going on in the mind of their prospects proactively, changed course fast, and turned the ship around.

But the true power of instinct is not just about studying others' past successes and failures. Rather it's your ability to create extraordinary success yourself. With your new worldview, you are now empowered to diagnose what's hurting any brand—be it a business, nonprofit, personal brand, political candidate, college applicant, or career—and have the principles for fixing it. If financial growth or fundraising has stalled, you know you likely have a salience problem, and there are negative associations brewing, holding you back.

This new perspective doesn't start and end in the business world. Next election, whether for a local congressperson or for president of the United States, think about the candidates' connectomes. You should be able to predict which candidates are most likely to win their party's nomination based on who has the most established Brand Connectomes. Can a lesser-known candidate swoop onto the scene and unseat a more established player? Possibly, but only if they follow Obama's playbook. And next time you find yourself getting into a heated argument with friends or family over politics, take a deep breath. The person you're arguing with is neither an idiot nor evil. They simply have the mirror image of your Democrat and Republican connectomes (connectomes that are the reverse of yours)—with positive associations where yours are negative and negative associations where yours are positive. You can also now consider the strengths and weaknesses of social causes and know how to fuel them. When you choose sides, take a moment to reflect on what, in your own connectome, caused you to do so.

This is the playbook for the next generation of marketing. It overturns the old rules, replacing them with the new rules of instinct based on the science of how the brain works. You now know that distinctiveness is more powerful than uniqueness, that fantasy triumphs over reality, and that distinctive brand assets, bolstered by supercharged cues, build memory structure faster than you can say Daniel Kahneman. You know to question traditional theories such as the product life cycle, segmentation, and the funnel because they go against the way the brain really works. What you see is not what you get. The truth behind people's decisions is not the tip of the iceberg but what lies beneath the waterline, in their physical memory structure. Instead of bombarding, arguing, or incentivizing, you can move away from conscious persuasion and focus on how people actually make choices. Think of it as a process of making the invisible visible, diving below the surface to inspect that massive iceberg and expose the true levers of people's decisions.

If your company's or organization's results have softened, there's likely a problem below the waterline—either an abundance of negative associations weighing down the Brand Connectome or a sparse network with insufficient positive associations. The result is the same: your growth will be hindered. That's why you need to remain a brand arborist, tending to your tree, watering its roots, giving it the necessary nutrients, and making sure any dead leaves or branches are quickly removed. If you don't, the negative associations will continue to fester and your brand will shrink, never reaching the level of salience needed to make an impact.

It all comes down to growth. Growing your brand, your business, the causes you care about, the candidate you support, your ideas at work or at home. Your own brain. Without growth, all of these cease to exist. But with growth, all of them—brands, businesses, causes, candidates, ideas, thoughts—can thrive. Despite any external factors, growth can happen; if anyone tells you otherwise, don't believe them. Yes, you will face ups and downs in the market. Economies change. Society goes through cultural trends. Natural disasters occur, and so do pandemics. There are supply shortages, distribution problems, and a host of other factors that may affect your brand—but they will only tank your brand if you let them.

If you're blaming these for poor performance or a declining customer base, you're spending too much time looking outward and not enough looking inward. What's really going on is a problem with your connectome. Knowing this gives you the power to get your brand back on track. By supercharging your content with Growth Triggers, you can convert people faster and create customers for life. While the rest of the world is attacking the conscious mind, trying to cajole, bombard, and argue, hoping to influence the mere 5 percent of the choices made by the conscious mind, you can step back and focus on the 95 percent of decisions that come from the unconscious mind. That's where you'll find growth.

And growth's what we need most today, though maybe not in the way you'd expect. Business growth, financial growth, growth in influence or prestige—these are all great, but we also need personal growth, how we understand each other and the evolving world around us. New branches sprouting, creating vast connectomes, are really the birth of new ideas, education, and knowledge. When it comes down to it, this process is all about learning. We need to learn from each other. We need to educate ourselves on all sides of an issue, allowing connectomes to grow that we have left untended. When we understand other points of view, those connectomes become stronger, and we become more tolerant. If we only look at a sliver of information, a tiny snippet of what's out there, our brains contract.

The tools throughout this book can help you inspect, or reinspect, where your ideas come from, why you make the choices you do, and how to become a more tolerant, understanding, and empathetic person. It all comes down to expansion, connecting the dots in your mind and in others'. With these tools, you can look at every situation and ask, "What's holding my business back? What's holding me back? What are the positive associations? What are the negatives? What connections can I make in people's lives? What Growth Triggers can I use to accelerate acceptance and growth of other people's ideas, causes, or values?"

And in finding the answers to these questions, we can make leaps and bounds together. This is the new playbook for the Age of Instinct—a set of counterintuitive principles that leverages how the world actually works, enabling you to take the path of least resistance to growth. Going forward, in any endeavor, you will have a new kind of power, the power of instinct, which, as it turns out, is the key to success in business and in life.

ACKNOWLEDGMENTS

This book is the culmination of everything I've learned throughout my career about how to make marketing the engine of growth. That's why these acknowledgments include not just the people who were instrumental in helping me write this book but also those who have mentored and supported me over the past thirty years and longer. My greatest gratitude goes out to the following, without whom this book would have been impossible.

Lynn Johnston, my agent, who believed in this book and its potential before anyone else. My keen-eyed editor at Hachette Book Group's PublicAffairs, Colleen Lawrie, who took a chance on a first-time author based on her belief in the broad appeal of the book. She deserves an award for surviving countless debates with my niggling tendencies—her patience knows no bounds! Thanks to Lindsay Fradkoff and Brooke Parson, Jocelynn Pedro, Mark Fortier, Matt Wendell, and Rebecca Bender for their marketing, public relations, and social media expertise. All were fabulous to work with. Big thanks to designer Pete Garceau for his radiant cover. And special thanks to Zach Gajewski, a brilliantly talented editor and collaborator who went above and beyond, providing thoughtful, concise input throughout the development of the manuscript.

I've been fortunate enough to work with some of the best brains in marketing at Triggers Brand Consulting. Their commitment to what we do is relentless bar none, and each of them brings a distinctive gift to our special company. Thank you to Heather Coyle, Morgan Seamark, Tom Gosline, Kelsey Sullivan, Mindy Harris, Jeffrey

McElnea, Sara Haim, Stephanie Veraghen, Jolene LaBelle, Dave Silcock, Kyra Meringer, Michelle Rhoades, and Celeste Stone. Additional thanks go to the folks behind the scenes—Steve Zanon, Darren Cohen, and Betty Graumlich—who have been supporting our company for decades.

In addition to my Triggers colleagues, there were a handful of people who generously helped me with various aspects of the book, willing to drop everything to have a conversation with me—even at strange hours—about any topic at all. Their insights and creativity have had an indelible impact on me, and their unswerving support on a personal level lifts me up. They are Elyse Kane, Lisa Mirchin, and Victoria Perla Guyardo. Wharton professor Michael Platt and CEO of Farmer & Company, and former Bain partner, Michael Farmer, provided not just input for the book but ongoing help whenever I had a question in their areas of expertise. Jill Tipograph, Lisa Gable, Christi Botello, and Jennefer Witter are always there providing invaluable assistance.

Without our clients, some of whom go back three decades with us, and the ability to work on the most amazing brands on the planet, this book would not have been possible. These leaders fuel our determination to push the boundaries of the unknown, make the invisible visible, and help them achieve their lofty goals. But we are further blessed at Triggers because the business leaders we work with are not only visionaries; they also happen to be amazing human beings—a rare combination. Many thanks to Greg Lyons, Michael Roberts, Ann Mukherjee, David Edelman, Wes Wilkes, Umi Patel, JP Bittencourt, Doug Healy, Pam Forbus, Jaime Friedman, Kevin Moeller, Kyle Lazarus, Dan O'Leary, Mark Mandell, Barry Tatelman, Paul Guyardo, Helen Cai, Keira Krausz, Kathy Price, Michaela Pardubicka-Jenkins, Zach Harris, Darrin Rahn, Koley Corte, Steve Caracappa, Joahne Carter, April Jeffries, Robin Kaminsky, and Geri Yoshioka.

In addition to great clients and colleagues, I had the luck of wonderful mentors early in my career, including Kathy Dwyer, Michael

White, Don Petit, and Libby Daniel. These gifted individuals took me under their wing, influencing my overall thinking, especially with regard to visual and verbal nuance, and how brands and business-building work in the first place.

Then there are those people who, book or no book, are always in my corner. I have been incredibly fortunate to count Richard Nanula, Scott Delman, Doron Grosman, and Paul Cusenza among my cherished friends. Their encouraging presence and advice have been a constant in my life. Additional thanks to my NYC HBS Forum and Scarsdale "Sisterhood" Forum (you know who you are) for their advice, friendship, and cheerleading. And special gratitude to Karen Strauss, my lifelong best friend, whose enormous emotional support I rely on in general in my life, and whose fingerprints are on this book cover.

Last but not least, my family, including my incredible sister, Liz Hirsh, and in-laws; powerhouse mom, Charlotte Picot, a community leader in Forest Hills; and my cherished father, Pierre Picot, who passed away in 2015. My dad's expertise in military intelligence, insights about human psychology, and astute visual sense all trickled into my genes, yet manifested in a different sphere. My biggest champions, my parents raised me to work hard, think for myself, and brush off failure—teaching me that nothing is out of reach if you're persistent.

Finally, my husband, Andrew Zane, put up with not seeing me for over two years—maybe more—as I hashed out this book late at night, early in the morning, and many a weekend. A heartfelt thank you, Andy, for being the perfect husband for a determined woman and for always having my back no matter what new ambitious and "zany" escapade I take on. And lastly, thanks to my grown sons, Dylan and Austen, whose wisdom and insight surpass their years and who, without fail, provide the honest answers I need to hear (and occasionally, ones I wish I hadn't asked for).

BIBLIOGRAPHY

INTRODUCTION

Milmo, Dan. "ChatGPT Reaches 100 Million Users Two Months After Launch." *The Guardian*, February 2, 2023. https://theguardian.com/technology/2023/feb/02/chatgpt-100-million-users-open-ai-fastest-growing-app.

Morse, Gardiner. "Hidden Minds." *Harvard Business Review*, June 2002. https://hbr.org/2002/06/hidden-minds.

Roach, Tom. "Most Marketing Is Bad Because It Ignores the Most Basic Data." TheTomRoach.com, November 10, 2020. https://thetomroach.com/2020/11/10/most-marketing-is-bad-because-it-ignores-the-most-basic-data.

Sharp, Byron. *How Brands Grow: What Marketers Don't Know*. New York: Oxford University Press, 2010.

Wendel, Stephen. "Who Is Doing Applied Behavioral Science? Results from a Global Survey of Behavioral Teams." *Behavioral Scientist*, October 5, 2020. http://behavioralscientist.org/who-is-doing-applied-behavioral-science-results-from-a-global-survey-of-behavioral-teams.

CHAPTER 1: THE CONSCIOUS MARKETING MODEL IS DEAD

"#1 New York Yankees." *Forbes*, March 2023. https://forbes.com/teams/new-york-yankees.

Bernacchi, Chris, Julio Aguilar, Kelsey Grant, and David Madison. "Baseball's Most Valuable Teams 2022: Yankees Hit $6 Billion as New CBA Creates New Revenue Streams." *Forbes*, March 24, 2022. https://forbes.com/sites/mikeozanian/2022/03/24/baseballs-most-valuable-teams-2022-yankees-hit-6-billion-as-new-cba-creates-new-revenue-streams.

"The Bigger Brains of London Taxi Drivers." *National Geographic*, May 29, 2013. https://nationalgeographic.com/culture/article/the-bigger-brains-of-london-taxi-drivers.

Chen, Quanjing, Haichuan Yang, Brian Rooks, et al. "Autonomic Flexibility Reflects Learning and Associated Neuroplasticity in Old Age." *Human Brain Mapping* 41, no. 13 (September 2020): 3608–3619. https://doi.org/10.1002/hbm.25034.

Cherry, Kendra. "What Is Neuroplasticity?" Verywell Mind, November 8, 2022. https://verywellmind.com/what-is-brain-plasticity-2794886#toc-how-neuroplasticity-was-discovered.

Cooke, Kirsty. "Mastering Momentum: Fewer Than One Percent of Brands Master Growth Momentum." Kantar, 2019. https://kantar.com/north-america/inspiration/brands/mastering-momentum-fewer-than-one-percent-of-brands-master-growth-momentum.

Day, Julia. "Nike: 'No Guarantee on Child Labour.'" *The Guardian*, October 19, 2001. https://theguardian.com/media/2001/oct/19/marketingandpr.

De Los Santos, Brian. "Sole Searching." *Mashable*. Accessed October 2023. https://mashable.com/feature/nike-snkrs-app-drops.

Fifield, Anna. "China Compels Uighurs to Work in Shoe Factory That Supplies Nike." *Washington Post*, February 29, 2020. https://washingtonpost.com/world/asia_pacific/china-compels-uighurs-to-work-in-shoe-factory-that-supplies-nike/2020/02/28/ebddf5f4-57b2-11ea-8efd-0f904bdd8057_story.html.

Flynn, Jack. "35+ Amazing Advertising Statistics [2023]: Data + Trends." Zippia, June 13, 2023. https://zippia.com/advice/advertising-statistics/#General_Digital_Advertising_Statistics.

Heaven, Will Douglas. "Geoffrey Hinton tells us why he's now scared of the tech he helped build." *MIT Technology Review*, May 2, 2023. www.technologyreview.com/2023/05/02/1072528/geoffrey-hinton-google-why-scared-ai.

Hinton, Geoffrey. "How Neural Networks Revolutionized AI." Interview by Brooke Gladstone. *On the Media*, WNYC, January 13, 2023. https://wnycstudios.org/podcasts/otm/segments/how-neural-networks-revolutionized-ai-on-the-media.

"How Nike Became Successful and the Leader in the Sports Product Market." Profitworks. Accessed August 2023. https://profitworks.ca/blog/marketing-strategy/545-nike-strategy-how-nike-became-successful-and-the-leader-in-the-sports-product-market.html.

Jabr, Ferris. "Cache Cab: Taxi Drivers' Brains Grow to Navigate London's Streets." *Scientific American*, December 8, 2011. https://scientificamerican.com/article/london-taxi-memory.

Jeopardy Productions. "Ken Jennings." *Jeopardy!*, 2022. www.jeopardy.com/about/cast/ken-jennings.

Leitch, Luke. "Nike at the Museum: Inside the Private View of Virgil Abloh's Design Legacy." *Vogue*, December 1, 2022. https://vogue.com/article/virgil-abloh-rubell-museum.

Mahoney, Manda. "The Subconscious Mind of the Consumer (and How to Reach It)." Working Knowledge, Harvard Business School, January 13, 2003. https://hbswk.hbs.edu/item/the-subconscious-mind-of-the-consumer-and-how-to-reach-it.

McLachlan, Stacey. "85+ Important Social Media Advertising Statistics to Know." Hootsuite, April 6, 2023. https://blog.hootsuite.com/social-media-advertising-stats.

Morse, Gardiner. "Hidden Minds." *Harvard Business Review*, June 2002. https://hbr.org/2002/06/hidden-minds.

Pusateri, Rich. "What is Neuromarketing with Dr. Michael Platt." Postal.com, August 5, 2021. www.postal.com/blog/what-is-neuromarketing-with-dr-michael-platt.

Queensland Brain Institute. "Adult Neurogenesis." University of Queensland, Australia, 2023. https://qbi.uq.edu.au/brain-basics/brain-physiology/adult-neurogenesis.

Queensland Brain Institute. "Understating the Brain: A Brief History." University of Queensland, Australia, 2023. https://qbi.uq.edu.au/brain/intelligent-machines/understanding-brain-brief-history.

Rosen, Jody. "The Knowledge, London's Legendary Taxi-Driver Test, Puts Up a Fight in the Age of GPS." *New York Times*, November 10, 2014. https://nytimes.com/2014/11/10/t-magazine/london-taxi-test-knowledge.html.

"Social Media Advertising—Worldwide." Statista, March 2023. https://statista.com/outlook/dmo/digital-advertising/social-media-advertising/worldwide.

Uddin, Lucina Q. "Salience Processing and Insular Cortical Function and Dysfunction." *Nature Reviews Neuroscience* 16 (2015): 55–61. https://nature.com/articles/nrn3857.

Weintraub, Karen. "The Adult Brain Does Grow New Neurons After All, Study Says." *Scientific American*, March 25, 2019. https://scientificamerican.com/article/the-adult-brain-does-grow-new-neurons-after-all-study-says.

Wolf, Cam. "'The Vibe of the Times': How Nike Became the Biggest Fashion Brand in the World." *GQ*, September 24, 2018. https://gq.com/story/how-nike-became-the-biggest-fashion-brand-in-the-world.

Woollett, Katherine, and Eleanor A. Maguire. "Navigational Expertise May Compromise Anterograde Associative Memory." *Neuropsychologia* 47, no. 4 (March 2009): 1088–1095. https://doi.org/10.1016/j.neuropsychologia.2008.12.036.

Yahr, Emily. "Ken Jennings Broke 'Jeopardy!' in 2004. In 2022, He Helped Save It." *Washington Post*, October 31, 2022. https://washingtonpost.com/arts-entertainment/2022/10/31/ken-jennings-jeopardy-host-interview.

CHAPTER 2: THE INSTINCT CENTER

Beadle, Robert. "All About Peanut M&Ms and More." Candy Retailer, September 11, 2021. https://candyretailer.com/blog/all-about-peanut-mms-and-more.

Bibel, Sara. "5 Little-Known Facts About How J.K. Rowling Brought Harry Potter to Life." *Biography*, May 13, 2020. https://biography.com/news/jk-rowling-harry-potter-facts.

"Election Results, 2020: Incumbent Win Rates by State." Ballotpedia, February 11, 2021. https://ballotpedia.org/Election_results,_2020:_Incumbent_win_rates_by_state.

Escobar, Natalie. "The Remarkable Influence of 'A Wrinkle in Time.'" *Smithsonian Magazine*, January 2018. https://smithsonianmag.com/arts-culture/remarkable-influence-wrinkle-in-time-180967509.

Griffiths, Chris. "Thimmamma Marrimanu: The World's Largest Single Tree Canopy." BBC, February 20, 2020. https://bbc.com/travel/article/20200219-thimmamma-marrimanu-the-worlds-largest-single-tree-canopy.

Hanna, Katie Terrell. "Mindshare (Share of Mind)." TechTarget. Accessed August 2023. www.techtarget.com/searchcustomerexperience/definition/mindshare-share-of-mind.

"Harry Potter Books Stats and Facts." WordsRated, October 19, 2021. https://wordsrated.com/harry-potter-stats.

"The Harry Potter Franchise's Magical Money-Making." LoveMoney, December 24, 2021. https://lovemoney.com/galleries/122033/the-harry-potter-franchises-magical-moneymaking.

Lindell, Crystal. "State of the Candy Industry 2021: Chocolate Bar Sales Are Up Overall Compared to Pre-pandemic Levels." Candy Industry, July 21, 2021. https://snackandbakery.com/articles/103255-state-of-the-candy-industry-chocolate-bar-sales-are-up-overall-compared-to-pre-pandemic-levels.

Livingston, Michael. "Burbank Public Library Offering Digital Copies of First 'Harry Potter' Novel to Recognize the Book's 20th anniversary." *Los Angeles Times, Burbank Leader*, September 4, 2018. https://latimes.com/socal/burbank-leader/news/tn-blr-me-burbank-library-harry-potter-20180831-story.html.

Nash Information Services. "Box Office History for Harry Potter Movies." The Numbers, 2023. https://the-numbers.com/movies/franchise/Harry-Potter.

Penn Medicine. "Penn Medicine Researchers Introduce New Brain Mapping Model Which Could Improve Effectiveness of Transcranial Magnetic Stimulation." News release, April 17, 2015. https://pennmedicine.org/news/news-releases/2015/april/penn-medicine-researchers-intr.

Popomaronis, Tom. "Google's Hiring Process Was Designed to Rule Out Toxic Hires—Here's How." LinkedIn, May 18, 2022. https://linkedin.com/pulse/googles-hiring-process-designed-rule-out-toxic-hires-how-popomaronis.

"Reelection Rates over the Years." OpenSecrets. Accessed August 2023. https://opensecrets.org/elections-overview/reelection-rates.

Santhanam, Laura. "Poll: Most Americans Don't Want Oprah to Run for President." *PBS NewsHour*, January 12, 2018. https://pbs.org/newshour/nation/poll-most-americans-dont-want-oprah-to-run-for-president.

Schumm, Laura. "Six Times M&Ms Made History." History, March 28, 2023. https://history.com/news/the-wartime-origins-of-the-mm.

Sharp, Byron. "How to Measure Brand Salience." *Marketing Science*, March 26, 2008. https://byronsharp.wordpress.com/2008/03/26/how-to-measure-brand-salience.

Sieczkowski, Cavan. "This Is the 'Harry Potter' Synopsis Publishers Rejected over 20 Years Ago." *HuffPost*, October 26, 2017. www.huffpost.com/entry/harry-potter-synopsis-jk-rowling_n_59f1e294e4b043885915a95c.

Smith, Morgan. "The 10 Best U.S. Places to Work in 2022, According to Glassdoor." CNBC, January 12, 2022. https://cnbc.com/2022/01/12/the-10-best-us-places-to-work-in-2022-according-to-glassdoor.html.

"Tolkein's Hobbit fetches £60,000." *BBC News*, March 18, 2008. http://news.bbc.co.uk/2/hi/uk_news/england/7302101.stm.

Weissmann, Jordan. "Stranger Than Fiction: Oprah Was Bad for Book Sales." *The Atlantic*, March 19, 2012. https://theatlantic.com/business/archive/2012/03/stranger-than-fiction-oprah-was-bad-for-book-sales/254733/.

Wunsch, Nils-Gerrit. "Market Share of Leading Chocolate Companies Worldwide in 2016." Statista, July 27, 2022. https://statista.com/statistics/629534/market-share-leading-chocolate-companies-worldwide.

Zane, Leslie, and Michael Platt. "Cracking the Code on Brand Growth." *Knowledge at Wharton*, Wharton School of the University of Pennsylvania, January 7, 2019.

https://knowledge.wharton.upenn.edu/podcast/knowledge-at-wharton-podcast
/cracking-code-brand-growth.

Zetlin, Minda. "You Need to Prove Your 'Googleyness' If You Want to Get a Job at Google. Here's How to Show Off this Most Desired Personality Trait During Your Interview." *Business Insider*, August 30, 2020. https://businessinsider.com /google-hiring-how-to-job-search-googleyness-personality-traits-2020-8.

CHAPTER 3: THE SHORTCUT TO INSTINCTIVE CHOICE

Bath & Body Works. "Bath & Body Works Celebrates 25th Anniversary of Nostalgic Icon, Cucumber Melon." Cision PR Newswire, June 1, 2023. www.prnewswire .com/news-releases/bath--body-works-celebrates-25th-anniversary-of -nostalgic-icon-cucumber-melon-301840063.html.

Callahan, Patricia. "Fruit Additions Spoon Out New Life for Cereal Players." *Wall Street Journal*, May 15, 2003. https://wsj.com/articles/SB105295323888157300.

Gillespie, Claire. "This Is Why We Associate Memories So Strongly with Specific Smells." Verywell Mind, October 4, 2021. https://verywellmind.com/why -do-we-associate-memories-so-strongly-with-specific-smells-5203963.

Humphrey, Judith. "5 Ways Women Can Be Heard More at Work." *Fast Company*, October 31, 2018. https://fastcompany.com/90256171/5-ways-for-women-can -be-heard-more-at-work.

Media Education Center. "Using Images Effectively in Media." Williams Office for Information Technology, February 2010. https://oit.williams.edu/files/2010/02 /using-images-effectively.pdf.

Quinton, Amy. "Cows and Climate Change: Making Cattle More Sustainable." In-Focus, UC Davis, June 27, 2019. https://ucdavis.edu/food/news/making-cattle -more-sustainable.

Richardson, Chris. "How Chick-fil-A Creates an Outstanding Customer Experience." Effective Retail Leader, November 2022. https://effectiveretailleader .com/effective-retail-leader/how-chick-fil-a-creates-an-outstanding-customer -experience.

Ross, Sean. "Financial Services: Sizing the Sector in the Global Economy." Investopedia, September 30, 2021. https://investopedia.com/ask/answers /030515/what-percentage-global-economy-comprised-financial-services-sector .asp.

"What Is the Picture Superiority Effect?" Simpleshow, August 9, 2017. https:// simpleshow.com/blog/picture-superiority-effect.

CHAPTER 4: THE CURSE OF NEGATIVE ASSOCIATIONS

Akhtar, Allana. "Wellness-Focused, 'Sober Curious' Consumers Are Driving Interest in Booze-Free Cocktails, a Relative Newcomer to the $180 Billion Beverage Industry." *Business Insider*, November 3, 2021. https://businessinsider.com /beverage-analysts-predict-non-alcoholic-spirits-to-grow-in-2022-2021-11.

"Animal Health & Welfare." McDonald's, updated 2022. https://corporate.mcdonalds .com/corpmcd/our-purpose-and-impact/food-quality-and-sourcing/animal -health-and-welfare.html.

"Are All the Eggs You Use Free Range?" McDonald's, May 21, 2018. https://mcdonalds.com/gb/en-gb/help/faq/are-all-the-eggs-you-use-free-range.html.

"Burgers FAQs." McDonald's, updated 2023. https://mcdonalds.com/us/en-us/faq/burgers.html.

"Churchill's Reputation in the 1930s." Churchill Archives Centre. Accessed August 2023. https://archives.chu.cam.ac.uk/education/churchill-era/exercises/appeasement/churchill-rearmament-and-appeasement/churchills-reputation-1930s.

CNN. "McDonald's Sets Record Straight on What's in a…" YouTube, February 5, 2014. https://youtube.com/watch?v=IjObCa9bXTo.

Courtesy Corporation—McDonald's. "McDonald's—Our Food, Your Questions—Beef." YouTube, February 16, 2015. https://youtube.com/live/Q6IMQaiYKeg.

Denworth, Lydia. "Conservative and Liberal Brains Might Have Some Real Differences." *Scientific American*, October 26, 2020. https://scientificamerican.com/article/conservative-and-liberal-brains-might-have-some-real-differences.

ESPN.com News Services. "Survey: Fewer Peers Believe Tiger Woods Will Win Another Major." ESPN, April 4, 2016. https://espn.com/golf/story/_/id/15129601/survey-shows-pga-tour-golfers-less-belief-tiger-woods-winning-another-major.

"Gathering Storm (1930s)." America's National Churchill Museum. Accessed August 2023. https://nationalchurchillmuseum.org/winston-churchill-and-the-gathering-storm.html.

Helling, Steve. "Tiger Woods and Ex-Wife Elin Nordegren 'Get Along Really Well' 9 Years After Scandal, Says Source." *People*, April 8, 2018. https://people.com/sports/tiger-woods-ex-wife-elin-nordegren-get-along-well-source.

Javed, Saman. "Negative Social Media Posts Get Twice as Much Engagement Than Positive Ones, Study Finds." *Independent*, June 22, 2021. https://independent.co.uk/life-style/social-media-facebook-twitter-politics-b1870628.html.

Klein, Christopher. "Winston Churchill's World War Disaster." History, May 21, 2014, updated September 3, 2018. https://history.com/news/winston-churchills-world-war-disaster.

Klein, Ezra. "How Technology Is Designed to Bring Out the Worst in Us." *Vox*, February 19, 2018. https://vox.com/technology/2018/2/19/17020310/tristan-harris-facebook-twitter-humane-tech-time.

"Kohl's—31 Year Stock Price History." Macrotrends. Accessed August 2023. https://macrotrends.net/stocks/charts/KSS/kohls/stock-price-history.

Maheshwari, Sapna. "Victoria's Secret Had Troubles, Even Before Jeffrey Epstein." *New York Times*, September 6, 2019, updated June 21, 2021. https://nytimes.com/2019/09/06/business/l-brands-victorias-secret-les-wexner-epstein.html.

McDonald's Canada. "McDonald's Burgers Don't Rot? McDonald's Canada Answers." YouTube, August 19, 2015. www.youtube.com/watch?v=gidsNjqoicw&t=57s.

McDonald's Canada. "Pink Goo in Chicken McNuggets? McDonald's Canada Answers." YouTube, January 31, 2014. www.youtube.com/watch?v=Ua5PaSqKD6k.

"McDonald's Food Suppliers." McDonald's, updated 2023. https://mcdonalds.com/us/en-us/about-our-food/meet-our-suppliers.html.

"Median Hourly Earnings of Female Wage and Salary Workers in the United States from 1979 to 2021." Statista, March 7, 2023. https://statista.com/statistics/185345/median-hourly-earnings-of-female-wage-and-salary-workers.

Meyersohn, Nathaniel. "How Kohl's Became Such a Mess." *CNN Business*, March 19, 2022. https://cnn.com/2022/03/19/business/kohls-stock-department-stores-activist-investor/index.html.

Meyersohn, Nathaniel. "How Kohl's Figured Out the Amazon Era." *CNN Business*, October 30, 2018. https://cnn.com/2018/10/30/business/kohls-stores-amazon-retail/index.html.

Morfit, Cameron. "Tiger Woods Wins TOUR Championship to Break Five-Year Win Drought." PGAtour.com, September 23, 2018. https://pgatour.com/article/news/latest/2018/09/23/tiger-woods-wins-2018-tour-championship-fedexcup-playoffs-east-lake.

"Number of Employed Women in the United States from 1990 to 2022." Statista, February 3, 2023. https://statista.com/statistics/192378/number-of-employed-women-in-the-us-since-1990.

O'Keefe, Michael. "Nearly a Quarter of Tiger Woods' PGA Tour Peers Thinks He Used Performance-Enhancing Drugs." *New York Daily News*, April 30, 2010. https://nydailynews.com/sports/more-sports/quarter-tiger-woods-pga-tour-peers-thinks-performance-enhancing-drugs-article-1.170007.

Pappas, Stephanie. "Republican Brains Differ from Democrats' in New FMRI Study." *HuffPost*, February 20, 2013, updated February 22, 2013. www.huffpost.com/entry/republican-democrat-brain-politics-fmri-study_n_2717731.

"Past Prime Ministers: Sir Winston Churchill." Gov.uk. Accessed August 2023. https://gov.uk/government/history/past-prime-ministers/winston-churchill.

"Percentage of the U.S. Population Who Have Completed Four Years of College or More from 1940 to 2022, by Gender." Statista, July 21, 2023. https://statista.com/statistics/184272/educational-attainment-of-college-diploma-or-higher-by-gender.

"Revenue for McDonald (MCD)." CompaniesMarketCap. Accessed August 2023. https://companiesmarketcap.com/mcdonald/revenue.

Robertson, Claire E., Nicolas Pröllochs, Kaoru Schwarzenegger, et al. "Negativity Drives Online News Consumption." *Nature Human Behaviour* 7 (2023): 812–822. https://nature.com/articles/s41562-023-01538-4.

Silver-Greenberg, Jessica, Katherine Rosman, Sapna Maheshwari, and James B. Stewart. "'Angels' in Hell: The Culture of Misogyny Inside Victoria's Secret." *New York Times*, February 1, 2020, updated June 16, 2021. https://nytimes.com/2020/02/01/business/victorias-secret-razek-harassment.html.

"Sir Winston Churchill." UK Parliament. Accessed August 2023. www.parliament.uk/about/living-heritage/transformingsociety/private-lives/yourcountry/collections/churchillexhibition/churchill-and-ww2/sir-winston-churchill.

Stein, Ed. "What Are McDonald's Chicken McNuggets Made Of." YouTube, December 12, 2014. www.youtube.com/watch?v=NCm6INQo9yY.

United States Securities and Exchange Commission. Form 10-K: Kohl's Corporation. Commission file number 1-11084. United States Securities and

Exchange Commission, 2018. https://sec.gov/Archives/edgar/data/885639 /000156459018006671/kss-10k_20180203.htm.

"Victoria's Secret Revenue." Zippia, July 21, 2023. https://zippia.com/victoria -s-secret-careers-1580221/revenue.

CHAPTER 5: THE SNOW-CAPPED MOUNTAIN EFFECT

"2020 State of the Beverage Industry: All Bottled Water Segments See Growth." *Beverage Industry*, June 24, 2020. https://bevindustry.com/articles/93226 -state-of-the-beverage-industry-all-bottled-water-segments-see-growth.

Andrivet, Marion. "What to Learn from Tropicana's Packaging Redesign Failure?" *Branding Journal*, March 9, 2022. https://thebrandingjournal.com/2015/05/what -to-learn-from-tropicanas-packaging-redesign-failure.

"Aquafina Logo." 1000 Logos, June 20, 2023. https://1000logos.net/aquafina-logo.

Göke, Niklas. "The Tropicana Rebranding Failure." *Better Marketing*, April 22, 2020. https://bettermarketing.pub/the-worst-rebrand-in-the-history -of-orange-juice-1fc68e99ad81.

Holcomb, Jay. "The DAWNing of Oiled Bird Washing." International Bird Rescue. YouTube, April 22, 2010. https://youtube.com/watch?v=axEpVTaK1-k.

Lucas, Amelia. "Consumer Brands Didn't Reap a Huge Windfall from Panic Buying, Are Adjusting to Life Under Lockdown." CNBC, April 22, 2020. https://cnbc .com/2020/04/22/coronavirus-consumer-brands-didnt-reap-a-windfall-from -panic-buying.html.

Mendelson, Scott. "'The Addams Family' Was One of Hollywood's First Successful Attempts at Replicating 'Batman.'" *Forbes*, October 7, 2019. https://forbes.com /sites/scottmendelson/2019/10/07/the-addams-family-was-one-of-hollywoods -first-successful-attempts-at-replicating-batman-oscar-isaac-charlize-theron -raul-julia-christina-ricci-terminator.

"Most Famous Logos with a Mountain." 1000 Logos, February 26, 2023. https://1000logos.net/most-famous-logos-with-a-mountain.

Newman, Andrew Adam. "Tough on Crude Oil, Soft on Ducklings." *New York Times*, September 24, 2009. https://nytimes.com/2009/09/25/business/media /25adco.html.

Parekh, Rupal. "End of an Era: Omnicom's Arnell Group to Close." *AdAge*, March 18, 2013. https://adage.com/article/agency-news/end-era-omnicom-s-arnell -group-close/240387.

"Peter Arnell Explains Failed Tropicana Package Design." *AdAge*, February 26, 2009. www.youtube.com/watch?v=WJ4yF4F74vc.

Porterfield, Carlie. "'Wednesday' Breaks Out: Scores Second-Highest Weekly Streaming Debut Ever for Netflix—Launches Viral Dance." *Forbes*, December 21, 2022. https://forbes.com/sites/carlieporterfield/2022/12/21/wednesday -breaks-out-scores-second-highest-weekly-streaming-debut-ever-for-netflix -launches-viral-dance.

Ridder, M. "Leading Brands of Refrigerated Orange Juice in the United States in 2022, Based on Sales." Statista, December 1, 2022. https://statista.com /statistics/188749/top-refrigerated-orange-juice-brands-in-the-united-states.

Rooks, Martha. "30,000 Different Products and Counting: The Average Grocery Store." International Council of Societies of Industrial Design, February 16, 2022. https://icsid.org/uncategorized/how-many-products-are-in-a-typical-grocery-store.

Sheridan, Adam. "The Power of You: Why Distinctive Brand Assets Are a Driving Force of Creative Effectiveness." Ipsos, February 2020. https://ipsos.com/sites/default/files/2022-03/power-of-you-ipsos.pdf.

Shogren, Elizabeth. "Why Dawn Is the Bird Cleaner of Choice in Oil Spills." *Morning Edition*, June 22, 2010. https://npr.org/2010/06/22/127999735/why-dawn-is-the-bird-cleaner-of-choice-in-oil-spills.

Solsman, Joan E. "'Wednesday' Is Netflix's No. 3 Most Watched Show of All Time (So Far)." CNET, December 13, 2022. https://cnet.com/culture/entertainment/wednesday-is-netflixs-no-3-most-watched-show-of-all-time-so-far.

Taylor, Erica. "Mother Daughter 'Wednesday Addams' Duo." TikTok, accessed August 2023. https://tiktok.com/@ericataylor2347/video/7184247045568384299.

"Top 50 Scanned: Dorito." Nutritionix. Accessed August 2023. https://nutritionix.com/grocery/category/chips/dorito/1669.

"Top 50 Scanned: Orange Juice." Nutritionix. Accessed August 2023. www.nutritionix.com/grocery/category/juice/orange-juice/271.

"Top Gun: Maverick." Box Office Mojo. Accessed August 2023. https://boxofficemojo.com/release/rl2500036097.

University of Glasgow. "What Our Eyes Can't See, the Brain Fills In." Medical Xpress, April 4, 2011. https://medicalxpress.com/news/2011-04-eyes-brain.html.

Whitten, Sarah. "'Top Gun: Maverick' and Disney Were the Box Office Leaders in an Otherwise Soft 2022." CNBC, January 10, 2023. https://cnbc.com/2023/01/10/top-gun-maverick-disney-top-box-office-2022.html.

"'You're Soaking in It!' Vintage Palmolive Ads Featuring Madge the Manicurist." Click Americana. Accessed 2023. https://clickamericana.com/topics/beauty-fashion/palmolive-ads-featuring-madge-the-manicurist.

CHAPTER 6: WHY LAYERING BEATS FOCUSING

Augustine, Amanda. "This Personality Trait Is an Interview Killer." *Fast Company*, September 4, 2019. https://fastcompany.com/90397790/this-personality-trait-is-an-interview-killer.

Barrett, Evie. "Unilever 'Misstepped' with Initial Purpose Message, Says Head of Comms." *PRWeek*. Accessed August 2023. https://prweek.com/article/1814096/unilever-misstepped-initial-purpose-message-says-head-comms.

Berk, Brett. "No Longer Boxed In, Volvo Wins Over Buyers with Its Sleeker Look." *New York Times*, October 22, 2021. https://nytimes.com/2021/10/22/business/volvo-electric-future-design-ipo.html.

"CeraVe to Launch Globally After L'Oréal Acquisition." *Cosmetics Business*, May 21, 2018. https://cosmeticsbusiness.com/news/article_page/CeraVe_to_launch_globally_after_LOreal_acquisition/143145.

DeSimone, Mike, and Jeff Jenssen. "While U.S. Wine Sales Are Expected to Decline, One Brand Is Defying the Trend." *Forbes*, May 23, 2019. https://forbes

.com/sites/theworldwineguys/2019/05/23/as-us-wine-sales-are-expected-to
-decline-one-wine-brand-defies-the-trend.

Hernandez, Morela. "The Impossibility of Focusing on Two Things at Once." *MIT Sloan Management Review*, April 9, 2018. https://sloanreview.mit.edu/article/the-impossibility-of-focusing-on-two-things-at-once.

IRI Worldwide. "Hand & Body Lotion, Facial Cleansers, Facial Moisturizers, Dollar Sales, Rolling 52 Weeks, Ending 03-21-21." IRI Market Research Data Report, 2021.

Kuncel, Nathan R., Deniz S. Ones, and David M. Klieger. "In Hiring, Algorithms Beat Instinct." *Harvard Business Review*, May 2014. https://hbr.org/2014/05/in-hiring-algorithms-beat-instinct.

L'Oréal. "CeraVe: A Simple, Accessible Dermatologist-Recommended Range." L'Oréal 2017 Annual Report, 2017. https://loreal-finance.com/en/annual-report-2017/active-cosmetics/cerave-acquisition-dermatologists.

L'Oréal Finance. "L'Oréal Signs Agreement with Valeant to Acquire CeraVe and Two Other Brands." News release, January 10, 2017. https://loreal-finance.com/eng/news-release/loreal-signs-agreement-valeant-acquire-cerave-and-two-other-brands.

Sandler, Emma. "CeraVe Head of Global Digital Marketing & VP Adam Kornblum: 2022 Top Marketer." *Glossy*, June 1, 2022. https://glossy.co/beauty/cerave-adam-kornblum-head-of-global-digital-marketing-vp-top-marketer.

Strugatz, Rachel. "The Content Creator Who Can Make or Break a Skin Care Brand." *New York Times*, September 8, 2020, updated December 2, 2020. https://nytimes.com/2020/09/08/style/Gen-Z-the-content-creator-who-can-make-or-break-your-skin-care-brand.html.

Voelk, Tom. "Crash Scene Investigations, with Automakers on the Case." *New York Times*, May 9, 2019. https://nytimes.com/2019/05/09/business/crash-scene-investigations.html.

White, Katherine, David J. Hardisty, and Rishad Habib. "The Elusive Green Consumer." *Harvard Business Review*, July–August 2019. https://hbr.org/2019/07/the-elusive-green-consumer.

Williams, Amy. "Unilever's Investor Backlash Illustrates the Need for Responsible Capitalism." *Adweek*, January 31, 2022. https://adweek.com/brand-marketing/unilevers-investor-backlash-illustrates-the-need-for-responsible-capitalism.

Willige, Andrea. "People Prefer Brands with Aligned Corporate Purpose and Values." World Economic Forum, December 17, 2021. https://weforum.org/agenda/2021/12/people-prefer-brands-with-aligned-corporate-purpose-and-values.

WineBusiness. "Josh Cellars Surpasses 5 Million Cases Annually." Press release, April 9, 2023. www.winebusiness.com/news/article/269463.

Womersley, James. "Hellmann's, Terry Smith and the Paradox of Purposeful Brands." Contagious, January 19, 2023. https://contagious.com/news-and-views/hellmanns-terry-smith-and-the-paradox-of-purposeful-brands.

Zanger, Doug. "10 Years After Setting 'Audacious Goals,' Unilever Shows How Purpose and Profit Can Coexist." *Adweek*, December 21, 2020. https://adweek.com/agencies/10-years-after-setting-audacious-goals-unilever-shows-how-purpose-and-profit-can-coexist.

CHAPTER 7: THE UNCONSCIOUS NEED FOR FANTASY

Associated Press. "Madoff Victims: Big Banks, Hedge Funds, Celebrities." CNBC, December 15, 2008, updated August 5, 2010. https://cnbc.com/id/28235916.

Atwal, Sanj. "Khaby Lame Overtakes Charli D'Amelio as Most Followed Person on TikTok." Guinness World Records, June 23, 2022. https://guinnessworldrecords.com/news/2022/6/khaby-lame-overtakes-charli-damelio-as-most-followed-person-on-tiktok-708392.

Ballew, Matthew, Sander van der Linden, Abel Gustafson, et al. "The Greta Thunberg Effect." Yale Program on Climate Change Communication, January 26, 2021. https://climatecommunication.yale.edu/publications/the-greta-thunberg-effect.

Berlinger, Joe, dir. *Madoff: The Monster of Wall Street*. RadicalMedia in association with Third Eye Motion Picture Company, 2023.

Bird, Deirdre, Helen Caldwell, and Mark DeFanti. "A Fragrance to Empower Women: The History of 'Charlie.'" *Marketing History in the New World* 15 (May 2011): 217–219. https://ojs.library.carleton.ca/index.php/pcharm/article/view/1434.

Bruyckere, Pedro de. "What's the Link Between Jennifer Anniston [*sic*] and How Our Memory Works?" *From Experience to Meaning...* Accessed August 2023. https://theeconomyofmeaning.com/2015/08/03/whats-the-link-between-jennifer-anniston-and-how-our-memory-works.

Clark, Lucy. "HGTV Confirms What We Suspected All Along About Home Renovation Shows." *House Digest*, February 2, 2022. https://housedigest.com/755007/hgtv-confirms-what-we-suspected-all-along-about-home-renovation-shows.

Clavin, Thomas. "The Good and Bad of Indulging in Fantasy and Daydreaming." *New York Times*, July 28, 1996. https://nytimes.com/1996/07/28/nyregion/the-good-and-bad-of-indulging-in-fantasy-and-daydreaming.html.

Douglas, Sylvie. "Gen Z's Dream Job in the Influencer Industry." *The Indicator from Planet Money*, NPR, April 26, 2023. https://npr.org/transcripts/1170524085.

Ducharme, Jamie. "Why People Are Obsessed with the Royals, According to Psychologists." *Time*, May 16, 2018. https://time.com/5253199/royal-obsession-psychology.

Editors of Encyclopaedia Britannica. "Bernie Madoff: American Hedge-Fund Investor." *Encyclopedia Britannica*. Accessed August 2023. https://britannica.com/biography/Bernie-Madoff.

"Finding Top Influencers: 4 Influencer Statistics to Look For." Traackr, March 16, 2023. https://traackr.com/blog/finding-top-influencers-influencer-statistics.

Golodryga, Bianna, and Jonann Brady. "Spielberg Among the Big Names Allegedly Burned by Madoff in $50 Billion Fraud Case." *ABC News*, December 15, 2008. https://abcnews.go.com/GMA/story?id=6463587.

Gordon, Marcy, and the Associated Press. "How Ponzi King Bernie Madoff Conned Investors and Seduced Regulators." *Fortune*, April 15, 2021. https://fortune.com/2021/04/15/how-ponzi-king-bernie-madoff-conned-investors-and-seduced-regulators.

Guggenheim, Davis, dir. *An Inconvenient Truth*. Paramount Classics and Participant Productions, 2006.

Hassabis, Demis, Dharshan Kumaran, and Eleanor A. Maguire. "Using Imagination to Understand the Neural Basis of Episodic Memory." *Journal of Neuroscience* 27, no. 52 (December 2007): 14365–74. https://doi.org/10.1523/JNEUROSCI.4549-07.2007.

Henrich, Joseph, and Francisco J. Gil-White. "The Evolution of Prestige: Freely Conferred Deference as a Mechanism for Enhancing the Benefits of Cultural Transmission." *Evolution and Human Behavior* 22, no. 3 (May 2001): 165–196. https://doi.org/10.1016/S1090-5138(00)00071-4.

Henriques, Diana B., and Alex Berenson. "The 17th Floor, Where Wealth Went to Vanish." *New York Times*, December 14, 2008. https://nytimes.com/2008/12/15/business/15madoff.html.

"In Depth: Topics A to Z—Environment." Gallup. Accessed August 2023. https://news.gallup.com/poll/1615/environment.aspx.

"Industry Demographics." Fantasy Sports & Gaming Association. Accessed August 2023. https://thefsga.org/industry-demographics.

The Influencer Report: Engaging Gen Z and Millennials. Morning Consult, November 2019. https://morningconsult.com/wp-content/uploads/2019/11/The-Influencer-Report-Engaging-Gen-Z-and-Millennials.pdf.

Israel, Sarah. "Top Influencers in 2023: Who to Watch and Why They're Great." Hootsuite, February 14, 2023. https://blog.hootsuite.com/top-influencers.

Johnston, Laura W. "How *An Inconvenient Truth* Expanded the Climate Change Dialogue and Reignited an Ethical Purpose in the United States." Master's thesis, Georgetown University, 2013. http://hdl.handle.net/10822/558371.

Kammerlohr, Emily. "How Home Renovation Shows Have Changed Homebuying Trends." *House Digest*, January 31, 2023. https://housedigest.com/723791/how-home-renovation-shows-have-changed-homebuying-trends.

Kiger, Patrick J. "What 'An Inconvenient Truth' Got Right (and Wrong) About Climate Change." HowStuffWorks, May 12, 2021. https://science.howstuffworks.com/environmental/conservation/conservationists/inconvenient-truth-sequel-al-gore.htm.

Kurzius, Rachel. "HGTV Is Making Our Homes Boring and Us Sad, One Study Says." *Washington Post*, July 7, 2023. https://washingtonpost.com/home/2023/07/07/hgtv-makes-homes-boring-sad.

Lefton, Terry. "The Story Behind Gatorade's Iconic Jordan Campaign." *Sports Business Journal*, October 11, 2021. https://sportsbusinessjournal.com/Journal/Issues/2021/10/11/In-Depth/Gatorade.

Majd, Azadeh Hosseini. "10 Best Makeup Influencers to Watch in 2023." Hoothemes, March 11, 2023. https://hoothemes.com/makeup-influencers.

"Market Size of the Fantasy Sports Sector in the United States from 2013 to 2022, with a Forecast for 2023." Statista, May 11, 2023. https://statista.com/statistics/1175890/fantasy-sports-service-industry-market-size-us.

Marlon, Jennifer, Liz Neyens, Martial Jefferson, Peter Howe, Matto Mildenberger, and Anthony Leiserowitz. "Yale Climate Opinion Maps 2021." Yale Program on Climate Change Communication, February 23, 2022. https://climatecommunication.yale.edu/visualizations-data/ycom-us.

McMarlin, Shirley. "How Popular Is Taylor Swift? It's the 2023 Version of Beat-lemania." *TribLive*, June 13, 2023. https://triblive.com/aande/music/theres -something-about-taylor-swift-fans-explain-singers-mass-appeal.

Moscatello, Caitlin. "Welcome to the Era of Very Earnest Parenting." *New York Times*, May 13, 2023, updated May 31, 2023. https://nytimes.com/2023/05/13 /style/millennial-earnest-parenting.html.

"Most Valuable Fashion Brands." FashionUnited. Accessed August 2023. https:// fashionunited.com/i/most-valuable-fashion-brands.

NPR Staff. "Transcript: Greta Thunberg's Speech at the U.N. Climate Action Sum-mit." NPR, September 23, 2019. https://npr.org/2019/09/23/763452863/transcript -greta-thunbergs-speech-at-the-u-n-climate-action-summit.

"Number of Fantasy Sports Players in the United States from 2015 to 2022." Statista, May 11, 2023. https://statista.com/statistics/820976/fantasy-sports -players-usa.

"Parahippocampal Gyrus." ScienceDirect. Accessed August 2023. https://sciencedirect .com/topics/neuroscience/parahippocampal-gyrus.

Pompliano, Joe. "How Four Scientists Created Gatorade and Became Billion-aires." *Huddle Up*, March 6, 2023. https://huddleup.substack.com/p/how-four -scientists-created-gatorade.

Saad, Lydia. "Global Warming Attitudes Frozen Since 2016." Gallup, April 5, 2021. https://news.gallup.com/poll/343025/global-warming-attitudes-frozen-2016 .aspx.

Sabherwal, Anandita, and Sander van der Linden. "Great Thunberg Effect: Peo-ple Familiar with Young Climate Activist May Be More Likely to Act." *The Conversation*, February 4, 2021. https://theconversation.com/greta-thunberg -effect-people-familiar-with-young-climate-activist-may-be-more-likely -to-act-154146.

Schaedler, Jeremy. "How Obsessed with Zillow Are You? A Survey." Surety First, April 7, 2021. www.californiacontractorbonds.com/house-hunting-zillow-users.

Sheridan, Adam. "The Power of You: Why Distinctive Brand Assets Are a Driving Force of Creative Effectiveness." Ipsos, February 2020. https://ipsos.com/sites /default/files/2022-03/power-of-you-ipsos.pdf.

Silver, Laura. "Americans See Different Global Threats Facing the Country Now Than in March 2020." Pew Research Center, June 6, 2022. https://pewresearch .org/short-reads/2022/06/06/americans-see-different-global-threats-facing -the-country-now-than-in-march-2020.

Target Corporation. "Target Corporation Reports Fourth Quarter and Full-Year 2022 Earnings." Press release, February 28, 2023. https://corporate.target.com /press/releases/2023/02/Target-Corporation-Reports-Fourth-Quarter-and-Full.

"Taylor Swift: The Eras Tour Onsale Explained." Ticketmaster Business, November 19, 2022. https://business.ticketmaster.com/business-solutions/taylor -swift-the-eras-tour-onsale-explained.

Terrell, Ellen. "The Black Monday Stock Market Crash." Library of Congress. Accessed August 2023. https://guides.loc.gov/this-month-in-business-history/october/black -monday-stock-market-crash.

"Then. Now. Always." Folgers. Accessed August 2023. https://folgerscoffee.com/our-story/history.

"US Influencer Marketing Spend (2019–2024)." Oberlo. Accessed August 2023. www.oberlo.com/statistics/influencer-marketing-spend.

Vann, Seralynne D., John P. Aggleton, and Eleanor A. Maguire. "What Does the Retrosplenial Cortex Do?" *Nature Reviews Neuroscience* 10 (2009): 792–802. https://doi.org/10.1038/nrn2733.

"Ventromedial Prefrontal Cortex." ScienceDirect. Accessed August 2023. https://sciencedirect.com/topics/neuroscience/ventromedial-prefrontal-cortex.

"What Were the Most Popular Perfumes in the '70s?" Fragrance Outlet. Accessed August 2023. https://fragranceoutlet.com/blogs/article/what-were-the-most-popular-perfumes-in-the-70s.

"When Was the Word 'Influencer' Added to the Dictionary?" Atisfyreach. Accessed August 2023. https://blog.atisfyreach.com/when-was-the-word-influencer-added-to-the-dictionary.

Wilson, Randy. "Maxwell House Coffee History." FoodEditorials. Accessed August 2023. www.streetdirectory.com/food_editorials/beverages/coffee/maxwell_house_coffee_history.html.

Yang, Stephanie. "5 Years Ago Bernie Madoff Was Sentenced to 150 Years in Prison—Here's How His Scheme Worked." *Business Insider India*, July 2, 2014. https://businessinsider.in/5-years-ago-bernie-madoff-was-sentenced-to-150-years-in-prison-heres-how-his-scheme-worked/articleshow/37604176.cms.

"Zillow.com." Similarweb. Accessed August 2023. https://similarweb.com/website/zillow.com/#traffic.

CHAPTER 8: BRING IN THE NEW

Ballard, John. "3 Reasons Lululemon's Growth Is Accelerating." *Motley Fool*, June 10, 2021. https://fool.com/investing/2021/06/10/3-reasons-lululemons-growth-is-accelerating.

Brusselmans, Guy, John Blasberg, and James Root. "The Biggest Contributor to Brand Growth." Bain & Company, March 19, 2014. https://bain.com/insights/the-biggest-contributor-to-brand-growth.

Evans, Jonathan. "Lululemon's ABC Pants Are a Cult Classic for a Reason." *Esquire*, October 26, 2022. https://esquire.com/style/mens-fashion/a41779660/lululemon-abc-pants-review-endorsement.

Faria, Julia. "Loyalty Management Market Size Worldwide from 2020 to 2029." Statista, July 18, 2023. https://statista.com/statistics/1295852/loyalty-management-market-size-world.

Gallagher, Jacob. "A Secret to Lululemon's Success? Men Who Are Obsessed with Its Pants." *Wall Street Journal*, August 15, 2022. https://wsj.com/articles/lululemon-mens-pants-abc-commission-customer-growth-11660345934.

"History." Lululemon. Accessed August 2023. https://info.lululemon.com/about/our-story/history.

Kavilanz, Parija. "Got a Stash of Bed Bath & Beyond Coupons? You'd Better Use Them Soon." *CNN Business*, January 6, 2023. https://cnn.com/2023/01/06/business/bed-bath-beyond-coupon-future/index.html.

Lululemon Athletica. "lululemon athletica inc. Announces Fourth Quarter and Full Year Fiscal 2022 Results." Press release, March 28, 2023. https://corporate .lululemon.com/media/press-releases/2023/03-28-2023-210523147.

Meyersohn, Nathaniel. "Bed Bath & Beyond Plans to Liquidate All Inventory and Go Out of Business." *CNN Business*, April 24, 2023. https://cnn.com/2023/04/23 /business/bed-bath-beyond-bankruptcy/index.html.

Morris, Chris. "Overstock Rebrands as Bed Bath & Beyond—and the Big Blue Coupon Lives On." *Fast Company*, August 1, 2023. https://fastcompany .com/90931179/overstock-branding-bed-bath-beyond-coupon-lives-on.

"Our Heritage—Celebrating the Last 75 Years." Tide. Accessed August 2023. https://tide.com/en-us/our-commitment/americas-number-one-detergent /our-heritage.

Petruzzi, Dominique. "Leading Home Care Brands' Household Penetration Rates in the United States in 2022." Statista, June 13, 2023. https://statista.com /statistics/945305/home-care-brands-household-penetration-rates-us.

Reichheld, Frederick F. "The One Number You Need to Grow." *Harvard Business Review*, December 2003. https://hbr.org/2003/12/the-one-number-you -need-to-grow.

Tighe, D. "Total Number of Lululemon Athletica Stores Worldwide from 2019 to 2022, by Country." Statista, May 11, 2023. https://statista.com/statistics/291231 /number-of-lululemon-stores-worldwide-by-country.

Wilson, Chip. "Lululemon Athletica: Chip Wilson." Interview by Guy Raz. *How I Built This*, NPR, June 18, 2018. https://npr.org/2018/06/14/620113439/lululemon -athletica-chip-wilson.

CHAPTER 9: DITCH THE FUNNEL

Blakely, Lindsay. "How a $4,500 YouTube Video Turned into a $1 Billion Company." *Inc.*, July 2017. https://inc.com/magazine/201707/lindsay-blakely/how-i -did-it-michael-dubin-dollar-shave-club.html.

Costa, Elísio, Anna Giardini, Magda Savin, et. al. "Interventional Tools to Improve Medication Adherence: Review of Literature." *Patient Preference and Adherence* 9 (September 2015): 1303–1314. https://doi.org/10.2147/PPA.S87551.

Dollar Shave Club. "Our Blades Are F***ing Great." YouTube, March 6, 2012. https://youtube.com/watch?v=ZUG9qYTJMsI.

George, Maureen, and Bruce Bender. "New Insights to Improve Treatment Adherence in Asthma and COPD." *Patient Preference and Adherence* 13 (2019): 1325–1334. https://doi.org/10.2147/PPA.S209532.

Handley, Rachel. "The Marketing Funnel: What It Is & How It Works." *Semrush Blog*, March 3, 2023. https://semrush.com/blog/marketing-funnel/#top -of-the-funnel-marketing.

Kim, Jennifer, Kelsy Combs, Jonathan Downs, and Frank Tillman III. "Medication Adherence: The Elephant in the Room." *U.S. Pharmacist*, November 2023. https:// uspharmacist.com/article/medication-adherence-the-elephant-in-the-room.

Klein, Dan. "Medication Non-adherence: A Common and Costly Problem." PAN Foundation, June 2, 2020. https://panfoundation.org/medication-non -adherence.

"Marketing Funnel." Sprout Social. Accessed August 2023. https://sproutsocial.com/glossary/marketing-funnel.

Matthews, Chris, and Andrea Mitchell. "'Hardball with Chris Matthews' for July 27 11 pm." *NBC News*, July 28, 2004. https://nbcnews.com/id/wbna5537683.

Obama, Barack. "Barack Obama's Keynote Address at the 2004 Democratic National Convention." *PBS NewsHour*, July 27, 2004. https://pbs.org/newshour/show/barack-obamas-keynote-address-at-the-2004-democratic-national-convention.

Parkes, Gary, Trisha Greenhalgh, Mark Griffin, and Richard Dent. "Effect on Smoking Quit Rate of Telling Patients Their Lung Age: The Step2quit Randomized Controlled Trial." *BMJ*, March 13, 2008. www.bmj.com/content/336/7644/598/rapid-responses.

Ritson, Mark. "If You Think the Sales Funnel Is Dead, You've Mistaken Tactics for Strategy." *MarketingWeek*, April 6, 2016. https://marketingweek.com/mark-ritson-if-you-think-the-sales-funnel-is-dead-youve-mistaken-tactics-for-strategy.

Ronald Reagan Presidential Foundation & Institute. "October 21, 1984: Reagan Quotes and Speeches: Debate Between the President and Former Vice President Walter F. Mondale in Kansas City, Missouri." Accessed August 2023. https://reaganfoundation.org/ronald-reagan/reagan-quotes-speeches/debate-between-the-president-and-former-vice-president-walter-f-mondale-in-kansas-city-missouri.

"Sales Funnel vs. Marketing Funnel: What's the Difference?" *LinkedIn Sales Blog*, July 13, 2022. https://linkedin.com/business/sales/blog/management/sales-funnel-versus-marketing-funnel.

Sepulvado, John. "Obama's 'Overnight Success' in 2004 Was a Year in the Making." *OPB*, May 19, 2016. https://opb.org/news/series/election-2016/president-barack-obama-2004-convention-speech-legacy.

"U.S. Razor Market." Prescient & Strategic Intelligence, June 2022. https://psmarketresearch.com/market-analysis/us-razor-market-demand.

Weissmann, Jordan. "Beyond the Bayonets: What Romney Had Right and Wrong About Our Navy." *The Atlantic*, October 23, 2012. https://theatlantic.com/business/archive/2012/10/beyond-the-bayonets-what-romney-had-right-and-wrong-about-our-navy/264025.

CHAPTER 10: THE IMMORTAL BRAND

Abelson, Reed. "Wal-Mart's Health Care Struggle Is Corporate America's, Too." *New York Times*, October 29, 2005. https://nytimes.com/2005/10/29/business/businessspecial2/walmarts-health-care-struggle-is-corporate.html.

"Axe." Unilever. Accessed August 2023. www.unileverusa.com/brands/personal-care/axe.

Baertlein, Lisa. "U.S. Grocers Add Plexiglass Sneeze Guards to Protect Cashiers from Coronavirus." Reuters, March 30, 2020. https://reuters.com/article/us-health-coronavirus-kroger/u-s-grocers-add-plexiglass-sneeze-guards-to-protect-cashiers-from-coronavirus-idUSKBN21H3G1.

Bibliography

Baker, Jackson, and Anjali Ayyappan. "Walmart's History and Economic Cycle." Sutori. Accessed August 2023. https://sutori.com/en/story/walmart-s-history-and-economic-cycle--FiQ3F95hiKoeeF41hWDmDYdD.

Barrera, Daniela. "Walmart Minimum Wages: How Much Did the Retail Giant Increase Their Employees' Wages By?" *AS USA*, May 9, 2023. https://en.as.com/latest_news/walmart-minimum-wages-how-much-did-the-retail-giant-increase-their-employees-wages-by-n.

Blodget, Henry. "Walmart Employs 1% of America. Should It Be Forced to Pay Its Employees More?" *Business Insider*, September 20, 2010. https://businessinsider.com/walmart-employees-pay.

Bomey, Nathan. "Walmart Boosts Minimum Wage Again, Hands Out $1,000 Bonuses." *USA Today*, January 11, 2018. https://usatoday.com/story/money/2018/01/11/walmart-boosts-minimum-wage-11-hands-out-bonuses-up-1-000-hourly-workers/1023606001.

Brown, Abram. "Facebook's New Metaverse Project Will Cost 'Billions' of Dollars." *Forbes*, July 28, 2021. https://forbes.com/sites/abrambrown/2021/07/28/facebook-metaverse.

Brown, Stillman. "Twenty 100+ Year Old American Brands Still Making Awesome, Authentic Products." *Primer*. Accessed August 2023. https://primermagazine.com/2020/learn/100-year-old-american-brands.

Church, Bianca. "Iconic Brands That Have Prospered for over 100 Years." *Truly Belong*, November 16, 2020. https://trulybelong.com/lifestyle/2020/11/16/iconic-brands-that-have-prospered-for-over-100-years.

Conick, Hal. "Philip Kotler, the Father of Modern Marketing, Will Never Retire." American Marketing Association, December 12, 2018. https://ama.org/marketing-news/philip-kotler-the-father-of-modern-marketing-will-never-retire.

Fitzpatrick, Alex and Erin Davis. "The Most Popular Grocery Stores in the U.S." *Axios*, April 20, 2023. https://axios.com/2023/04/20/most-popular-grocery-stores.

"Fortune 500: Walmart, Rank 1." *Fortune*. Accessed August 2023. https://fortune.com/company/walmart/fortune500.

Goddiess, Samantha. "10 Largest Paper Towel Brands in the United States." Zippia, June 16, 2021. https://zippia.com/advice/largest-paper-towel-brands.

Guest Writer Series. "The History of Old Spice." The Razor Company, May 10, 2023. https://therazorcompany.com/blogs/history-of-wet-shaving/the-history-of-old-spice.

Harris, Richard. "White House Announces New Social Distancing Guidelines Around Coronavirus." NPR, March 16, 2020. https://npr.org/2020/03/16/816658125/white-house-announces-new-social-distancing-guidelines-around-coronavirus.

Hern, Alex. "Mark Zuckerberg's Metaverse Vision Is Over. Can Apple Save It?" *The Guardian*, May 21, 2023. https://theguardian.com/technology/2023/may/21/mark-zuckerbergs-metaverse-vision-is-over-can-apple-save-it.

Hess, Amanda. "The Pandemic Ad Salutes You." *New York Times*, May 22, 2020, updated May 28, 2020. https://nytimes.com/2020/05/22/arts/pandemic-ads-salute-you.html.

Kim, Lisa. "Facebook Announces New Name: Meta." *Forbes*, October 28, 2021. https://forbes.com/sites/lisakim/2021/10/28/facebook-announces-new-name-meta.

Kurtzleben, Danielle. "Walmart Struggles to Overcome Environmental Criticism." *U.S. News & World Report*, April 20, 2012. https://usnews.com/news/articles/2012/04/20/walmart-struggles-to-overcome-environmental-criticism.

Leone, Chris. "How Much Should You Budget for Marketing in 2023?" WebStrategies, November 11, 2022. https://webstrategiesinc.com/blog/how-much-budget-for-online-marketing.

"Location Facts." Walmart Corporate. Accessed August 2023. https://corporate.walmart.com/about/location-facts.

Meisenzahl, Mary. "Walmart Grew Ecommerce Sales 24% in Q2." Digital Commerce 360, August 17, 2023. https://digitalcommerce360.com/article/walmart-online-sales.

Neff, Jack. "The Battle of the Brands: Old Spice vs. Axe." *AdAge*, November 17, 2008. https://adage.com/article/news/battle-brands-spice-axe/132559.

"Old Spice Guy Brings 107% Increase in Sales." Kinesis. Accessed August 2023. https://kinesisinc.com/old-spice-guy-brings-107-increase-in-sales.

"Old Spice: Smell Like a Man, Man." Wieden+Kennedy, February 2010. https://wk.com/work/old-spice-smell-like-a-man-man.

"The Procter & Gamble Company—Company Profile, Information, Business Description, History, Background Information on the Procter & Gamble Company." Reference for Business Company History Index. Accessed August 2023. https://referenceforbusiness.com/history2/83/The-Procter-Gamble-Company.html.

"Procter & Gamble Revenue 2010–2023 | PG." Macrotrends. Accessed August 2023. https://macrotrends.net/stocks/charts/PG/procter-gamble/revenue.

Rupe, Susan. "How Walmart Is Taking On the Cost of Employee Health Care with 'Innovation.'" *Insurance Newsnet*, March 16, 2023. https://insurancenewsnet.com/innarticle/how-walmart-is-taking-on-the-cost-of-employee-health-care-with-innovation.

Segal, Edward. "How Walmart Is Responding to Covid-Related Challenges." *Forbes*, September 1, 2021. https://forbes.com/sites/edwardsegal/2021/09/01/how-covid-repeatedly-put-walmart-to-the-test.

Smith, Matt. "Store and Club Associates Adapt After the First Week of Social Distancing." Walmart Corporate Affairs, March 24, 2020. https://corporate.walmart.com/newsroom/2020/03/24/store-and-club-associates-adapt-after-the-first-week-of-social-distancing.

Spector, Nicole. "100-Year-Old Companies Still in Business Today." GOBankingRates, June 5, 2023. https://gobankingrates.com/money/business/big-name-brands-around-century.

Tighe, D. "Leading 100 Retailers in the United States in 2022, Based on U.S. Retail Sales." Statista, July 12, 2023. https://statista.com/statistics/195992/usa-retail-sales-of-the-top-retailers.

"US Digital Ad Spend Grew Faster Last Year Than at Any Point in the Previous 15 Years." Marketing Charts, May 18, 2022. https://marketingcharts.com/advertising-trends/spending-and-spenders-225723.

Bibliography

Valinsky, Jordan. "Walmart, Albertsons, Kroger and Whole Foods are Adding Sneeze Guards to Checkout Lanes." *CNN Business*, November 23, 2020. https:// cnn.com/2020/03/25/business/walmart-kroger-changes-coronavirus-wellness /index.html.

"Walmart Revenue 2010–2023 | WMT." Macrotrends. Accessed August 2023. https:/macrotrends.net/stocks/charts/WMT/walmart/revenue.

INDEX